D0732615

Unlocking
Your
Giftedness

What Leaders Need to Know
To Develop Themselves and Others

formerly called
Developing Leadership Giftedness

**By
Dr. J. Robert Clinton
Dr. Richard W. Clinton**

Copyright © 1993, 1998 J. Robert Clinton, Richard W. Clinton All Rights Reserved

Published by Barnabas Publishers

No part of this book may be reproduced or transmitted, in whole or part, including illustrations, in any form or by any means, electronic or mechanical, including photocopying, recording, or by any information storage and retrieval systems, except as is permitted by sections 107 and 108 of the U.S. copyright law and as is permissible for published public reviews, without permission in writing from the publisher.

Barnabas Publishers

P.O. Box 6006
Altadena, CA 91003-6006

Printed in the United States of America

Cover Design by D.M. Battermann

TABLE OF CONTENTS

Part III. DEVELOPMENT PERSPECTIVES

PREFACE

There have been numerous books written on the subject of spiritual gifts. Nearly every major publishing company has published several books dealing with the topic. If dust covers can be believed, several of these books have sold over 100,000 copies. Nearly every denomination has its book on spiritual gifts which outlines its position on gifts along with its definitions.

The question is, "Why take the time, energy and money to write another piece of material on spiritual gifts?" We believe that this manual offers something distinctive that the other books on spiritual gifts do not. Here are a few of the distinctives that set this manual apart from the other books:

- we focus on leaders and leadership development as it relates to giftedness. This is a manual primarily for leaders.

- we bring a wealth of perspective about leadership development to our study of the topic. We draw on nearly 800 leadership case studies as a research base. These case studies provide a rich source of information on the process of development as it relates to giftedness.

- we talk about a leader's giftedness development which includes natural abilities, acquired skills and spiritual gifts rather than just spiritual gifts.

- we focus on the issue of development of maturity in giftedness as opposed to just focusing on definitions and identification of spiritual gifts.

- we try to help leaders become proactive in their own giftedness development as well as learning to help their followers develop in their development by building structures that enhance giftedness development.

THE HISTORY OF THIS PROJECT

There is a history behind the writing of this book. I (Bobby) have been concerned about spiritual gifts since 1968 when I had to write a paper for one of Dr. Robertson McQuilkin's classes at Columbia Bible College. The paper required me to identify and lay out a plan for developing my spiritual gift. I had to study the Scriptures to try to define spiritual gifts and identify my own. I set out a plan for development. The basic guidelines of that plan have been followed through the years.

My missionary experience in Jamaica included teaching about spiritual gifts to young pre-service students from all over the Caribbean. Each time I taught on the subject, I saw the need for a self-study manual on spiritual gifts that could be used in ministry. In 1975, I wrote this manual for use in ministry. I used this text in churches, house churches, classrooms, workshops and seminars to train people to identify and develop their spiritual gifts.

In 1983 I began my deliberate research on leadership development. Because my original gifts book was out of print, I published an expanded version in 1985. I used this text in my courses at Fuller's School of World Mission and began to systematically gather data about gifts as I researched leader's lives. Out of nearly 500 leadership case studies, 300 of them had specific data on gifts and giftedness. Comparative studies of this data forced me to discover helpful information which broadened my earlier research on gifts which was based on Biblical research alone.

Some helpful findings came out of that research. Here are just a few that will be elaborated on later in the book.

- All leaders have at least one word gift.{1} Knowing this is helpful in learning to identify, select, and develop emerging leaders.
- Most leaders operate in multiple gifts...a gift-mix.
- There is usually one dominant spiritual gift which is supported by others.
- Spiritual gifts are just one component of a person's giftedness set. Natural abilities and acquired skills make up the rest of the set.
- Any of the three components of the giftedness set can be the dominant element, called the focal element.
- Ultimately, ministry flows out of being. Character and giftedness are key components of our being.
- Most leaders use informal means of training to develop in their giftedness.
- Leaders who shape their "roles" to fit who they are in terms of giftedness will tend to be more effective over a lifetime.
- Knowledge about giftedness and development can be a major step forward in aiding a leader to develop that giftedness with intentionality and deliberateness.

In 1989, I began to teach a course on developing leadership gifts. This course was designed to get students to do research on how mid-career leaders can learn to identify and intentionally develop in their giftedness. The research data that has come out of this course has contributed greatly to the overall understanding of giftedness and development. I was able to test my ideas concerning gift-mix, giftedness set, and other crucial definitions and concepts. This course continues to be taught on a yearly basis and provides on-going research in this area.

Over the last three years, my son Richard and I have been working together in ministry in the field of leadership development. He has joined me in my efforts here at Fuller Theological Seminary as well as ministry in other locations. Over the last 10 years, he has operated in the charismatic renewal movement and brings a different perspective and experience in the area of giftedness development than my own. By working together, we have observed that God allows us to draw on the strengths of one another's experience and knowledge to form a balanced perspective on giftedness and development.

Our personal experiences, the development of our own giftedness sets, our teaching in this area and our leadership research have all combined to give us the information that is presented in this book. It has been gathered over a period of twenty-two years.

Layout of the Manual

We have organized that presentation as follows.

Part I will lay the foundation for what follows. It will give some motivational reasons why leaders should know about giftedness as well as give some of the Biblical rationale behind the development of a giftedness set. If you are already motivated and already have a solid Biblical rationale for developing

---

[1]Word gifts are one of three categories (word, power, love) which describe the function of spiritual gifts. These gifts all deal with clarifying who the unseen God is and what He is doing. Gifts such as apostleship, pastoring, evangelism, prophecy, teaching, exhortation, word of wisdom, word of knowledge, and sometimes faith are word gifts.

giftedness you may wish to move on to Part II directly and by-pass Part I.

Part II presents the giftedness set made of three elements: natural abilities, acquired skills, and spiritual gifts. There is a chapter on each component of the set. It concludes with a focus on the leadership gifts, a special sub-set of spiritual gifts which we identify with the Word cluster of spiritual gifts.

Part III will cover our findings on how leaders can develop their giftedness. It will suggest some basic ways that can help a leader be more proactive in development and not simply reactive, as is the case with many leaders.

A glossary will help you become familiar with the various concepts that are introduced. We will also include a bibliography of spiritual gift books. This bibliography covers a wide spectrum of views concerning spiritual gifts. Most authors have not or do not want to see how others who differ from their perspective are writing on the subject. We have found that an overall perspective in which a person pinpoints one's own viewpoint as it relates to others who have written on the subject, will bring balance as well as tolerance regarding giftedness. This allows both strengths and weaknesses to be determined.

While some may individually study this book, many will probably use this book in small groups or in classes. In either case, whether individually or in groups, serious readers will benefit from some exercises, including questions, discussion material, and personal sharing stimuli. With that in mind we have designed such exercises for each chapter covering the major concepts of the chapter. Doing these exercises and answering the questions will be a means of learning and will clarify your understanding of concepts. Some of the exercises require sharing with others and will not have answers. Most of the questions and exercises will have answers so that your can compare your efforts with our own. These self-study prompts are scattered throughout the presentation of the material.

We need to give a final word on the manual's title, The original title "Developing Leadership Giftedness" was chosen for semantic reasons. First, developing implies that there are deliberate steps, procedures, or plans that can be used to further one's leadership...that is, make one a more effective leader. And these deliberate steps focus on an important part of one's leadership—the area of giftedness. Secondly, leadership is used collectively to refer to any of God's people who are responsibly influencing groups of God's people toward accomplishing His purposes. They could be lay or full time. We are not just referring to full time Christian workers. However, we are not writing about the body as a whole, but those leaders who are exercising leadership with respect to the body. Third, we are dealing with giftedness, not just spiritual gifts. Our view on the stewardship model broadens our approach. We are not just dealing with spiritual gifts, important as they are, but on giftedness, a broader topic. The new title, "Unlocking Your Giftedness," was chosen for its suggestive implications.

We pray that God uses this manual to better equip, train and develop His leaders to operate in the maximum potential of giftedness that God has measured out to each one.

CHAPTER ONE:
MOTIVATING LEADERS TO STUDY GIFTEDNESS

INTRODUCTION

We have been involved in the study of **leaders** and leadership over the past 10 years. We have learned a great deal about how God develops **leaders** over their lifetime. One of our goals which motivates our studies is the attempt to discover how we can become more effective **leaders** for the Lord Jesus. We have learned many things that will make **leaders** effective in their leadership. *One of the keys to leadership effectiveness is knowing about, developing and operating in your giftedness.*

Notice I said *giftedness*. In this material we will be making a distinction between a person's spiritual gift or gifts and a person's giftedness. This distinction is very helpful when we talk about a **leader** developing a focused ministry, which we will do later.

Definition:
A spiritual gift is a God-given unique capacity which is given to each believer for the purpose of releasing a Holy Spirit empowered ministry either in a situation or to be repeated again and again.

Definition:
A leader's giftedness set refers to three elements seen in the leader's life: natural abilities, acquired skills, and spiritual gifts.

We have developed this material with **leaders** in mind. As a result, we will be directing most of our attention towards leaders. However, we believe that everyone can benefit from this material. Whether you are a **leader** or not, God wants you to operate in your giftedness so that you might reach the maximum potential that God has for you. God is primarily concerned that each one of us walk in obedience to Him. God has invested in you! He has a plan for you! He has things for you to do!

No matter what level of Christian service that you are called to, it is important to know that you are responsible to God for your life. Jesus taught clearly that each one of us will be held accountable for the results of our lives and our service in His Kingdom. The Bible also teaches clearly that leaders are going to be held especially accountable for their actions. Each one of us ought to eagerly desire to learn about our own giftedness so that we can operate more effectively in our service in the Kingdom. Then, on that day, we can stand before our King and Judge without fear and hear the "Well done my good and faithful servant" that each one of us wants to hear. What follows are two case studies which emphasize two different levels of Christian service. Yet an understanding of giftedness is important to both **leaders**— for different reasons.

LEADERS AND GIFTEDNESS: TWO CASE STUDIES

Recently I (Bobby) had a day of prayer and fasting. But not a normal one. It was interrupted by two visits. Both visits had something in common. They were visits discussing the future of leaders. Each of these incidents formed the basis for the two cases which follow.

One visit was with a very competent mission executive named Dean. He has about 17 years of experience, two years as a pioneering church planter and 15 years as a missionary. During this time he had about five different major ministry assignments.

The other visit was with a gifted young leader, Ray. He has had two major ministry assignments both of which were pastoral in nature. He had about 7 years of ministry experience. Both of these leaders were seeking advice as well as affirmation for their future. Both were in the process of making decisions. These decisions would affect their ministry for the rest of their lives.

CASE 1. DEAN AND A MAJOR DECISION

I spent about 3 hours with Dean. He is 38 years old. He had spent the last 15 years with a mission and had served as the general director for the last few years. Before joining the mission, he had planted a church amongst drug addicts. After joining the mission, he had worked his way up through the ranks. His ministry experience included school teaching among aboriginal peoples, church planting among slum dwellers in a major city, running non-formal and informal training programs for inter-city leader and finally directing the mission. He is well on his way toward introducing renewal into the mission that is 60 years old.

The thrust of our talk was an evaluation of a major career decision that looms on the horizon for dean. His decision, which needed to made in the next two months could take him away from the top leadership position in the mission. I already knew most of his background because I had met him during one of my trips to the mission field. He had taken several leadership courses in an extension setting and had eventually come on campus to finish his masters in missiology in the leadership concentration. One of the courses that he took from me was Leadership Emergence Patterns. In this course, each student does an in-depth leadership study on his/her life. I had read his study and knew much of his background before our visit.

During the 3 hours, I would listen and probe him with some questions as he talked through the possibilities and ramifications of his decision. The first questions that I asked were fairly standard questions concerning the guidance that he had received up to this point in the process. He had been grappling with this decision for the past 18 months.

Next I began to push him toward thinking about insights and perspectives that were important for the long term career plans. My questions were purposeful, catalytic and esoteric. Fortunately, Dean had studied with me so he understood what I meant by asking questions about destiny processing, mini-convergence factors, ideal roles, ideal influence-mix, and his potential ultimate contribution set.[1] All of these questions require a person to really know something about his/her giftedness. Because Dean had studied with me, he understood his giftedness set. He knew the strengths that flowed from his natural abilities as well as his weaknesses. He could articulate the skills that he had acquired along the way that supplemented his natural abilities and his spiritual gifts. He knew his gift-mix and could point out the dominant gift. During our talk, I continually tried to help clarify what kind of roles could best fit his giftedness set, his destiny processing, his ideal influence-mix and the areas of ultimate contribution that God was calling him to.

---

[1] For a detailed explination of these concepts please see the <u>Leadership Emergence Theory</u> manual published by Barnabas Publishers.

One other thing happened over the course of the three hours. Dean related several incidents that had happened to him during his recent ministry assignment as general director of the mission. Most of them had to do with learning to assess personnel and shifting them to roles that fit their giftedness. Some of the incidents were sad situations in which people were not developing in their giftedness. Some were improperly matched with roles that their giftedness was not suited to. Fortunately, he had some good experiences in which some of the leaders were developing in their giftedness and were moved into roles that challenged them to develop and expand in their giftedness.

As Dean and I chatted, I was aware of how much he knew about giftedness and used it in his position as head of the mission. His awareness of his own personal giftedness allowed him to:

- recruit to his weaknesses on his executive leadership team, and
- helped him choose the ministry tasks that he accepted.

As director of the mission, he was continually besieged by invitations and opportunities.

His awareness of giftedness in general helped him to:

- assign missionaries to field situations,
- move various personnel around to roles that better suited them,
- recruit new people to the mission to fill roles that he perceived.

I was struck anew by the idea that *leaders who are responsible for accomplishing God's work in the context of an organization* need to be **knowledgeable about giftedness** and **how people develop in their giftedness** if they are going to use the resources that God has given them. **People are the primary resource that God gives to leaders.**

CASE 2. RAY IN A TIME OF TRANSITION

Ray's visit also lasted about 3 hours. I had been meeting with him on a regular basis for the past several months. Those months had been a critical time in his life. A major decision was being made in his life. I was continually giving advice all along the way. Ray was a part of a pastoral staff in a large church. The church was going through a time of major transition. The leadership at the top of the structure had recently changed and the new leaders were bringing their ideas and leadership structures into the church. Ray was caught in what I call a regime turnover. The new regime was confused about exactly where it was going. The only thing that was clear was that changes were going to be made.

The new leadership began to recruit its own staff to fill positions of leadership. There was no role that was being developed for Ray that he could see. He was being throttled in the situation. What might be a next ministry assignment that could develop Ray's giftedness? That was my task as a mentor counselor. I worked to affirm and confirm to Ray that he was gifted in ministry and that whatever the next assignment was, God was in it and wanted to develop him in his giftedness, leadership abilities and relationship to God.

My knowledge of Ray's giftedness set enabled me to point out:

- the relationship between his natural abilities and spiritual gifts (he was a talented musician but also gifted in exposing the Scriptures in an applicational way),

- what kind of role would best develop him in these areas of strength,

- some experiences that might help him discover other parts of his giftedness.

I have just touched the surface of these two visits. I could relate many other similar stories concerning young leaders, mid-career leaders and older leaders who have come to me with questions seeking perspective about God and themselves.

Some were frustrated with roles that they were in.
Some were plateaued in their growth.
Some were struggling to understand themselves and what God was doing with them.

All of the leaders that come to me share a common desire. They want to grow and develop but most of all, they want their lives and ministries to count for God. And I must confess my answers very frequently have to do with an assessment of their giftedness and God's guidance toward roles that will make them more effective.

As a result of comparative studies of many leaders, Biblical, historical, and contemporary, I have synthesized the following definition of a leader.

definition   *A leader is a person with God-given capacity, and God-given responsibility who is influencing some of God's people towards God's purposes.*

Giftedness deals with a leader's God-given capacity—the first major concept in the definition of a leader.   Over a lifetime leaders need to develop that capacity and use it in order to accomplish God's purposes.   Let me summarize what I have been hinting at by sharing the two case studies with Dean and Ray.

7 Reasons Why Leaders Need to Know About Giftedness

- **Give Perspective To Followers**
  A leader is responsible to give perspective concerning giftedness and developing that giftedness to the followers that God has given him/her responsibility over. This is especially important if there needs to be any correction concerning problems with giftedness. (Frequently problems with spiritual gifts and how they operate in a given context come up.)

- **Recognize and Develop Leadership Potential**
  Leaders are to be involved in selecting and training emerging leaders. Giftedness is a major indicator of leadership potential. It should be identified as early in the process of training as possible so that opportunities and roles can be created that will help develop the emerging leader along his/her giftedness.

- **Placement of Leaders in Roles**

  A leader often influences decisions on the placement of people and should allow their understanding of giftedness and its development to shape their decisions.

- **Accountability**
  Leaders are going to be held accountable at a higher standard than followers for using their God-given capacities. This implies that leaders need to have a good grasp of giftedness and development.

- **Facilitate A Proactive Stance Toward Development**
  The recognition and identification of giftedness is an important part of moving toward a focused ministry that includes deliberateness, intentionality and development toward optimum potential. Identification can move a person toward operating in gifted power as he/she cooperates with the Holy Spirit. The failure to recognize giftedness may hinder a person from moving along to higher stages of realized potential in terms of giftedness.

- **Move Toward Focused Lives**
  Leaders need to be moving towards convergence in their own lives. Convergence in leadership development describes a phase during which the leader is operating in peak efficiency and effectiveness in his/her ministry. Operating in maturity in one's giftedness is a major part of reaching convergence.

- **Balanced Profile**
  As leaders, we are responsible for the health of the body we are working with. We ought to be able to recognize gift vacuums in groups.[2] When we recognize a gift vacuum, or an unbalanced situation regarding giftedness that our followers are manifesting, we should influence followers to use their giftedness to meet those missing needs. (There is the assumption that the Holy Spirit will give the necessary gifts to meet the needs of the group.)

SUMMARY

Giftedness development is at the heart of our own understanding of leadership development. Ministry ultimately flows out of our beingness. Over our lifetime, God is actively initiating various types of shaping activities which He uses to mold us into a unique being. He uses that uniqueness or that beingness to serve His purposes in His Kingdom. Giftedness is a major component of that beingness.

As leaders, we need to know and study our own giftedness in order to get insights as to how God develops giftedness in people. This manual will provide material to help you analyze your own giftedness. Once you understand the process of giftedness development, you will be able to help others develop in their own giftedness.

---

[2] A given group of God's people will corporately manifest gifts which will function *to explain who God is and what He has said and what He wants to do* (**called Word Gifts**). They will also manifest gifts which *demonstrate the reality of the unseen God in our world today* (**Power Gifts**). And they will demonstrate the *reality of knowing this God in terms of its effect upon their lives and their relationships with others* (**Love Gifts**). A given group will manifest these three clusters to differing degrees. The resulting profile of the three as seen in the body may be out of balance or even have one or more of these clusters missing. If so we are talking about a gift vacuum. Leader's should be able to recognize present profiles and what is needed to minister to the current situation they are in.

CHAPTER FEEDBACK

1. Glance again at the *7 reasons Why Leaders Need to Know about Giftedness* given below.

___ a. Leaders need to be able to give **Perspective To Followers** concerning giftedness and development.

___ b. Leaders need to recognize and **Develop Leadership Potential** in emerging leaders—of which giftedness is a major indicator.

___ c. A leader often influences decisions on the placement of people and should allow an **understanding of giftedness and its development to shape those important decisions**—that crucially affect people's lives.

___ d. Leaders are going to be **held accountable** at a higher standard than followers for using their God-given capacities. This implies that leaders need to personally have a good grasp of their own giftedness and development.

___ e. The recognition and identification of giftedness is an important part of **moving toward a focused ministry.**

___ f. Leaders need to be moving towards convergence in their own lives. **Operating in maturity** (role compatibility, discernment and power) in one's giftedness is a major part of reaching convergence.

___ g. As leaders, we are **responsible for the health** of the body we are working with including correction of abuses of giftedness as well as imbalances.

At this point in your own personal development as a leader, which one of the above seven reasons are most important to you (Mark with M—most important)? Which one is least important to you (Mark with L—least important)?

2. Though we have not developed it, we have mentioned a distinction between spiritual gifts and giftedness. Which is the broader concept?

___ a. spiritual gifts
___ b. giftedness

ANSWERS —————-

1. Your choice. For me _M_ c. _L_ g.

2. _x_ b.

CHAPTER 2.
PHILOSOPHICAL FOUNDATIONS FOR DEVELOPING GIFTEDNESS

INTRODUCTION

Our first title for the book, Developing Leadership Giftedness, presupposes that you have a basic understanding of leadership definitions. Perhaps you do. If so, you may want to skip this chapter and go directly to chapter 3. But if you don't, you should ransack this chapter to understand the basic leadership definitions that are assumed as well as see the Biblical rationale for the stewardship model—a key to the notion of development.

Our understanding of giftedness, as regards the emphasis of development, is based on several New Testament philosophical leadership models. In this chapter, we will introduce you to some of the foundational leadership concepts which will help you interpret some of our basic thinking and approach to leadership and how leaders operate in ministry. We will spend the bulk of this chapter looking at four basic New Testament philosophical models for leadership. These philosophical models provide the foundation for our emphasis on developing your giftedness. Two of the models, Harvest and Shepherd, are closely related to giftedness. Two, stewardship and servant leader, carry strong leadership values that also affect our views on giftedness. We will look at the issue of accountability, which flows from the Stewardship Model, by focusing on two key parables, Talents and Pounds, that Jesus taught. The combination of all of these pieces of material will provide you with the understanding of the philosophical foundations that underlie our approach to giftedness.

The key concepts in this chapter will be written using information mapping, sometimes followed by narrative commentary. Information mapping is the technical name for a referential learning layout which unpacks information into focused units which are individually labeled and easy to refer to later. You can, at a glance, identify a major concept and all its related parts. You can then read those you need to and skip those which you already know. Many of these important concepts will have feedback sections which are questions and exercise (along with answers) that will help you assess your learning of the concepts.

To go on to chapter three you should have met the objectives of this chapter which include familiarization with the following definitions and concepts:

- leadership act (p. 12),
- leader (p. 14),
- leadership (p. 18),
- 3 major high-level leadership functions (giftedness correlates somewhat to these three functions) (p. 20, 21),
- The Stewardship Model (responsibility for development correlates to this model) (p. 25),
- The Servant Leader Model (responsibility for using giftedness correlates to this model) (p. 27),
- The Shepherd Leader Model (certain of the leadership gifts relate to this model) (p. 29),
- The Harvest Model (certain of the leadership gifts relate to this model) (p. 31),
- The Central Truth of the Parable of the Talents (p. 34),
- The Central Truth of the Parable of the Pounds (Gold Coins) (p. 35).

LEADERSHIP ACT   **synonym: group influence**

introduction   A leadership act occurs when a given person influences a group, in terms of behavioral acts or perception, so that the group acts or thinks differently as a group than before the instance of influence. While the process may be complex and difficult to assess, nevertheless, leadership can be seen to happen and be composed essentially of influencer, group, influence means, and resulting change of direction by the group. People who so influence, whether full time or not, are the target group for this manual. They are leaders. They are the ones who we say can develop in giftedness.

definition   A leadership act is the specific instance at a given point in time of the leadership influence process between a given influencer (person said to be influencing) and follower(s) (person or persons being influenced) in which the followers are influenced toward some goal.

example   Barnabas, Acts 9:26-30 (not a full time Christian worker here),

example   Barnabas, Acts 11:22-24

example   Barnabas, Acts 11:25-26

example   Agabus, Acts 11:27-28 (probably an itinerant full-time worker), spiritual gift identified (prophecy),

example   leaders, whole church: Acts 11:29-30

example   Paul, Barnabas, apostles and elders in Jerusalem, Peter, James: Acts 15:1-21

comment   One can differentiate between a momentary instance of leadership which I call a leadership act, as defined above, and leadership as an ongoing process which I call leadership. The momentary leadership act recognizes the reciprocal nature of leadership (that is, the impact of gifts that all have) for any group in a given situation. The repeated persistence of leadership acts by a given person indicates the permanence of a leader in a group context and specifies leadership, such as we are focusing on in this manual.

comment   A major difference in one who influences momentarily in a group and one who persistently influences over time is the emergence of vision and sense of responsibility for seeing that vision fulfilled.

comment   Notice that ordination, position, or full time work or not do not essentially affect this leadership act definition. Influence is the key element.

FEEDBACK EXERCISES ON LEADERSHIP ACT

1. Examine the leadership act given in Acts 9:26-30. Identify the four major parts of the leadership act.

    a.   leader—

    b.   followers—

    c.   influence means-

    d.   the influence goal (resulting change)—

2. For the leadership act in Acts 9:26-30, was the leader successful in this leadership act? If not, why not? If so, why do you think the leader was successful?

3. Describe a recent leadership act you have observed in connection with some ministry you are involved in. Describe,

    a.   leader—

    b.   followers—

    c.   influence means—

    d.   results—

ANSWERS—————
1. a. leader—Barnabas b. followers—apostles in Jerusalem, unnamed but most likely including Peter, James, John et al. c. influence means—persuasion backed by credibility. d. the goal was to have Saul recognized as a legitimate Christian and to have him accepted by the apostles.

2. In my opinion, yes. Verse 28 describing Saul's staying in Jerusalem and his ministry there indicates that Barnabas was successful.

3. Your choice. In doing this exercise you will probably note that leadership acts in life are generally much more complex than the biblical example given above (that one was probably complex but we only have a selected summary of it). For one thing, there is usually multiple influence going on in the group. That is, it may not be easy to identify only one leader. For another thing influence goals are not always straightforward or understood by leaders and followers. Sometimes there are differing groups of followers within the same leadership act.

LEADER

introduction	One who persists in leadership acts is a leader. Such an influencer is said to demonstrate leadership. From a study of many leaders in both the Old and New Testaments the following perspectives are offered as a synthesis of a biblical leader.
definition	A **leader**, as defined from a study of Biblical leadership, and for whom we are interested in tracing leadership development is a person,

1) with God-given capacity AND
2) with God-given responsibility
WHO IS INFLUENCING
3) a specific group of God's people
4) toward God's purposes for the group.

Biblical examples	Joseph, Moses, Joshua, Jephthah, Samuel, David, Daniel, Paul, Peter, Barnabas, Timothy, Titus
historical examples	William Carey, J. Hudson Taylor, J. O. Fraser, Cameron Townsend, Charles Simeon, Henrietta Mears, Phineas Bresee, Simon Kimbangi, Livingston Sohn, John Sung, Samuel Mills
central ethic	The *central ethic* of Biblical leadership is, INFLUENCING TOWARD GOD'S PURPOSES. That is, the prime function of leadership is the influencing of groups so as to accomplish God's purposes involving the group. This requires vision. This external direction is what distinguishes a Christian leader from a secular leader.
comment capacity	The *God-given capacity* denotes giftedness capacity (whether an actual spiritual gift or natural talent or acquired skill). The capacity of a leader relates to the ability to influence. It also connotes leadership character, as well as the concept of the potential that is yet to be developed.
comment responsibility	The *God-given responsibility* denotes two major ideas concerning a sense of accountability with God for leadership. 1) There is a downward sense of responsibility (a burden from God) to influence others for God. 2) There is an upward sense of responsibility (to God) for the people being influenced.
comment specific group	Leadership is concerned with the persistent specific influence of a leader upon *specific groups*. It is this group (the followers) for which the leader will be responsible and will discern God's purposes.

FEEDBACK ON LEADER

1. Give Biblical evidence for each of the four significant points in the definition of leader.

2. Choose any of the leaders mentioned in the examples (or any other one that you want to use) and illustrate how each of the significant points in the leadership definition is fulfilled.

3. Explain how you personally interpret the concept of *God-given capacity to influence?*

ANSWERS————

1. I'll just touch on some answers. There is much more in the Bible. You probably have other answers than those I've hastily jotted down. Concept 1: see Ephesians 4:7-11, and passages on spiritual gifts of ruling, administration, apostleship, and pastoring. Concept 2: see Acts 20:28, Hebrews 13:17. Concept 3: see Acts 20:28, I Peter 5:2. Concept 4: see Acts 20:17-38. The whole passage is Paul's example of this very concept; his letters to churches illustrate this.

2. A study of Samuel Mills' leadership development (Maranville 1982) reveals that he was gifted to foster mission organizations. He had an amazing ability to organize and administer and to motivate others to take over the organizations. His influence was greatly felt in the early years of mission activity in the United States in the early 1800s. He demonstrated traits usually identified with the spiritual gifts of apostleship and administration. A study of Mills' whole life-time seems to indicate that God gave him a national *responsibility* to motivate North American Christians toward involvement in missions. The groups of people for whom he was responsible (indirectly) were *those people already involved in churches but not in missions*—which was the majority of Christians in North America. In terms of God's purposes, time and time again Mills saw the need for an organization or a movement which would recruit and activate God's people into *missions' involvement.* He was able to sense God's timing in events and happenings and develop plans and organizations based on what he saw.

3. I interpret the phrase "God-given capacity to influence" to mean that the person is born with natural abilities for leadership as well as potential to acquire skills that will enable influence. A leader has also been imparted spiritual gifts which are important for influencing. I consider spiritual leadership gifts (that is, those gifts which allow for influence) to include what I call the word gifts. Primary word gifts include teaching, prophecy, exhortation, Secondary word gifts include: apostleship, evangelism and pastoring (and ruling). Tertiary word gifts include word of wisdom and word of knowledge and faith.

COMMENTARY ON LEADER

position
or
influence

Frequently missionaries, nationals and particularly women coming to the School of World Mission, where we teach, identify a leader as a person having a formal position of leadership. Notice that the focus of our leader definition is not on status or position but on functionality. That is, a leader is one who influences others. It is true that there are leaders who are influencing people toward God's purposes who may not have formal positions. It is also true that there are people holding formal positions who are not really functioning as leaders. One can exercise leadership even in situations where structures prohibit them from having formal positions. This manual will go further than just influence when talking about leaders; it will identify certain kinds of spiritual gifts, natural abilities, and acquired skills which relate to the central ethic of leadership, influencing people.

women
in
leadership

Frequently, women students do not think of themselves as leaders. This can occur primarily for two reasons. One, some Christian leaders have convictions against women in leadership and teach against it. Some women who have sat under this kind of teaching find it difficult to freely see themselves as leaders. Two, many women come from male dominated cultures in which formal leadership structures are open only to males. My own conviction allows for women who are gifted and developed by God for leadership to lead; the same for men. My definition of a leader can apply broadly to those who hold my conviction or not—since it is an influence based definition, not a formal/positional one. Sometimes women who study leadership emergence theory go through a paradigm shift in which they move from viewing themselves as not being leaders to being leaders. The real problem, once one admits that God has gifted one to lead, is how to exercise that leadership in terms of the cultural structures and roles available. Our study of leadership giftedness indicates that both females and males receive giftedness for leadership including natural abilities, acquired skills, and spiritual gifts needed for leadership.

elements
of
emergence

Though potential leaders are born, effective leaders are made as a result of, 1) opportunity, 2) training and 3) experience. These three components do not automatically guarantee that one will rise to become a great leader. But without them it is not likely that one will realize maximum potential. Awareness of leadership giftedness will help one recognize what is happening in their experience and help them focus on deliberately seeking opportunity and training.

essential
difference
leaders and
followers

Both leaders and followers actually influence in church and para-church situations. When Christians use their gifts with others, these impact so as to influence. In small groups, the sharing of both leaders and followers will influence. There is a mutuality of leadership in group situations. Sometimes followers spontaneously exert influence that is significant to a group. Le Peau (1983) stresses that anyone can lead. He describes paths along which anyone can develop as a leader. My understanding of leaders and leadership disagrees somewhat with his approach. I do allow for anyone to lead (that is, exert influence) in the sense of a leadership act. But I want to strongly point out that this is different from on-going leadership. When I think of a leader as defined herein I am thinking of permanency, a continuing on-going influence that can build toward accomplishment of vision (a la Ephesians 4:7ff, Christ's

COMMENTARY ON LEADER CONTINUED

gifts to the church for leadership). I am talking about people who have a sense, inherent or instilled, of responsibility to carry out some aspect of God's work and to give an account to God for others. This sense of vertical accountability differentiates *casual leadership* from *permanent on-going leadership*. Those who do not have this sense of accountability are basically followers.

calling
and
leadership

Leaders need a strong sense of destiny. A call is one manifestation of that but not the only one. Even without a supernatural call the stewardship model can provide a pseudo-call to those who see the implications of the model. The model, itself, is enough to give one a sense of destiny toward leadership. If God has given capacity, then inherent in it is the destiny to use it. Leadership giftedness, itself, can be a means of awareness toward a destiny.

LEADERSHIP

introduction	Leadership is essentially the ongoing persistence of leadership acts by one person. One who consistently exerts influence over a group is said to manifest leadership. Leadership is then seen to be an ongoing process involving several complex items.
definition	Leadership is a dynamic process over an extended period of time in various situations in which a leader utilizing leadership resources, and by specific leadership behaviors, influences followers, toward accomplishment of aims mutually beneficial for leaders and followers.
example	Barnabas' leadership: Acts 4:32-36; 9:26-30; 11:22-24; 11:25-26; 15:1-21. Here Barnabas is seen to exercise influence in various situations over a long period of time. He used various resource means to accomplish this influence.
example	Paul's leadership (a few leadership acts cited): Acts 11:25,26; 13:9-12; 13:13-43; 13:44-48; 14:21-23; 20:17-38.
comment	The major items in the leadership process include:

1. It is a dynamic process over an extended period of time.

2. It is exercised in various situations.

3. It is identified with a leader, one who persists in exercising influence.

4. It involves the use of leadership resources which include various power bases for influencing.

5. It is seen overtly in leadership behaviors which contribute to the influence process.

6. Its nature is seen as motivating followers so that the group responds differently than would be the case without the influence.

7. It is seen as purposeful (directive). That is, influence which moves followers, toward accomplishment of aims which may originate with the leader, the followers, or some combination of both.

8. Ideally, it results in mutual benefit for the leader, the followers, and the situation of which they are a part.

comment	Point eight is an ideal not always seen in secular leadership.

FEEDBACK ON LEADERSHIP

1. I have stated in the examples that Barnabas exercised leadership. I pointed out several leadership acts: Acts 4:32-36, 9:26-30, 11:22-24, 11:25-26, 15:1-21. Do you agree? Quickly scan the biblical passages giving these leadership acts. How many of the major items of the leadership process are seen in these leadership acts examined as a whole? Check the leadership elements which you feel can be seen in these acts.

___ a. It is a dynamic process over an extended period of time.
___ b. It is exercised in various situations.
___ c. It is identified with a leader, one who persists in exercising influence.
___ d. It involves the use of leadership resources which include various power bases for influencing.
___ e. It is seen overtly in leadership behaviors which contribute to the influence process.
___ f. Its nature is seen as changing the followers thoughts and/or behavior so that the groups respond differently than would be the case without the influence.
___ g. It is seen as purposeful (directive). That is, influence which affects the thoughts and activity of followers, toward accomplishment of aims which may originate with the leader, the followers, or some combination of both.
___ h. It results in mutual benefit for the leader, the followers, and the macro context of which they are a part.

2. Take any two of the leadership elements you checked above and explain them. That is, show what you saw in scripture that prompted you to select the leadership element as being present.

3. If you were to examine an autocratic leader, Hitler, in terms of his leadership acts which of the following leadership elements most likely would not be demonstrated.

___ a. His leadership was demonstrated in various situations.
___ b. He used various power bases for influencing.
___ c. One of the overt behaviors which was tremendously effective was his public oratory.
___ d. His leadership was purposeful (directive). Influence which affected the thoughts and activity of followers, toward accomplishment of aims which were primarily his own.
___ e. It resulted in mutual benefit for the leader, the followers, and the macro context.

ANSWERS————
1. I checked all of them. "g" is least easiest to demonstrate.

2. I'll explain what I saw concerning (e) and (h). Barnabas used persuasive oratory to convince apostles to accept Saul in Acts 9:26-30. He used modeling as well as oratory to influence behavior in Acts 11:22-24. Barnabas' influence resulted in Paul being accepted as a Christian leader which significantly altered the course of history. His ministry at Antioch provided the base for cross-cultural missionary effort which began the worldwide expansion of the Gospel.

3. e. My opinion of course.

3 GENERAL LEADERSHIP FUNCTIONS

introduction   High level Christian leaders perform many leadership functions. In addition to direct ministry functions based on giftedness there are those additional functions that are the responsibility of leaders simply because they are people of responsibility for others. The inspirational functions are part of this added responsibility of Christian leaders. Note that the giftedness of the leader, that is, the direct ministry functions can occur in any of the three major categories. In the commentary which follows I will suggest that certain giftedness correlates to one or more of these major functions.

description   **Leadership functions** describe general activities that leaders must do and/or be responsible for in their influence responsibilities with followers.

description   **Consideration functions,** (relational behaviors) are those things leaders do to provide an atmosphere congenial to accomplishment of work, affirmation of persons, and development of persons.

description   **Initiation of structure functions,** (task behaviors) are those things leaders do to focus on accomplishing the organization's mission such as clarifying goals, forming organizational units, and holding people accountable for achieving.

description   **Inspirational functions** are those leadership activities that leaders do to motivate people to work together and to accomplish the ends of the organization.

comment   Leadership Research at Ohio State during the years, 1948-1967 reduced the many observed functions of secular leadership by factor analysis to two major generic categories: consideration and initiation of structure.

comment   *Consideration* is the Ohio State term which groups all of those activities which a leader does to affirm followers, to provide an atmosphere congenial to accomplishing work, to give emotional and spiritual support for followers so that they can mature, in short, *to act relationally* with followers in order to enable them to develop and be effective in their contribution to the organization. We will popularize this function's name to *relational behaviors.*

comment   *Initiation of structure* is the Ohio State term which groups all of those activities which a leader does to accomplish the task or vision for which the group exists. We will popularize this function's name to *task behaviors.* Task behaviors involve clarifying goals, setting up structures to help reach them, holding people accountable, disciplining where necessary and in short, to act responsibly to accomplish goals.

comment   Christian leadership is externally directed. God's touch on a life is what motivates such a leader. And such a leader in turn *inspires* followership because of that external direction from God. That is a major unique difference between secular leadership and spiritual leadership. That is, leadership goals result from vision from God. That kind of leadership, *inspirational leadership,* must move followers toward recognition of, acceptance of, and participation in bringing about that God-given vision or those goals.

LISTING THE THREE LEADERSHIP FUNCTIONS

Consideration Functions (relationship behaviors)
Christian leaders,
1. must continually be involved in knowing their *people* so that the selection, development, and release of emerging leaders occurs.
2. are continually called upon to solve crises which involve relationships between *people*.
3. will be called upon for decision making focusing on *people*.
4. must do routine *people* related problem solving.
5. will coordinate with *people* including subordinates, peers, and superiors.
6. must facilitate *people* into leadership tasks, roles, functions—that is, make sure transition happens; their own and others.
7. must do direct ministry relating to *people* (extent depends on giftedness).

Initiation of Structure Functions (task behaviors)
Christian leaders,
1. must provide *structures* which facilitate accomplishment of vision, that is, there must organization of units and allocation of tasks to them to realize the vision,
2. will be involved in crisis resolution which hinders achievement and is brought about due to *structural* issues—either poor organization or lack of it.
3. will do routine problem solving concerning *structural* issues.
4. will adjust *structures* where necessary to facilitate leadership transitions.
5. must do direct ministry relating maintaining and changing *structures* (extent depends on giftedness).

Inspirational Functions (motivating toward following God)
Christian leaders,
1. must *motivate* followers toward vision.
2. must *encourage* perseverance and faith of followers.
3. are responsible for the *corporate integrity* of the structures and organizations of which they are a part.
4. are responsible for developing and maintaining the *welfare* of the corporate culture of the organization.
5. (especially higher level) are responsible for promoting the *public image* of the organization.
6. (especially higher level) are responsible for the *financial welfare* of the organization.
7. are responsible for direct ministry along lines of giftedness which relate to inspirational functions.
8. must model (knowing, being, and doing) so as to inspire followers toward the reality of God's intervention in lives.
9. have *corporate accountability* to God for the organizations in which they operate.

FEEDBACK ON LEADERSHIP FUNCTIONS

1. The two Ohio State behavioral functions of consideration and initiation of structure are commonly referred to in the leadership concentration as relational behavior and task behavior. The Ohio State findings indicated that the two were independent of each other. That is, a given leader could operate freely in both functional areas. Fiedler (1967) and others generally disagreed and posited that leaders usually are bent toward one or the other as dominant in their leadership. What has been your experience? Are leaders in your culture generally task oriented or relationally oriented or some combination? Explain.

2. Give here the name of a leader that you have known who is highly task oriented. Give also an example of a task which has driven this leader.

    a. leader—

    b. cultural origin—

    c. culture ministering in—

    d. illustration of task—

3. Give here the name of a leader that you have known who is relationally oriented. Give an example of relational behavior from that leader's ministry.

    a. leader—

    b. cultural origin—

    c. culture ministering in—

    d. illustration of relational behavior—

4. Give here the name of a leader that you have known who operates well in the inspirational functions. Identify a specific inspirational function and illustrate it.

    a. leader—

    b. cultural origin—

    c. culture ministering in—

    d. illustration of inspirational function—

ANSWERS————

1.   In my culture I have experienced a mix of both although task behavior seems to be more valued and espoused by leadership in general. In the West Indies I found the reverse was more generally true. In either case leaders were not usually both task and relational—one usually dominated to the detriment of the other.

2. your choice. 3. your choice. 4. your choice.

COMMENTARY ON LEADERSHIP FUNCTIONS

essentials   There are common activities and unique activities for the three categories of leadership functions. Listing them in a single list helps identify the essential activities of Christian leaders.

1. Utilize their giftedness for direct ministry for all those within their sphere of influence.
2. Solve crises.
3. Make decisions.
4. Do routine problem solving.
5. Coordinate people, goals, and structures.
6. Select and develop leaders.
7. Facilitate leadership transition (adjustments with people and structures) at all levels.
8. Facilitate structures to accomplish vision.
9. Motivate followers toward vision. This usually involves changing what is, and providing/ promoting a sense of progress.
10. Must encourage perseverance and faith of followers by maintaining what is and creating a sense of stability. This is usually in dynamic tension with activity 9.
11. Accept responsibility for corporate functions of integrity, culture, finances, and accountability.
12. Must inspire followers toward the reality of God's intervention in lives and history.

direct versus indirect   Direct ministry involves ministry which produces growth such as evangelism (quantitative growth) or teaching (qualitative growth). Usually the word gifts (apostleship, prophesy, evangelism, pastoring, teaching, exhortation) are thought of as involving primarily direct ministry. Indirect ministry involves activities which enable direct ministry to happen. While it is true that most of the activities on the condensed list above involve both direct and indirect ministry it is also true that the larger majority are dominantly indirect. As leaders move along the Typology continuum1 they will increasingly be involved in more indirect ministry and will embrace it as primary because of their understanding of capacity entrusted them. The enablement of others to do direct ministry is the thrust of indirect ministry. This means creating and keeping healthy organizations and structures through which it can happen.

gifts and major leadership functions   Certain spiritual gifts tend toward realization of one or more of the major leadership functions. Apostleship, evangelism, and prophecy tend to correlate with task functions. They also relate to inspirational functions. Pastoring tends to relate to relational functions as do mercy and helps and sometimes governments. Teaching can go both ways. Inspirational functions, except as noted above, tend to be related more to natural abilities or even acquired skills. That is, people with various gifts can inspire if they have certain inherent natural abilities or have picked up skills to carry out inspirational functions.

---

1 The typology continuum is a linear listing from smaller influence to larger influence which identifies 5 types of leaders: Type A and B which refer to local church influence (inward and outward); Type C, full time leadership influencing a whole local church or a whole region influenced by that church; Type D, large regional or national influence; Type E, international influence. On the typology continuum the move from Type B to C involves a shift toward indirect ministry. The shift from C to D is a major shift toward indirect ministry. Processing which develops a leader for these shifts focuses on the first two elements of the leader definition—capacity and responsibility.

4 BIBLICAL LEADERSHIP MODELS

introduction   More New Testament philosophical models may exist, but the following four models
are the most important ones noted in Christian literature. These models are not ex-
haustively treated in one unified source in the New Testament. Much of the descriptive
analysis comes as much from observations of practice of New Testament leaders as
from explanatory passages. The diagram below relates the various models in terms of
foundational and superstructural issues. It also relates the superstructural with gifts.
The framework is built on a premise that foundational models have more widespread
application, while superstructural models apply less widely. The foundational models
apply to all leaders. The superstructural models apply somewhat to all leaders but more
specifically to certain gifted leaders.

FOUR BIBLICAL LEADERSHIP MODELS

Gifts: Apostleship   Pastoral
                Evangelism   Teaching
                Faith   Governments
                            Exhortation
                            Prophecy
                            Leadership

Harvest Model	Shepherd Model
(applies to some leaders)	(applies to some leaders)
Outward thrust of the	Inward trust of the
Great Commission	Great Commission
Based on giftedness.	Based on giftedness.

Servant Model
(applies to all leaders)
Based on Biblical leadership values.

Stewardship Model
(applies to every Christian)
Based on Biblical values for each believer.

MINISTRY PHILOSOPHY MODEL
THE STEWARDSHIP MODEL   SYNONYM: ACCOUNTABILITY MODEL

introduction   Ministry philosophy refers to a related set of values that underlies a leader's perception and behavior in his/her ministry. The values may be ideas, principles, guidelines or the like which are implicit (not actually recognized but part of perceptive set of the leader) or explicit (recognized, identified, articulated). For any given leader a ministry philosophy is unique. It is dynamic and related to three major elements: Biblical dynamics, giftedness, and situation. Though a ministry philosophy is dynamic there are core issues which are stable and apply to all leaders. The stewardship model is one such set of stable Biblical values.

definition   *Ministry philosophy* refers to ideas, values, and principles whether implicit or explicit which a leader uses as guidelines for decision making, for exercising influence, and for evaluating his/her ministry.

definition   *The stewardship model* is a philosophical model which is founded on the central thrust of several accountability passages, that is, that a leader must give account of his/her ministry to God.

passages   Accountability parables: Matthew 20 Laborers in the Vineyard, Matthew 24 The Waiting Servants, Matthew 25 The Ten Virgins, Matthew 25 The Ten Talents, Luke 16 The Worldly Wise Steward, Luke 19 The Pounds.

General Judgment Passages: Romans 14:11,12, I Corinthians 3:5-9,12-15, II Corinthians 5:10, Philippians 2:10,11, Hebrews 9:27.

Special Leadership Responsibility: James 3:1, Daniel 12:1-3, Hebrews 13:17.

Other Passages Indicating Accountability/ Rewards: I Corinthians 4:1-5, II Corinthians 4:1-6, Acts 20:17-38, I Peter 5:1-4.

BASIC VALUES

1. Ministry challenges, tasks, and assignments ultimately come from God.
2. God holds a leader accountable for leadership influence and for growth and conduct of followers.
3. There will be an ultimate accounting of a leader to God in eternity for one's performance in leadership.
4. Leaders will receive rewards for faithfulness to their ministry in terms of abilities, skills, gifts and opportunities.
5. Leaders are expected to build upon abilities, skills, and gifts to maximize potential and use for God.
6. Leaders will be uniquely gifted both as to gifts and the degree to which the gift can be used effectively.
7. Leaders will receive rewards for their productivity and for zealously using abilities, skills, gifts, and opportunities for God.
8. Leaders frequently must hold to higher standards than followers due to "the above reproach" and modeling impact they must have on followers.

IMPLICATIONS

1. Leaders must maintain a learning posture all of their lives—growing, expanding, developing.
2. Leaders must make certain of ministry tasks, challenges, and assignments in terms of God's guidance (calling) for them.
3. Leaders must perform in ministry as unto the Lord in all aspects of ministry.

comment   The Stewardship Model is the most general of the New Testament Philosophical models in that it applies to followers as well as leaders. Servant leadership applies only to leaders as does the Shepherd and Harvest Models.

FEEDBACK ON STEWARDSHIP MODEL

1. Scan the list of values for the Stewardship Model. Assess your own personal preference for these values by placing an "x" in the appropriate column for each value. (MP = my personal ministry philosophy)

values	Column 1 Does not affect MP	Column 2 Loosely Held in MP	Column 3 Definitely affects MP	Column 4 Deliberately used and vital to MP
1.				
2.				
3.				
4.				
5.				
6.				
7.				
8.				

2. What other values has God taught you that are not listed but somewhat compatible with the central thrust of this philosophical model?

3. For any one of the values in exercise 1 for which you checked the right most column (deliberately used and vital to my personal ministry philosophy) suggest implications of this value for your ministry.

    Value Number   Implication for Me:

4. Which of the values or implications of this model do you think God is impressing upon you, especially at this time in your life, to learn more about or apply more definitely in your life?

ANSWERS————
1. all of mine are column 4.
2. your choice.
3. Value 8. Implication: Particularly in disputed practices I must sometimes forego a Christian liberty for the benefit of others. That is, I must adhere to a more strict standard than I think is Biblical. This is necessary because my actions as a leader are constantly under scrutiny by followers and may be harmful to a weaker brother.
4. Values 1 and 7.

The Servant Leader Model

introduction — Ministry philosophy refers to a related set of values that underlies a leader's perception and behavior in his/her ministry. The values may be ideas, principles, guidelines or the like. Each Christian leader will have a unique ministry philosophy that generally differs from others due to values God has taught experientially. But there will be some items in common with other leaders. The Servant Leader Model provides a set of values that should be common to the ministry philosophy of each Christian leader. Its central thrust says in essence that a leader's main focus is to use leadership to serve God by serving followers. A leader is great whose leadership capacities are used in service vertically to God and horizontally to followers.

definition — The servant leader model is a philosophical model which is founded on the central thrust of Jesus' teaching on the major quality of great Kingdom leaders. That is, a leader uses leadership to serve followers. This is demonstrated in Jesus' own ministry.

passages — Matthew 20:20-28, Mark 10:35-45.

secondary passages — Parable of the Waiting Servant—Matthew 24:42-51, Luke 12:35-40, 41-48 Parable of the Unprofitable Servant—Luke 17:7-10. Isaiah's suffering Servant—Isaiah 52:13-53:12.

Basic Values

1. Leadership is exercised primarily as service first of all to God and secondarily as service to God's people.
2. Service will require sacrifice on the leader's part.
3. Servant leadership is dominated by an imitation modeling leadership style. That is, the dominant form of influence is modeling for the followers and setting expectancies for them to do the same.
4. Abuse of authority, Lording it over followers in order to demonstrate one's importance, is incompatible with servant leadership.
5. A major motivational issue for leadership is anticipation of the Lord's return.
6. One ministers as a duty expected because of giftedness. Hence, there is no expectancy or demand or coercion for remuneration—no demanding one's due.

Implications

1. A servant leader does not demand rights or expect others to see him/her as one with special privileges and status.
2. A servant leader can expect God to give ministry affirmation and does not demand it from followers.
3. A servant leader expects to sacrifice. Personal desires, personal time, and personal financial security will frequently be overridden by needs of service in ministry.
4. The dominant leadership style to be cultivated is imitation modeling. While there is a place for other more authoritarian styles this style will dominate.
5. Spiritual authority, with its earned credibility, will be the dominant element of one's power-mix.
6. Leadership functions are performed always with a   watchful spirit anticipating the Lord's return.
7. Finances will not dominate decision making with regard to acceptance of ministry.

comment — Balance is important, for the servant leader must lead and must serve. The servant leader must maintain a dynamic tension by recognizing Butt's (1975) assertion that a leader leads by serving and serves by leading.

comment — The servanthood Model is a general leadership model applying to all leaders.

FEEDBACK ON THE SERVANT LEADER

1. Scan the list of values for the Servant Leader Model. Assess your own personal preference for these values by placing an "x" in the appropriate column for each value. (MP = my personal ministry philosophy)

values	Column 1 Does not affect MP	Column 2 Loosely Held in MP	Column 3 Definitely affects MP	Column 4 Deliberately used and vital to MP
1.				
2.				
3.				
4.				
5.				
6.				

2. What other values has God taught you that are not listed but somewhat compatible with the central thrust of this philosophical model?

3. For any one of the values in exercise 1 for which you checked the right most column (deliberately used and vital to my personal ministry philosophy) suggest implications of this value for your ministry.

Value   Implication for Me:

4. Which of the values or implications of this model do you think God is impressing upon you especially at this time to learn more about or apply more definitely in your life?

ANSWERS————

1. Column 1 = value 5. Column 2 = values 2, 6. Column 3 = value 1. Column 4 = values 3, 4.
2. Your choice.
3. Value 3—I must deliberately use what happens in my life (positive and negative lessons) as a means towards influencing my students.
4. In reviewing the values and implications for this model I have been impressed by how little the Servant Model has affected my leadership. There is much improvement for me in making the values and implications of this model real for me.

THE SHEPHERD LEADER MODEL

introduction	Each Christian leader will have a unique ministry philosophy that generally differs from others due to values God has taught experientially. Leaders whose giftedness and calling line up with the central function of the Shepherd Leader Model will find that its values are enmeshed in their own unique ministry philosophy. Leaders not so gifted may or may not have had shaping experiences imparting these particular ministry philosophy values. In any case the values are worth evaluation. Shepherd leaders tend to have a leadership style bent which is fundamentally relational in nature.
definition	The shepherd leader model is a philosophical model which is founded on the central thrust of Jesus' own teaching and modeling concerning the responsibilities of leadership in caring for followers as seen in the various Shepherd/ Sheep metaphors in scripture.
central thrust	Its central thrust is concern and care for the welfare of followers—that is, growth and development in the Kingdom so that they know God's rule in their lives and hence bring God's righteousness in society. This model is concerned primarily with the inward aspects of the Great Commission—teach them to obey all that I have commanded.
primary passages	Matthew 28:19,20, Great Commission, Inward Aspect. Matthew 9:36,37 Shepherd Aspect of the Analogy. Matthew 18:12 Parable of Lost Sheep, Luke 15:1-7 Parable of Lost Sheep. John 10:1-18 The Good Shepherd, John 21:15-17 Feed My Sheep. I Peter 5:1-4 Peter's View, Shepherd Leadership. Acts 20:17-38 Paul's View, Watching for the Flock.
archetypes	Peter and Barnabas are significant examples of shepherd leaders.

VALUES

1. Shepherd leaders value personal kingdom growth in each follower. That is, they have a strong desire to see realization of kingdom truth in followers that is, they have a drive to see followers increasingly experiencing the rule of God in their lives. (Matthew 28:20, John 21, Acts 20)
2. Shepherd leaders have a strong empathy with followers which seeks to assess where they are and to help meet their needs in order to develop them toward their potential for the kingdom. (Matthew 9:36,37)
3. Shepherd leaders value each follower as important to the whole body and want to keep them incorporated in the body. (Acts 20:28 Luke 15:1-7, Matthew 18:12,13)
4. Shepherd leaders value a personal relationship with followers. (John 10:3, 4, 14)
5. Shepherd leaders give personal guidance to followers by setting examples—particularly in the area of kingdom values. They value the importance of imitation modeling as an influence means with followers. (John 10:4)
6. Shepherd leaders protect followers from deviant teaching by giving positive truth that will aid them in assessing counterfeit teaching. (John 10:5, 10, 12 Acts 20:28)
7. Shepherd leaders want followers to experience abundant life in Christ. (John 10:10)
8. Shepherd leaders are willing to sacrifice and know that personal desires, personal time, and personal financial security will frequently be overridden by needs of service in ministry. (John 10:11)
9. Shepherd leaders are willing to persevere through persecution or hard times in order to better the condition of followers. (John 10:11)
10. Shepherd leaders transparently expose weaknesses, strengths and their heart with followers. (John 10:14)
11. Shepherd leaders value unity in body and wider body. (John 10:16)
12. Shepherd leaders willingly take responsibility for followers. (I Peter 5:2)
13. Financial gain is secondary to performing ministry in the values of a Shepherd leader. I Peter 5:2)

comment	Gift-mixes of leaders which correlate strongly with the Shepherd Leader model include the various combinations of: the word gifts of pastor and teaching; the love gifts of mercy and helps and governments; the power gifts of healing and word of wisdom.
comment	The word gifts of prophecy and exhortation and leadership can operate with both Shepherd and Harvest leader models.

FEEDBACK ON SHEPHERD MODEL

1.   Scan the list of values for the Shepherd Model. Assess your own personal preference for these values by placing an "x" in the appropriate column for each value. (MP = my personal ministry philosophy)

values	Column 1 Does not affect MP	Column 2 Loosely Held in MP	Column 3 Definitely affects MP	Column 4 Deliberately used and vital to MP
1.				
2.				
3.				
4.				
5.				
6.				
7.				
8.				
9.				
10.				
11.				
12.				
13.				

2.   Suggest one or two implications that in your opinion are necessitated if one is to hold these values with a high preference.

3.   Is God impressing a need for you to learn more about or apply more definitely in your life one or more of the values or implications of this model? If so which?

ANSWERS————
1.   No Column 1 entries. Column 2 = values 3, 6, 9, 13. Column 3 = values 8, 11. Column 4 = values 1, 2, 4, 5, 7, 10, 12.
2.   Implication of value 10: Leaders must share openly of God's processing in their lives. Implication of Value 4 (in my culture): Leaders must be on a first name basis with as many followers as practical.
3.   Value 7 has been reaffirmed for me. Just this summer God gave a special word to me on this.

HARVEST MODEL

introduction   Ministry philosophy refers to a related set of values that underlies a leader's perception and behavior in his/her ministry. The values may be ideas, principles, guidelines or the like. Each Christian leader will have a unique ministry philosophy that generally differs from others due to values God has taught experientially. Leaders whose giftedness and calling line up with the central function of the Harvest Leader Model will find that its values are enmeshed in their own unique ministry philosophy. Leaders not so gifted may or may not have been shaped toward these particular ministry values. In any case the values are worth evaluation. Harvest leaders tend to have a leadership style bent which is fundamentally task oriented in nature.

definition   The harvest leader model is a philosophical model founded on the central thrust of Jesus' teaching to expand the Kingdom by winning new members into it as demonstrated in the agricultural metaphors of growth in scripture.

central   Its central concern is with expansion of Kingdom so as to bring new members
thrust   into the Kingdom as forcefully commanded in the outward aspect of the Great Commission—Go ye into all the world and make disciples of all people groups.

primary   Matthew 28:19,20: Great Commission—Outward Aspect. (See also Mark
passages   16:15, Luke 24:46,47, John 20:21, Acts 1:8).
                 Kingdom Growth Parables:
                        Matthew 13:24-30 Tares.
                        Matthew 13:31,32 Mustard Seed; Mark 4:30-32 Mustard Seed.
                        Matthew 13:33-35 Leaven; Luke 13:33-35 Leaven.
                        Mark 4:26-29 Mysterious Growth of Seed.
                        Sending Passage: Luke 10:1-12 Sending of 70.

archetype   Paul is the archetype of a harvest leader in the New Testament.

VALUES

1.   Harvest leaders have a strong concern for those outside the kingdom and want to give them a choice to hear and enter the kingdom. (Great Commission Passages)
2.   Harvest leaders have a strong desire to motivate followers to take the kingdom message to others. (Luke 10:1-12)
3.   Harvest leaders have a strong concern for power in ministry—they know the value of power to gain a hearing for the gospel of the kingdom. (Matthew 28:20, Mark 16:16,17, Luke 24:49, Acts 1:8)
4.   Harvest leaders are more concerned with the ultimate destiny of those outside the kingdom than the present state of those in the kingdom. (Matthew 28:19 emphasis on outward not inward)
5.   Harvest leaders recognize that Kingdom expansion means will not always sift out the real from the unreal but know that ultimately there will be resolution. (Matthew 13:24-30)
6.   Harvest leaders by and large exercise faith. They believe God will accomplish His expansion work and hence are not afraid of small beginnings. (Matthew 13:31,32, Mark 4:30-32)
7.   Harvest leaders recognize the evangelistic mandate as taking priority over the cultural mandate since the cultural mandate will require large numbers before impact on a non-kingdom society can be made. (Matthew 13:33-35, Luke 13:20-21)
8.   Harvest leaders value receptivity testing in order to discover movements of God. (Mark 4:26-29)

comment   Gift-mixes which correlate strongly with the Harvest Leader model include the various combinations of: the word gifts of apostle, faith, evangelist; the love gifts of mercy; the power gifts of healing, miracles, word of knowledge.

Feedback On Harvest Model

1. Scan the list of values for the Harvest Model. Assess your own personal preference for these values by placing an "x" in the appropriate column for each value. (MP = my personal ministry philosophy)

values	Column 1 Does not affect MP	Column 2 Loosely Held in MP	Column 3 Definitely affects MP	Column 4 Deliberately used and vital to MP
1.				
2.				
3.				
4.				
5.				
6.				
7.				
8.				

2. What other values has God taught you that are not listed but somewhat compatible with the central thrust of this philosophical model?

3. Suggest one or two implications that in your opinion are necessitated if one is to hold these values with a high preference.

4. Is God impressing a need for you to learn more about or apply more definitely in your life one or more of the values or implications of this model? If so which?

ANSWERS————

1. Column 1 = value 4. Column 2 = values 1, 2, 3, 6. Column 3 = value 7, 8. Column 4 = value 5 (Used in a negative way. I am vitally concerned with the sifting process. My strong bias to the Shepherd Leader Model makes me want to assess genuineness of those professing to be in the kingdom.)
2. Your choice.
3. If one held value 8 on receptivity high then that person would by necessity do studies in futurology—future trends, since receptivity is often correlated with various trends.
4. Your choice. For me—No, I don't think so.

NOTION OF DEVELOPMENT INHERENT IN THE ACCOUNTABILITY PARABLES

We want to take a look at two specific parables because of their importance to the subject of giftedness and giftedness development. The Stewardship model has the following values. Note especially values 4, 5, 6, and 7 which relate to awareness of giftedness and development of same.

1. Ministry challenges, tasks, and assignments ultimately come from God.
2. God holds a leader accountable for leadership influence and for growth and conduct of followers.
3. There will be an ultimate accounting of a leader to God in eternity for one's performance in leadership.
√ 4. Leaders will receive rewards for faithfulness to their ministry in terms of abilities, skills, gifts and opportunities.
√ 5. Leaders are expected to build upon abilities, skills, and gifts to maximize potential and use for God.
√ 6. Leaders will be uniquely gifted both as to gifts and the degree to which the gift can be used effectively.
√ 7. Leaders will receive rewards for their productivity and for zealously using abilities, skills, gifts, and opportunities for God.
8. Leaders frequently must hold to higher standards than followers due to the above reproach and modeling impact they must have on followers.

Since we are concentrating on the concept of development of leadership giftedness these values are extremely important. Perhaps we should examine in depth two major parables from which these values are drawn.

Jesus often taught by using parables. Nearly 50% of His teaching comes to us in parabolic forms. A parable is a true to life narrative which teaches a central truth by using one or more comparisons. We are going to look at two parables which have to do with accountability because they form the biblical basis for motivating our study of giftedness. Most of us are familiar with these two parables already but we feel that they deserve a closer look because together they provide a clear picture of accountability.

Remember that a parable is a true-to-life story which teaches a central truth by use of one or more comparisons. It is the central truth that we are after. The whole parable is given to illustrate that central truth with impact. To interpret a parable one carefully observes the observable elements: setting, story, sequel. Having done, so one can identify the comparisons between story elements and the actual life setting as well as identify the central truth which usually is identified with the punch of the story. And we must remember that not all points in the story are comparisons. Some are needed to make the story complete.

Once we have identified the central truth we can then explore its implications for application to other life settings as well as the Biblical context in which it occurred.

THE PARABLE OF THE TALENTS: MATTHEW 25:14-30

Setting: This parable occurs in a series of interconnected parables which are explaining what
                Jesus' expectations were for his followers in the interim between his resurrection and
                His second coming. This parable is given to motivate the disciples to minister during
                the time before the second coming.

Story: The lord of the house was going to leave on a long trip. He left varying amounts of
                resources with 3 of his servants. One was left 5 talents, another 2 talents and another 1
                talent. They were to manage his property until he returned from his trip. When he
                returned from his trip, he called the servants to settle accounts with him. The one with
                five talents had earned 5 more. He was blessed by his master. The one with two talents
                earned 2 more. He was blessed by his master. The third servant returned the one talent
                to his master. He didn't invest it for fear of losing it. He was rebuked by his master and
                thrown out.

Comparisons:

lord of the household	= Christ
leaving home on a trip	= Jesus going away to heaven
3 servants	= kingdom followers
5 talent servant	= person with large resources
2 talent servant	= person with less resources
1 talent servant	= person with relatively small resources
another country	= heaven or eternity
talents	= total resources: opportunity, abilities, gifts, influence, power, time, etc. That is, anything that a person has which can be used for the Kingdom
coming back	= 2nd coming
settling accounts	= time of judgment or a time of accountability

Central truth:

You should recognize that you will be held accountable and rewarded on the basis of your service according to your faithfulness as it relates to your own gifts, abilities, and opportunities and not in terms of comparison with others.

Or another way to say it.

You wise kingdom followers must recognize your accountability for I will reward you at my second coming on the basis of service rendered according to your faithfulness to your gifts, abilities, and opportunities, and in terms of equal rewards for equal faithfulness.

Four Implications of this parable:
1)   Don't compare your giftedness with others.
2)   Don't be envious of someone else's giftedness.
3)   Be faithful to what God has given you; God never expects out of us more than we are capable of
        doing.
4)   The major basis of rewards is your faithfulness. Productivity is important but is secondary. If you
        are faithful in your efforts, you will normally be productive.
5)   You will be held accountable for your giftedness and its development to maximum potential.

THE PARABLE OF THE GOLD COINS: LUKE 19:1-27

Setting: The story of Zaccheus just precedes this parable. This parable is given to correct the notion that the Kingdom of God was going to appear immediately. Jesus was giving this parable to encourage his hearers to work hard.

Story: There was a man of high rank who was going on a trip to be made king and then he was going to return home. Before he left he called ten of his servants in and gave them each a gold coin. He instructed them to see what they could earn with it. When he returned he settled accounts with the servants. Three servants report to the king. One had earned 10 more gold coins, one had earned 5 more gold coins and one returned the one gold coin that he had been given. The first two servants were blessed and given rewards over cities equal to what they had earned. The third servant had his coin taken away and given to the first servant. He was rebuked.

Comparisons:

Man of high standing   = Jesus
Citizens who detested him   = Jews who were rejecting Christ
Servants   = kingdom followers
gold coin   = service opportunities
king returning   = the second coming of Jesus
settling of accounts   = judgment or accountability

Central truth:

My kingdom is not coming right away. Do not lose heart in your service for I expect you to take advantage of opportunities to serve in the kingdom with zeal. I will reward you according to your zealous efforts and your results.

Implications of this parable:

1.   All believers have the same chance to prove their zealousness.
2.   Results in response to the ministry opportunities are important and will be evaluated.
3.   We must use what we have to the very best of our ability.

Lessons concerning Accountability And Development

The parable of the talents stresses the concept of faithfulness. We are to be faithful with what God has given us. Each of us are given different abilities and gifts and are responsible to be faithful to what we have been given. If given more we should produce more. If given less we will produce less.

The parable of the gold coins stresses the concept of zealousness and results. Jesus expects us to take advantage of service opportunities, our abilities and gifts with a zealous attitude. We are accountable to produce tangible results before He returns.

When these parables are placed side by side, there is a certain tension that we must face in regards to accountability. On the one hand, we can take comfort that we will only be held accountable for what God has given us. He doesn't expect more out of us than we are capable of. On the other hand, the other parable stresses that fact that we are to push, learn and grow so that we can take advantage of every opportunity. We are not to be complacent. We are not to plateau in our growth. We will be held accountable to show tangible results in the ministry situation that God has given us. These two parables both point out different aspects of our accountability before God. We need to hold them in balance with one another.

Our notion of development in leadership giftedness resonates with the general teachings of these parables as related to giftedness as well as the specific teaching on development about spiritual gifts given in Romans 12.

Summary

In this chapter, we have set out to describe some basic leadership concepts which influence our understanding of development as well as articulate what leaders are to do as they influence followers. These basic leadership definitions and concepts have come out of our research on leadership. They provide the background as we come to the issue of giftedness and its development. Giftedness is a major component of the God-given capacity which leaders use to exercise influence among their followers. The generic leadership functions describe the basic activities that leaders do as they influence their followers. It is in the context of these activities that giftedness is exercised.

We have also articulated 4 basic leadership philosophical models that have emerged from our study of leadership in the Bible. These models provide the philosophical motivation behind our approach to giftedness and its development. This is especially true of the Stewardship Model. The stewardship model applies to every leader and teaches us that we, as leaders will be accountable to God for our life and our leadership in His Kingdom. This accountability will be measured in different ways. Faithfulness will certainly be one measurement. The development of what God has given us is another important measurement. We are to grow, develop and mature in all that God gives us. We are to produce results in ministry which demonstrate faithfulness as well as growth. This type of accountability provides the philosophical motivation behind our approach to giftedness and its development.

We have also implied that certain spiritual gifts are in harmony with the shepherd model and the harvest model. People having these gifts will naturally be drawn to the values inherent in the given model whether or not the model or gifts are actually explicitly known. Spiritual gifts of Apostleship, Evangelism, and sometimes faith are repeatedly seen to go hand-in-hand with the Harvest Model values. Pastoral, teaching and governments gifts often are reflected in those who operate strongly out of Shepherd Model values. Some gifts are swing-gifts. The word gifts of prophecy and exhortation and leadership can operate with both Harvest and Shepherd leader models.

We have sought to show that giftedness development closely relates to a number of leadership concepts. In a later chapter we will talk about identify of giftedness. May we suggest that you take a closer look at your answers to the feedback exercises for Harvest and Shepherd Models. Frequently, these feedbacks, especially question 1, have helped people identify spiritual gifts they have. Where the values of a model are dominant in your experience and attitude it is most likely true that the gifts that go along with that model as we have identified them are probably yours too.

For Further Study

Three helpful books on Harvest Model values include Wagner's **Leading Your Church To Growth, Church Growth** and **The Whole Gospel** and Alan Tippett's **Verdict Theology in Missionary Thought.**

CHAPTER 3:
BASIC GIFTEDNESS CONCEPTS

INTRODUCTION

This chapter introduces you to the overall framework for understanding giftedness and its development. Chapter 1 was motivational. You should learn about giftedness! It is important to leaders—for a number of reasons! But is it Biblical?! Chapter 2 says emphatically, yes! It laid the Biblical and philosophical framework for the importance of giftedness and its development. Now this chapter gives the key definitions involved in giftedness—what it is and the basic patterns for how it develops.

Remember in chapter 1 we said that we will make a distinction between spiritual gifts and giftedness? Well, this is the chapter that does that. This is a crucial distinction for leaders who want to develop and want to help others develop.[1] What are the basic concepts which shape our understanding of giftedness? There are several:

- the general notion of the giftedness set (p. 40),
- the giftedness awareness continuum (p. 42),
- the focal element of the giftedness set (p. 44),
- the notion of gift-mix (p. 46),
- the notion of gift-cluster (p. 46),
- the processes through which a leader discovers giftedness (p. 51),
- the standard pattern describing this discovery and development of giftedness (p. 53),
- the giftedness time-line, the method for displaying ones discovery and development (p. 55),
- several patterns (like-attracts-like, complementary giftedness need, giftedness drift, forced role/ gift enablement) which help leaders pinpoint identification of gifts (p. 59-62).

These concepts will give the overall framework within which we will work.[2] Later chapters will give details of each of these important concepts. This chapter will introduce them.

By the time you complete this chapter you should be able to relate these concepts generally to your own personal situation. That is, you should generally be aware of your own giftedness set and which element is focal. You should be comfortable in recognizing God's enabling of your endowments—whether natural, acquired, or spiritual gifts. You should be familiar with the way giftedness develops over a lifetime. You won't have constructed your own giftedness developmental time-line yet (but you will be rarIng to do so) since you need more detailed information. But you will later.

---

[1] This is so philosophically since we hold a presupposition that **ministry flows out of being** and that God has **created each of us uniquely** (i.e. special beings) for His special purposes (Ephesians 2:10). We can better take advantage of our uniqueness, the being that we are, when we describe it in terms of the giftedness set—the whole range of endowments which include natural abilities, acquired skills, and spiritual gifts.

[2] These concepts have been derived from our observations of many leader's history of giftedness development. Don't be afraid of the new terminology. It flows from real life experience. Though they seem complicated at first, they will be easily learned because they relate to real experience and give pegs to hang things on which you will have experienced and seen. You will get some *aha* flashes as you read and study these labels.

THE GIFTEDNESS SET[3]

introduction   Because our thinking is shaped by our understanding of the stewardship model, we recognize that we will have to be accountable to God for everything that He has entrusted to us. Accountability will be measured in part by our faithfulness, our growth and development and the results of our ministry. The giftedness set takes into account the three components that make up the set: natural abilities, acquired skills, and spiritual gifts.

definition   *The Giftedness Set* refers to the threefold collection of giftedness elements: natural abilities, acquired skills, and spiritual gifts.

definition   *Natural abilities* refer to those capacities, skills, talents or aptitudes which are *innate* in a person and allow him/her to accomplish things.

examples   analytical bent, persevering attitude, relational aptitude

definition   *Acquired skills* refer to those capacities, skills, talents or aptitudes which have been *learned* by a person in order to allow him/her to accomplish something.

example   writing, oral motivational skills, frameworks for thinking and analysis

definition   A *spiritual gift* is a *God-given* unique capacity imparted to each believer for the purpose of releasing a Holy Spirit empowered ministry via that believer.

example   discernings of spirits, kinds of healings, teaching, exhortation, prophecy

comment   Natural abilities may be reflected in a spiritual gift. That is, a spiritual gift may relate to or be based on a previously recognized natural ability. The Holy Spirit releases the gift through the individual in such a way that his/her natural ability is enhanced with the power of the Spirit.

comment   Acquired skills often act as enhancements to either natural abilities and/or spiritual gifts. It is in the area of acquired skills that we can focus our growth and development efforts. Once we begin to identify our natural abilities and spiritual gifts, we can be intentional about learning skills that we need in order to enhance our effectiveness.

comment   Sometimes there may be no direct correlation between natural abilities and spiritual gifts, e.g. a person prior to conversion and empowerment by the Holy Spirit may have had no teaching bent but subsequently begins to teach with power. Sometimes it is difficult to say whether something is natural or acquired or some combination of both. The giftedness awareness continuum helps us relate natural abilities, acquired skills, and spiritual gifts.

comment   Each of these elements of the giftedness set, natural abilities, acquired skills, and spiritual gifts will be defined with much more detail in chapters which follow. They are simply introduced here so that you will catch the notion of the giftedness set.

---

[3] A set is a mathematical concept describing a collection of items. The essential question about sets is, "Does something belong to a set or not?" We will use this notion of set a number of times.

FEEDBACK ON GIFTEDNESS SET

1. Check any of the following which reflect correct teaching on giftedness.

____a.   Spiritual gifts represent the most important element in the giftedness set.

____b.   Most leaders have only one of the elements of the giftedness set.

____c.   Natural abilities never are reflected in a spiritual gift—the two are distinct.

____d.   Acquired skills often act as enhancements to either natural abilities or spiritual gifts.

____e.   None of the above were given in the teaching on giftedness.

2. Why does our approach to giftedness differ from the usual approach which focuses only on spiritual gifts?

3. Sometimes there may be no direct correlation between natural abilities and spiritual gifts and at other times there can be relationships.

    a. That is, sometimes a spiritual gift appears which seems not to fit in with the background and natural abilities of a person. Can you think of a Biblical illustration of this?

    b. Or, sometimes a spiritual gift seems to build upon a persons background and natural abilities of a person. Can you think of a Biblical illustration of this?

ANSWERS————

1. d

2. Because our thinking is shaped by our understanding of the stewardship model, we recognize that we will have to be accountable to God for everything that He has entrusted to us. Accountability will be measured in part by our faithfulness, our growth and development and the results of our ministry. The giftedness set takes into account the three components that make up the set: natural abilities, acquired skills, and spiritual gifts. Spiritual gifts are important to us too. The majority of leaders will have spiritual gifts as the focal element of their set. However, we are concerned with developing the whole person so that their ministry flows out of who they are, that is, who God made them to be.

3. a. Peter
    b. Paul

The Giftedness Awareness Continuum[4]

introduction   The stewardship philosophical model points out that we are going to answer to God for all that He has given us. Identifying the three elements of a person's giftedness set helps that person know what he/she is going to be accountable for. This continuum helps a person see that God is involved in each component of our giftedness set although we may be more aware of certain aspects than we are of other aspects. And because God is involved we can use what we have no matter where it occurs along the continuum, by faith, believing that God will empower. And we do not necessarily have to know exactly where we are on the continuum—the old is it a natural ability or acquired skill or spiritual gift question which perplexes some leaders—in order to freely use it for God.

THE GIFTEDNESS AWARENESS CONTINUUM

Spiritual Gifts	Natural Abilities	Expanded Natural Abilities	Acquired Skills

|——|

Level of Awareness of God's Involvement

<————— Increases   Decreases —————>

SOVEREIGN   PROVIDENTIAL
INTERVENTION   OVERSIGHT

comment   This continuum helps a person recognize how God superintends indirectly or intervenes more directly in the origin and use of the elements of the giftedness set. Most people can easily see how God was involved in releasing spiritual gifts but have increasing difficulty in recognizing God's involvement in their acquired skills. The application of the stewardship model allows us to more deliberately count upon God's involvement whether direct or indirect. By faith we can see God's power all along the continuum.

comment   Understanding the giftedness set and how each element interrelates is complex. There is usually overlap between the elements. Often, one element such as a spiritual gift is based on or builds on a natural ability or an acquired skill enhances or builds on a natural ability. Acquired skills often enhance natural abilities or spiritual gifts. However, it is possible to acquire skill in areas that you are not naturally gifted in or have spiritual gifts operating in. For example, I (Richard) have had to acquire skills in organization and administration because various roles that I have had required it. I am the first one to admit that I don't have natural abilities or spiritual gifts operating in this area.

---

[4] A continuum is a way of explaining and relating the notion of moving from one extreme to another extreme by a continuous movement from one to the other in which one extreme becomes less and the other becomes more. In the middle of the continuum there is some of each involved. This can be seen by analogy by a single shower head control which goes from hot to cold in a single motion. All the way counterclockwise is very hot (no cold) and all the way clockwise is very cold (no hot). As you move the handle in one direction or the other you have various degrees of hot and cold. A continuum is a both/and kind of concept rather than an either/ or concept. Along the continuum there is some of both in differing degrees. This notion of continuum is very helpful in describing a number of development concepts such as the one here—the relationship between natural abilities, acquired skills, and spiritual gifts.

Feedback On Giftedness Awareness Continuum

1. What is the significance of the word **Awareness** in the title of the continuum—*The Giftedness Awareness Continuum*? To arrive at your answer, examine again the continuum noting each item, its location, and especially the fundamental notion of the criterion for location of an item on the continuum.

2. The continuum serves two major teaching purposes in giftedness theory. Each of the comments touches on one of the reasons for the importance of the continuum in giftedness theory. Read again these two important comments. Can you summarize each of these purposes and then formulate a question which the purpose deals with?

   a. purpose 1:

   Question being answered by this purpose:

   b. purpose 2:

   Question(s) being answered by this purpose:

ANSWERS————

1. The more we are aware that God is involved in every aspect of our personal resources for ministry — the more we can authoritatively use them. In effect, by deliberately describing the continuum we are not only alerting you to God's involvement in making you who you are but we are seeking to move all of the items more to the left of the continuum so that you by faith see God's power in these resources (easily done with spiritual gifts—especially the more so-called ones, but not so easily done for some acquired skill that we learned *by ourselves*—??)

2. a. Purpose 1. (The most important one). It gives one authoritative backing for using every element of the giftedness set in a ministry for it focuses on the divine involvement.

   Question: Why should we study natural abilities and acquired skills? Aren't spiritual gifts more important, since they are God-given?

   b. Purpose 2. It releases one from the sometimes confusing pressure to identify distinctions between these elements by bypassing the questions altogether and getting to the main issue—use of giftedness not identification.

   Question: How can I tell whether something is a spiritual gift or a natural ability? or the similar question, how can I tell whether something is a natural ability or an acquired skill? The continuum says you don't have to. You may not be able to but that's all right as long as you can see that God is in it. Use it with God's backing, that's what's important.

THE FOCAL ELEMENT

introduction

As we studied various leader's giftedness sets, we discovered that each one was unique. We also discovered that usually one of the three components was more dominant that the other two. Our initial assumption about leaders and giftedness was that the spiritual gifts would be the dominant element. As we studied the giftedness sets of various leaders, we discovered that any one of the three elements could be the dominant element. We call the dominant element the focal element. It is the recognition of this dominant element and seeing the synergistic[5] relationship of the other two which truly frees up a leader to minister out of being. The giftedness set and especially the notion of the focal element are two of the most liberating concepts in all of our teaching.

definition

The *focal element* refers to the element of a person's giftedness set that is dominant and to which the other two elements operate in a supportive way which enhances the dominant element.

example

Philip Bliss, important evangelistic song leader and hymn composer during the mid 1800s--**natural abilities** were his focal element.

example

G. Campbell Morgan, leading Bible Expositor during the first half of the 20th Century—**spiritual gifts** (teaching, prophetical and exhortation) were his focal element.

example

Henry Venn, mission statesperson—19th century, **acquired skills** (organizational frameworks).

comment

It is possible to be an effective leader and have any of the three elements as the focal element. Philip Bliss who was used by God as a songwriter had **natural abilities** as the focal element. Acquired skills in music enhanced his natural musical abilities. God released the gift of exhortation and evangelism through the lyrics that he wrote. God uses other leaders whose focal element is in **acquired skills** in powerful ways. Counselors who have been trained in certain counseling methodologies often have acquired skills as their focal element. The counseling methodology, an acquired skill, usually dominates how they operate in ministry. There spiritual gifts and natural abilities will flow through that methodology. Also, leaders who have primarily administrative or organizational positions often have their acquired skills dominate how they operate in ministry. Usually they have learned certain management paradigms or tools which they use to operate in ministry.

comment

A common wrong assumption about leaders is that their spiritual gifts should dominate in their ministry. In many circles, certain spiritual gifts are required or projected on to leaders. If you are a leader, then you should be able to _____ (fill in the blank). This creates difficulty for those leaders whose gifting does not match the expected ones. Often, they move on to other groups or places that affirm who they are.

comment

The focal element usually remains the same throughout the entire time of ministry. The exception to this occurs when spiritual gifts are late in being identified (late bloomer or late adult conversion).

---

[5] Synergism and its related words (synergistic, synergistically) all refer to a process in which items work together to produce a united effort which is greater than just the sum of the individual efforts.

FEEDBACK ON THE FOCAL ELEMENT

1. Consider the two following possibilities:

   a. A leader with a focal element of natural abilities supported by spiritual gifts and acquired skills. For example: creative musical ability dominates though there is a strong natural ability (charismatic kind of person) to lead, strong helps gift, music theory is part of acquired skills.

   b. A leader with a focal element of acquired skills supported by natural abilities and spiritual gifts. For example: a person with an organizational framework with strong tendencies toward strategic planning, job analysis and descriptions, goal setting, accountability, etc. supported with an innate ability to put things in order, and a spiritual gift of teaching.

   Now suppose that each of these persons is put into a ministry ambiance in which leaders who are affirmed, supported, and given the best ministry assignments have spiritual gifts dominant—for example: prophecy. Natural abilities and acquired skills are not even acknowledged as being important.

   What do you think will happen to the leader of situation a? the leader of situation b? How will the leader in each case view what is happening? How will the leadership over them view the situation?

2. What is the basic problem we are dealing with in situations a and b?

ANSWERS————

1. In both cases the leaders will probably either attempt to get the spiritual gift of prophecy or minister as if they had it or will be frustrated and eventually leave the ministry situation and move to an environment more suited to who they are. Leader a will most likely try to fit in and sublimate creative music drives to giving supportive atmosphere for the prophetical ministry. But creativity in music will be thwarted. Leader b will be even more frustrated that leader a. For the prophecy ambiance will usually have associated with it an intuitive approach to planning or organizational matters or none at all. Leader b will see the lack of coordinated purpose, no accountability. He/she will want to organize things, will see the need for structures, etc. In both cases, leadership will see both leader a and b as weak leaders who do not hear from God and can not minister with power.

2. We are dealing with the concept of **gift projection**, that is, the tendency of strong gifted leaders to lay expectations (even guilt trips) on followers to operate in the same gifts in which these leaders are strong. Leaders with strong evangelism gifts want all to have evangelism. Leaders with strong teaching gifts want all to teach the Bible like they do. Leaders with healing gifts want all followers to be able to heal. This is not a new problem. Paul dealt with it in the Corinthian church in which gift projecting by some leaders (tongues) was taking place. The end result of gift projections is that those emerging leaders without the necessary gifts being projected are made to feel like second class leaders—self-image is affected.

GIFT-MIX, GIFT CLUSTER AND DOMINANT GIFT

introduction
All Christians have at least one spiritual gift. While we have found this true for the body in general, we have also found that leaders usually are multi-gifted. Over their time of ministry experience at any one given time they will be repeatedly exercising a combination of gifts. The set of gifts that a leader is demonstrating at any given time is important. We give it a special label. For leaders who have spiritual gifts as the focal element, there will usually be a maturing of the set of gifts they have so that the gifts operate synergistically together. We have a name for that effective use of gifts. One of the gifts of that set will usually be stronger than the others. They will complement it so that it becomes enhanced.

definition
A *gift-mix* is a label that refers to the set of spiritual gifts being used by a leader at any given time in his/her ministry.

definition
A *gift-cluster* refers to a person's gift-mix which has matured in such a way that one gift is dominant and the other gifts harmonize with that gift in order to maximize the person's effectiveness.

definition
Dominant gift refers to that gift in the gift-mix or gift-cluster which is more central to the person's ministry.

example
Early on G. Campbell Morgan demonstrated evangelism, teaching, and some exhortation (maybe mercy) in his gift-mix. From competent ministry onward his gift-mix matured into a gift-cluster including *teaching*, exhortation, and prophecy. These were repeatedly used with power. Teaching was the dominant gift in the gift-cluster

comment
When we refer to a person's **giftedness**, we are referring to the combination of natural abilities, acquired skills, and spiritual gifts. When we refer to a person's **gift-mix**, we are referring specifically to the person's **spiritual gifts**. It is possible to talk about development of either or both—a person's giftedness and/or the person's gift-mix.

comment
A person's gift-mix may change over time. Sometimes certain roles in ministry require certain types of spiritual gifts to be operating. God will often release those gifts to the person in order to meet the needs in the ministry. Later as the person moves out of that role those gifts drop away. Also, God often releases and develops gifts over a period of time in a person's life. From the person's perspective, there could be a new discovery of a gift as he/she matures and develops. But over the long haul, 1-3 gifts will be seen to be repeatedly used. It is this set of gifts that will be identified with the gift-cluster.

comment
A person's gift-cluster is a label used to describe the gift-mix that has stabilized and is operating in maturity. Other spiritual gifts may come and go depending on the various roles and needs of the ministry but certain gifts are constant in each situation. It is the interrelationship of these gifts as they operate in maturity that make up a gift-cluster. When listing a gift-mix or gift-cluster the dominant gift in the cluster is usually indicated by underlining it.

FEEDBACK ON GIFT-MIX, GIFT CLUSTER AND DOMINANT GIFT

1. What is the basis for talking about a gift-mix? That is, the Bible mentions that the Spirit gives to each member of the body a spiritual gift. What is our warrant then for even talking about multiple gifts for leaders?

2. Distinguish between the following terminology. That is, how are we using them in this material.

    a. giftedness—
    b. gifts—
    c. abilities—
    d. talents—
    e. gifting—
    f. spiritual gifts—
    g. skills—
    h. acquired skills—

3. We make the statement that a person's gift-mix may change over time. Do you have any observations from ministry situations and leaders that you have observed which seems to confirm this observation? Any that seem to deny it?

ANSWERS————

1. Twofold. (1) Empirical studies of historical and contemporary leaders reveal that all have multiple gifts. (2) Studies of Bible characters like Paul and Peter also indicate multi-giftedness. But it is true that we don't have direct Biblical teaching or a command that indicates multiple gifts for leaders.

2. a. giftedness—broadest concept; includes natural abilities, acquired skills, spiritual gifts
    b. gifts—shorthand notation for spiritual gifts
    c. natural abilities—innate resources in an individual due to birth or early environmental conditioning
    d. abilities—short hand notation for natural abilities
    e. talents—another short hand notation for natural abilities
    f. gifting—used usually to mean spiritual gifts but sometimes used like giftedness; ambiguous; check context to see how used
    g. spiritual gifts—Spirit engendered capacity specifically in terms of a limited list of activities/results given in Scriptural passages on spiritual gifts
    h. acquired skills—learned behaviors that may supplement natural abilities or spiritual gifts
    i. skills—short hand notation for acquired skills

3. I have observed in campus ministries that workers up to age 30 usually have evangelism dominant in their gift-mix. After that time there is usually a transition into some ministry which does not focus on evangelism with a result that evangelism drops out of the gift-mix altogether or is certainly not dominant. An exception to this would be the founder of Campus Crusade who has demonstrated evangelism at every stage of his ministry.

COMMENTARY ON GIFTEDNESS CONCEPTS

introduction

We have covered a number of important concepts which are fundamental to the notion of development of a leader in giftedness. You really need the detailed concepts of chapters 4, 5, 6, 7 to truly understand these fundamental concepts. But you also need these concepts to properly understand those chapters. My suggestion is, after you finish chapters 4,5,6,7, come back and go through this chapter again in a much more detailed fashion. This will enhance your learning and help insure that you will use these concepts later in ministry. The commentary which follows is a miscellaneous hodgepodge of ideas which flow out of my interactions with people studying giftedness.

value of
stewardship
model and
notion of
giftedness
set

When we are studying giftedness concepts with various groups of people there are many people who immediately identify their focal element and have no problem in distinguishing between a natural ability and a spiritual gift. But there are others who frequently pose a question like. I'm not sure whether teaching is a natural ability, acquired skill, or spiritual gift. This is particularly true of people who may have studied education in college. I do two things to help them understand. I always question them this way. Did you have symptoms of teaching as a child? If you taught as a child—tendency to always explain to others or even play teach—then teaching may well be a natural ability. If not I explore the idea of the acquired skill of teaching. The basic difference between the acquired skill of teaching and the spiritual gift of teaching is an inner drive to communicate Biblical ideas to people. A person with a spiritual gift of teaching will have this drive as well as some complementary symptoms—Bible study disciplines and desire to learn abut the Bible. A person with an acquired skill of teaching may be very competent to organize teaching but not have these inner drives. So the basic questions are when did you first note symptoms of the potential gift (like teaching)? And what are the complementary symptoms or drive underlying. Of course it is also possible to have a natural ability, acquired skill and spiritual gift of teaching. I finally close by asserting and affirming, if you have trouble distinguishing, don't worry whether you can distinguish or not. The most important thing is to acknowledge the gifting under question as from God and as part of your resources to be used for Him. Then use it even more deliberately and in faith expecting God to empower it whether it is a natural ability or acquired skill or spiritual gift. The stewardship model gives us assurance that we can and must use what we have. And we must develop those resources. So don't get bogged down in the identification—but instead exult in what you have and use it for God.

focal element
a freeing
concept

The notions of *ministering out of being* and the *focal element* of the giftedness set, which is strongly tied to being, have been the most freeing concepts of our teaching on giftedness. In our classes, workshops, and seminars on giftedness on the average about 60% of leaders have spiritual gifts as their focal element. About 25% have natural abilities as their focal element. Another 15% have acquired skills. For those with natural abilities and acquired skills as focal elements this teaching has been especially freeing. Folks with those focal elements are released to be themselves, because they see God has created them that way for His purposes. They are free to deliberately pursue ministry which centers around their focal element. In short, they are freed up to pursue ministry which flows out of being—that resonates in their inner souls with who they are.

correction to gift projection	A second major effect of our broader emphasis on giftedness teaching has to do with giftedness projection. There are a number of leaders out there who have been harmed by ministry situations in which gifts were projected which were not compatible with their own gifting. Some of these have self-image problems now because they have labored under the false premise that they can not measure up to demands and expectations of others about giftings which they don't have. Our teaching has an emotional release effect upon many of these wounded soldiers. They don't have to measure up to others expectations. They are free to use what they have for God's purposes.
Venn Diagrams	Later we shall introduce the concept of Venn diagrams. A Venn diagram is especially helpful for picturing a person's giftedness set. We use symbols to represent the various elements of the giftedness set—circles for spiritual gifts, triangles for acquired skills, and rectangles for natural abilities. The size of the symbol indicates its dominance—larger symbols indicate more dominant gifting. The exercise of identifying and relating these elements helps clarify commonalties in the three kinds of elements as well as distinct differences. More on this later.
bi-focal	The very large majority of leaders we have studied have one focal element but a very few are bi-focal in their giftedness. You should assume you have a single focal element in your initial attempts at identification. But if there seems to be a difficulty in resolving then perhaps you are one of those with two focal elements.
application of giftedness awareness continuum	The notion of the Giftedness Awareness continuum can be applied individually to a number of gifts. I will do three so you can get the idea. This is a freeing concept which will allow you to move in ministry with confidence. For each of these continuums recognize that a person can minister all along the continuum.

|——|

Word of Knowledge   Accumulated Knowledge

(spiritual gift—spontaneous   (natural ability to gain,   (use of research skills,
revelation from God)   organize and use knowledge)   frameworks for
                                                                                                organizing knowledge,
                                                                                                knowledge gained via
                                                                                                experience over the years)

A given leader may be one who continually operates to the right of the continuum. Another given leader may be one who operates far to the left. Still another leader may be one who operates mostly to the right but occasionally to the left. All three cases are appropriate. The thing to recognize is that God is involved as you use knowledge for Him no matter from what part of the continuum a given use arises. Frequently, one can not even tell where on the continuum the use of giftedness is coming from.

COMMENTARY ON GIFTEDNESS CONCEPTS CONTINUED

|———|

Discernings of Spirits	Natural Abilities	Analytical Skill of Discernment
(spontaneous—intuitive-like discovery without always reasoned out explanation)	(intuitive-like instincts to see things)	(strong use of skills to arrive at a reasoned explanation, or deductions drawn from experience gained over the years)

A given leader may be one who continually operates to the right of the continuum. Another given leader may be one who operates far to the left. Still another leader may be one who operates mostly to the right but occasionally to the left. All three cases are appropriate. Frequently one operating to the far left will know something without having the reasoning to see why it is so. But they know it. Later after reflection and perhaps time to mull it over—like weeks, they will see the logical reasoning behind it (i.e. see it from the right of the continuum). The thing to recognize is that God is involved as you use knowledge for Him no matter from what part of the continuum a given use arises. Frequently, one can not even tell where on the continuum the use of gift is coming from.

|———|

Word of Wisdom	Natural Abilities	Use of Accumulated Wisdom
(spontaneous—intuitive-like grasp of truth to be applied to a situation)	(intuitive-like instinct to see solutions to situations and problems)	(application of solutions to a situation which are based on deductions drawn from past use of wisdom)

I relate to this diagram personally. I have learned much over the years which provide a reservoir of resources for me to draw on when I face situations and problems. That is, I operate on the right part of the diagram quite a bit. But sometimes I move to the far left. I am given a *wise* solution which I can not necessarily identify with anything from my past experience. I have learned to recognize these as words of wisdom (if confirmed by the other party). I now expect to operate in a given situation anywhere along the continuum.

Giftedness Discovery Process Item

introduction	Apart from acquisition of general leadership knowledge and skills, the most important development during the first 10 years of ministry involves giftedness, especially in regards to discovery of spiritual gifts and confident use of them.[6] The focus of this process item[7] is the discovery of giftedness and how development occurs.
definition	The *giftedness discovery process item* refers to any significant advancement along the giftedness development pattern and the event, person or reflection process that was instrumental in bringing about the discovery.
Barnabas spiritual gift discovery	Barnabas discovered his exhortation gift early in his ministry. A destiny experience affirmed this discovery and set life-time expectations for using it. (See Acts 4:32-37.) Later significant discoveries in Acts 9 and Acts 11 brought out manifestations of his apostleship gift. The Galatians 2:6-10 affirmation was another step forward in giftedness discovery.
comment	Giftedness development occurs through the identifying, adding to, and building upon one's natural abilities, acquired skills, and spiritual gifts.
comment	Usually this process of development occurs in a fairly generic way. There is a general pattern of development which tends to flow from an emphasis on natural abilities to acquired skills to spiritual gifts to adding supplemental skills which enhance effectiveness. These are the basic stages of discovery and development which nearly everyone goes through. Some stages may overlap; some may be skipped but in genral the flow is from natural abilities to acquired skills to spiritual gifts.
comment	Discovery of **spiritual gifts** flows out of ministry experience. Small group activities allow for ministry experience at a most basic and non-threatening level. Usually spiritual gifts can not be determined prior to ministry experience by taking tests since most tests are based on experience and not symptoms of gifts.
comment	Discovery of **natural abilities** is usually not explicit. Usually we simply use natural abilities without really acknowledging their place in our lives—certainly not the divine impartation of them for His purposes.
comment	**Acquired skills** are not so much discovered as they are learned. But to see *how they fit and their importance in our ministry* is usually a discovery process.
comment	Some break-through discoveries come later and involve identification of dominant element and dominant gift and synergistic use of giftedness.

---

[6] A close second is the discovery of ministry insights, that is, ways to effectively deliver one's ministry appropriate to gifting. The ministry insights process item is usually a breakthrough concept involving a paradigm shift.

[7] Process item is a technical term used in Leadership Emergence Theory which describes the shaping activity of God. This shaping activity usually involves three kinds of formation: spiritual formation (leadership character), ministerial formation (leadership skills), and strategic formation (leadership values and direction). The development of giftedness relates most closely with ministerial formation. God will use people, activities, events, circumstances and the like to put a leader in situations where giftedness can be discovered. The means whereby the discovery comes is what is described by the giftedness discovery process item.

FEEDBACK ON GIFTEDNESS DISCOVERY PROCESS ITEM

1.   List here 3 or 4 discovery causes that God has used to help you discover something about your
      giftedness.

2.   What is the central feature of most of these causes?

ANSWERS————

1.   Your choice. Here are some for me: various ministry experiences (some were negative—showed
      me I was not gifted), people telling me I had some gift, study about gifts, observation of results of
      ministry experience, attracted to certain people in ministry, etc.

2.   experience—that is, use

GIFTEDNESS DEVELOPMENT PATTERN

introduction   We have described the giftedness development pattern broadly—from natural abilities to acquired skills to spiritual gifts to advanced acquired skills. Here are more details. The age span is at best only approximate.

Stage	Age Span	Label	Explanation
1.	1-14	Natural abilities	Natural abilities, sometimes in seed form manifest themselves. The form the core of ones being whether implicit or whether known.
2.	6-22	Basic Skills	Basic skills are acquired both in the social environment and the educational environment. Some of the things learned in the educational environment will resonate with one's beingness. Others will be forced and not become a part of one's useful repertoire.
3.	16-21	Spiritual Gift Symptoms	Early spiritual gift indications begin to emerge as the leader gets started in ministry. Though being used, knowledge of spiritual gifts is usually only implicit.
4.	16-28	Complementary	Further acquired skills are added in order to enhance the leader's effectiveness in ministry. Some of these will be suggested by the early symptoms of spiritual gifts.
5.	20-25	Gifts explicit.	Early explicit identification of spiritual gift(s) happens as a leader gets more ministry experience and has some awareness of spiritual gifts are and how they work.
6.	30+	Latent Abilities	In some cases, there can be a late discovery of some latent natural ability. Especially true for late bloomers.
7.	25-40	Added gifts	There can be the identification of other spiritual gifts as diverse ministry happens or roles force enablement.
8.	30-40	Gift-Mix Forms	The identification of several spiritual gifts leads to the identification of the leader's gift-mix.
9.	30-40	Giftedness Set	The leader initially identifies his/her giftedness set along with the focal element and proactively moves towards development and operating in maturity.
10.	30-50	Advanced Skills	In order to enhance effectiveness, the leader acquires additional skills.
11.	35-50	Gift-Cluster	The leader develops maturity in his/her spiritual gifts which leads to the identification of the gift-cluster. This usually involves role adaptation.
12.	45-65	Convergence	The leader experiences convergence in his/her giftedness. This means that he/she is operating in maximum potential in all that God has given him/her.

FEEDBACK ON GIFTEDNESS DEVELOPMENT PATTERN

1. Glance again at the stages in the giftedness development pattern given below. Check any of the stages where you have discovered something about your giftedness.

Stage	Age Span	Label
____1.	1-14	Natural abilities
____2.	6-22	Basic Skills
____3.	16-21	Spiritual Gift Symptoms
____4.	16-28	Complementary
____5.	20-25	Gifts explicit
____6.	30+	Latent Abilities
____7.	25-40	Added gifts
____8.	30-40	Gift-Mix Forms
____9.	30-40	Giftedness Set
____10.	30-50	Advanced Skills
____11.	35-50	Gift-Cluster
____12.	45-65	Convergence

2. Choose one of the stages that you checked above and comment on something about that stage.

ANSWERS————

1. Your choice. I have checked down through 11 for myself.

2. Stage 4. Complementary. I was challenged by one of my buddies, Jeff Imbach to study Mager's **Preparing Instructional Objectives.** This was a programmed text (a self-study methodology) teaching about how teachers should be able to write objectives for what they were teaching and be able to measure them. This was a good complementary skill to my teaching. It forced me to become more focused about what I was teaching and showed me the initial steps for finding out if my teaching was effective.

GIFTEDNESS TIME-LINE: DISPLAYING THE PROCESS OF DISCOVERY

introduction   Most people do not keep a running journal of how they discovered their natural abilities, acquired skills and spiritual gifts. Most leaders need to go through an exercise of reflection and evaluation in order to identify the various abilities, skills and gifts which they have discovered. This is a profitable exercise which can lead one to forcefully move to the later stages of the development pattern. The following time-line lays out the basic flow of time as it relates to giftedness discovery and development. The years of ministry are estimates. You may not fit this general pattern so feel free to be unique. However, for the most part, our research on leadership development reveals this time frame is fairly normal. Below I show the general giftedness time-line; then I give an actual example.

description   A *giftedness time-line* is a horizontal display of the discovery and acquisition of natural abilities, acquired skills, and spiritual gifts by identifying the actual date in which there was some recognition or discovery.

GENERAL GIFTEDNESS TIME-LINE

|<—Foundations—> <———————————— Ministry Development ————————————>

| Early   Middle   Mature
| First 5 years   Next 10 years   The rest of ministry
|—————————————|————————————|————————————|————————————|

1. Natural Abilities
  2. Basic Skills   3. Early Spiritual Gift Indicators
              4. Acquired Skills
                  5. Spiritual Gifts
                    6. Late Natural Abilities
                      7. More Spiritual Gifts
                        8. Gift-Mix
                          9. Giftedness Set Identified
                            10. Further Acquired Skills
                              11. Gift-Cluster
                                12. Convergence

Example: Mo Whitworth (1989a)

1959	1964 - 1977 [K-12 grade]	1977-1981 college	1982 work	1983	1984	1985	1987-1989 grad. ed.
1)optimism		2)analytical thinking	2)resource linking	2)prayer 5)faith	5)teaching	5)giving 5)word of knowledge	7)discernings of spirits
1)perseverance							
1)high commitment			3)governments	5)prophecy	exhortation		
1)compassionate		2)writing					8)gift-mix
1)diversity of interests		2)self-discipline	3)faith	5)pastoring		3)miracles 10)small	identified
2)organizational skills				5)ruling		business skills	9) giftedness set
2)group dynamics skills		1)see overall picture				10)event coordination	tentatively seen
3)prophetic impressions							

FEEDBACK ON GIFTEDNESS TIME-LINE

1. Examine closely the Whitworth example of the giftedness time-line. Then check below stages for which she gives giftedness indications. What stages are missing.

Stage	Age Span	Label
____1.	1-14	Natural abilities
____2.	6-22	Basic Skills
____3.	16-21	Spiritual Gift Symptoms
____4.	16-28	Complementary
____5.	20-25	Gifts explicit
____6.	30+	Latent Abilities
____7.	25-40	Added gifts
____8.	30-40	Gift-Mix Forms
____9.	30-40	Giftedness Set
____10.	30-50	Advanced Skills
____11.	35-50	Gift-Cluster
____12.	45-65	Convergence

2. According to her age what is the furthermost stage she should be?

3. Note in the period 1977-1981 she lists a natural ability, see overall picture. Natural abilities are usually discovered between ages 1-14. What do you think she means by this natural ability and why discovered there?

4. **Just from the information given** here could you tell what is Whitworth's focal element?

ANSWERS————

1. I checked off 1-8 omitting 6.

2. She was 30 when she did this analysis. According to that, if we went by the suggested ages given for each stage she should probably be in 6 or 7. She actually shows herself as being in 8.

3. You may have your own ideas about this. Here are mine. She probably means the ability to synthesize from parts to the whole. To get a big perspective and use it to integrate findings. She does not identify this as an acquired skill (like analytical thinking—of which it is certainly an example). But instead she puts it in the category of natural ability. I surmise that during her studies in college she noted across her courses that she had an ability to see and integrate things. It was not something she learned in any course but a general ability. This probably prompted her to think back and recognize that even in her childhood this trend was there. Perhaps the way she was always asking questions or wanting to know things.

4. This would be difficult to do just from this information. Her spiritual gifts are just beginning to be seen to form a gift-mix. From what is given, I would say natural abilities (ideation, discernment, analytical abilities) seem to dominate.

COMMENTARY ON GIFTEDNESS DEVELOPMENT

introduction   Let me illustrate the process of giftedness development in my (Bobby) own experience. I consider myself a late bloomer—late adult commitment to leadership, late learner, etc.

CASE STUDY—ILLUSTRATING THE PROCESS OF DISCOVERY

I (Bobby) will illustrate part of the process of discovery as it relates to my spiritual gifts. I want you to get a feel for how giftedness emerges over time and how the three elements of the giftedness relate to one another. See if you can follow the basic giftedness pattern.

My first gift discovered was teaching in 1965. It came about through a series of ministry tasks relating to home Bible classes that were assigned by Pastor Thompson. Pastor Thompson was a Bible teachers with a strong teaching gift. His many home Bible classes during the week provided opportunity for many like myself to observe a master at work and to get practical experience via small assignments and eventually taking over the whole Bible study. Later we will identify the like-attracts-like pattern. This is a specific illustration of it. I increasingly accepted openings to teach. I did not know about spiritual gifts at the time. I simply was doing ministry and doing what I could do best. In the early years I taught children classes, teen-age boy's classes, teen-age girl's classes, high-schoolers, collegiate classes, couple's classes, single's classes, and old people's classes.

My early training and acquisition of disciplines—especially Bible study, from the Navigators fit hand-in-glove with the development of my teaching gift. My focus on learning the Bible for myself and yearly goals of memory work, reading through the Bible and book analyses, etc. aided my teaching gift even though I did not even know about spiritual gifts at the time.

I saw my effectiveness in teaching improve as I continued to have numerous opportunities to teach. I gained a better understanding in regards to teaching methods by acquiring skills and learning various teaching tools which enhanced my teaching gift as well as observe good teachers for methodology. As I experienced personal growth and maturity in my Christian development, I had more to draw on in terms of my teaching ministry.

In 1968 I did a spiritual gifts paper for Dr. J. R. McQuilkin entitled, "My Spiritual Gift and How I Intend to Develop It." This paper outlined steps for development of my teaching gift which I have followed and added to since that time. As a result of this paper I deliberately began to study books on practical communication as well as hermeneutics and writing skills so as to improve the effectiveness of the teaching gift. I got into the educational technology scene—reading all of Mager's very practical books. These added to my understanding of how to focus my teaching and measure its effectiveness. These deliberate and proactive decisions to develop immensely aided me in my teaching gift.

I chose a role (rather, guided by God) which let me use my teaching in a formal way. My time at the Jamaica Bible College, greatly stimulated my development as a teacher. It was there, in 1973,74 in conjunction with my study into spiritual gifts, that I recognized that I had the gift of exhortation (primarily the admonition thrust). I understood that there were three basic thrusts in the use of exhortation: admonition, encouragement and comfort. As I continued to utilize my teaching gift, I began to see that my exhortation gift dominated all that I did in teaching. I found that I had already made significant efforts towards developing my exhortation gift because of my diligence in applying truth to my own life. Over time, I was increasingly shifting the admonition thrust to the encouraging thrust so that my exercise of that gift was more balanced. Today I have seen that God has also further balanced my exhortation gift into a comfort thrust as well. I was beginning to catch the notion of a dominant gift in a gift-mix, though I had no terminology or labels for these concepts.

In 1975,76 I began to increasingly notice, especially in small group settings, that I often would speak a word of wisdom for situations. I first noticed this gift in another member of the executive team of which I was a part. I then saw that I too was operating in this same way from time to time. My continued study of gifts identified this as the word of wisdom gift. In the past[8] I have been very careful about this gift and would seek outside confirmation. Increasingly in recent times I have been more free to use it and even try to put myself in situations where I can, by faith, expect to use that gift.

Let me summarize. Since 1979 I have recognized a gift-mix of exhortation, teaching, and word of wisdom with exhortation being dominant. I have had occasional uses of other gifts from time-to-time.

Since my study of giftedness, beginning with 1985. I have recognized that spiritual gifts is my focal element. But I have seen how my natural analytical abilities and leadership have fitted with my gift-mix. I have seen how my engineering background has given skills which buttress my natural analytical ability and help me organize my frameworks for understanding and using concepts.

The cluster has begun to take shape. I am learning how to release these gifts with greater effectiveness and gifted power. The teaching gift provides the base from which exhortation takes off. Ideas arising in teaching stir people and open them for change.
Exhortation strongly moves people toward use of ideas. Follow-up counseling after application leads to opportunity for word of wisdom. My analytical skill and research skills provide me with new insights into leadership which flow back into my teaching.

The challenge that lies before me is that of adapting my role in light of what I know about my giftedness. This means learning to say no to ministry situations which do not fit with my giftedness. It means careful design of my teaching situations to flow with my giftedness.

---

[8] Not coming from a charismatic background, I am not comfortable with prefacing my statements with "God is saying, or God said, or God told me, or God gave me this word for you..." So I have been extremely cautious (maybe overly so) with regards to this gift, word of wisdom. But continued use has helped me identify those unusual times when I know God is prompting me with ideas for someone. By confirmation I mean—I would suggest something to a person about the word I was receiving without identifying it as such. If it were really a word from God then I would usually get a strong affirmation from the person who would resonate with what I was saying and accept it as coming from God for them.

THE LIKE-ATTRACTS-LIKE GIFT INDICATOR PATTERN

introduction

Effective leaders recognize that leadership selection and development is a priority function. They learn to recognize very early in the life of a potential leader symptoms and tendencies which indicate leadership. They then plan for training activities which will confirm, clarify or invalidate those early *selection guesses*. An early ministry selection pattern is the like-attracts-like pattern. Potential leaders tend to be challenged by and attracted to experienced leaders who contain giftedness elements similar to their own embryonic giftedness. This can be true for natural abilities, acquired skills, and spiritual gifts—especially spiritual gifts.

description

The *Like-Attracts-Like* gift pattern describes an early giftedness recognition pattern frequently seen in potential leaders in which those potential leaders are intuitively attracted to leaders who have like giftedness even though the giftedness in the potential leader may be very embryonic.

examples

I (Bobby) was drawn early to Pastor Thompson (teaching gift) and to Professor Buck Hatch (teaching, analytical/synthesis skills), and Professor Frank Sells (teaching gift with dominant exhortation gift). I wanted to be around them. I went to many Bible classes and learned much from Pastor Thompson both in techniques of teaching and in the power of the Word when exposed. I learned the importance of knowing a subject well, the whole subject from Professor Hatch. I saw the importance of giving learners a perspective from which to view a subject. From Professor Sells I learned the importance of teaching for affect and volition as well as for cognition. In short, I wanted to learn what they were teaching and I wanted to learn how they taught. These men affected my teaching gift.

applies
to

This pattern is helpful for both mentors who tend to attract protégés with like giftedness and for emerging leaders as they seek to evaluate their own giftedness.

2 uses

A leader aware of this pattern can use it in at least two ways. **One,** the leader who knows well his or her own giftedness (especially spiritual gifts) can observe those people who are drawn to that leader's person and ministry and assume that there is the possibility of that person having one or more of those known gifts. The leader can then suggest ministry tasks which will aid development of those suspected gifts. The leader can also suggest disciplined self-study personal growth projects that personally helped his/her own development. **Two,** the leader can recognize that people drawn to another leader may well have one or more gifts of that leader. Again the same deliberate process of activities and growth projects can be suggested (except of course they should fit that other leader's gift development).

disclaimer

This is not an absolute pattern but only a suggested guideline. It must be confirmed by other means. There are other reasons besides giftedness why people are attracted to others.

The Complementary Giftedness-Need Indicator Pattern

introduction   An early ministry selection pattern is the like-attracts-like pattern. Potential leaders tend to be challenged by and attracted to experienced leaders who contain giftedness elements similar to their own embryonic giftedness. This can be true for natural abilities, acquired skills, and spiritual gifts—especially spiritual gifts. But this pattern is not the only reason why potential leaders might be attracted to leaders. The flip side of this pattern also occurs. Frequently, in a leader operating in ministry there are holes in his/her ministry, that is, areas which are being overlooked or done poorly due to a lack of giftedness in that area. Certain people gifted in those areas where the leader is weak are often drawn to them in order to help them in those weak areas. This is true even when the potential leader operates only implicitly with gifting in the needed area. So then, in addition to a leader using the like-attracts-like pattern as a gift indicator, wise leaders who know their weaknesses, will look for the complementary gift needed pattern as a gift indicator. They ought to be proactively doing this anyway simply because of the principle of recruit to your weaknesses—one way of adapting a role to move toward more effective ministry.

description   The *complementary giftedness-need* indicator pattern describes a giftedness recognition pattern frequently seen in potential leaders in which those potential leaders are intuitively attracted to leaders who due to weaknesses in ministry need giftedness which the potential leader has; the giftedness may be very embryonic.

example   May Brown had good organizational, administrative support skills and natural relational abilities. In addition she had the spiritual gift of helps. At one point in her early development she attended a church in which a young pastor with strong evangelistic gifts was reaching many people for Christ. The church was growing rapidly by radical (adult) conversions. Over a period of 16 months May observed that many were attracted to this ministry but also many dropped through the cracks because there was not a sufficient follow-up program to engage them in nurture and firmly connect them to the on-going ministry of the church. She was able to work with Pastor McCrae, who welcomed her efforts, in order to develop a small group program which not only incorporated new believers into the life of the church but firmly grounded them in discipleship skills. May did not have the teaching or exhortation gifts needed to do the actual small group work. But she did have organizational abilities and her relational abilities combined with the Pastor's support enabled her to recruit people with the needed gifts to fit into the small group program which she organized. Her helps gift was the underlying motivational thrust behind the whole venture.

applies to   This pattern is helpful to leaders caught up in ministry situations that are overwhelming, especially with needs which they themself are not gifted. Recognition of this pattern is often a first step in recruiting to one's weakness.

major use   The leader who knows well his or her own weaknesses can expect to draw people to the minsitry who can meet those weaknesses.

disclaimer   This is not an absolute pattern but only a suggested guideline. It must be confirmed by other means. There are other reasons besides giftedness why people are attracted to others.

THE GIFTEDNESS DRIFT PATTERN

introduction | Effective leaders recognize that leadership selection and development is a priority function. They learn to recognize very early in the life of a potential leader symptoms and tendencies which indicate leadership. They then plan for training activities which will confirm, clarify or invalidate those early *selection guesses*. The tendency for a potential leader, if given freedom or choice, to naturally drift toward ministry roles or functions which utilize that leader's embryonic giftedness (even though these may not be explicitly known at the time) is helpful in early identification of giftedness. An early alternate pattern is the forced recruitment into roles and ministry tasks which do not fit giftedness and which give negative experience forcing avoidance of those kinds of future ministry tasks. These negative experiences are frequently a reason for drifting into those situations and tasks which may fit.

description | The *Giftedness Drift* pattern describes the tendency of a potential leader to most naturally respond to ministry challenges and assignments either that fit prior experience or acquired skills or perception of natural ability or intuitively, a spiritual gift.

example | A young aspiring lay leader, Jeffrey Roberts, wanted to develop in the area of teaching. As a youngster growing up he had been in church situations which featured good Bible teaching. His natural inclinations were that way. He loved to study. He contributed in adult Sunday School classes being a responsive learner.   In small groups, he often studied beyond the basic required materials and was helpful in explaining ideas to the group. The leader of the group saw this attitude and allowed Jeffrey to substitute from time-to-time. Jeffrey was relocated several times in the first five years of his early Christian growth experience due to job shifts. In each church, Jeffrey and his wife Lola got involved in Bible classes and small groups. Wherever he could Jeffrey took on teaching responsibilities. He even started a small group Bible study at work.

heuristic value | This should encourage those who are emerging to attempt ministry roles and activities toward which they feel drawn as they will most likely stimulate use of a latent gift or natural ability or point out the need to acquire a skill.

selection hint | This tendency should also point out to mid career leaders where and how to look for potential leaders. People tend to want to minister out of being—that is they intuitively want to do those things that resonate with how they are made.

warning | Forcing people to do things that do not fit them may implant avoidance tendencies that spill over to other things beside the actual assignment. They may turn off in general on the church and its leadership because they have no confidence in the leader's ability to discern and to empower people in ministry.

central notion | This tendency is central to the notion of the giftedness development pattern which says that giftedness identification correlates strongly to ministry experience (particularly positive ministry experience).

The Forced Role/Gift Enablement Pattern

introduction	Effective leaders focus on leadership selection and development. Tendencies and embryonic gifts are not the only thing a leader looks for in identifying gifts in a potential leader. Latent giftedness emerges, or acquisition of new aspects of giftedness sometimes happen, when God clearly leads a potential leader or developed leader into a role which requires giftedness not seen in past ministry. If God clearly leads into a role then a leader can expect enablement for that role.[9] The needed giftdedness may come to the leader (direct) or others associated with that leader (indirect).
description	The *Forced Role/Gift Enablement* pattern describes the not so frequent pattern in which a person is placed in a role which requires some specific giftedness (especially a spiritual gift) not previously known or demonstrated and in that role is met by the Holy Spirit so as to demonstrates one or more of those needed gifts while the role is active.
example	II Timothy 4:5. Paul's admonition to Timothy concerning evangelism, may illustrate this.
guidance implication	Normally guidance into a position or role is confirmed by some past experience. That is, we usually make decisions for the future which agree with what we have positively experienced in the past. However, if God has, by other guidance, clearly led one to a role or function, not with standing former experience or demonstrated giftedness, then the leader can expect that giftedness will be given in the situation.
warning	Frequently, leaders and potential leaders refuse assignments with the basic reasoning, "I don't have the giftedness for that." This may be true or may not be true. For God frequently uses situations of this nature in order to give giftedness or draw out a latent ability or gifting which would not otherwise be known apart from this experience. Earlier in ministry, especially before a gift-mix is carefully identified and confirmed, I would recommend that a leader try to take on a number of diverse assignments in order to discover if God may want to give or bring out giftedness not hither to known. On the one hand, do move toward roles which enhance your known giftedness. However, in special situations don't use known giftedness as a cop out which may cause you to miss out on something special God has for you. This is a dynamic tension that is hard to give any fixed rule on.
related to tertiary gifting	The forced role/ gift enablement observation seems to correlate with the notion of tertiary spiritual gifting. A spiritual gift is spoken of as vested if it appears repeatedly in a person's ministry over an extended period of time. A gift is spoken of as non-vested if it appears only situationally and is not repeated in the normal course of ministry. A gift is primary if it is a vested gift and currently being demonstrated as a significant part of the gift-mix or gift-cluster. A gift is secondary if at one time it was a vested gift but is now not demonstrated as part of the current gift-mix or gift-cluster. A gift is tertiary if it has been or is a non-vested gift or if it was manifested as necessitated by *role* responsibility in the past and is not now viewed as vested.

---

[9] At least the leader can expect God to provide someone in the body with the needed giftedness if not directly to the leader forced into the role.

FEEDBACK ON BASIC GIFTEDNESS PATTERNS

1. Which of the following basic giftedness patterns have you experienced personally? Check any that you experienced.

___a. Like-Attracts-Like Gift Indicator Pattern
___b. The Complementary Giftedness-Need Indicator Pattern
___c. The Giftedness Drift Pattern
___d. The Forced Role/ Gift Enablement Pattern

2. For any that you checked in exercise 1 list what you learned about your giftedness. Don't worry about correct names for natural abilities, acquired skills, or spiritual gifts. Use your own wording. Later we will redo this exercise after you have studied a number of defintions.

___a.The Like-Attracts-Like Gift Indicator Pattern

   Giftedness indications:

___b.The Complementary Giftedness-Need Indicator Pattern

   Giftedness indications:

___c. The Giftedness Drift Pattern

   Giftedness indications:

___d.The Forced Role/ Gift Enablement Pattern

   Giftedness indications:

ANSWERS————

1. Mine were a, c. d. yours will differ, of course.
2. **a. teaching, exhortation**

    c. teaching. I have moved toward edification roles in ministry which have used teaching and exhortation from spiritual gifts or leadereship roles which used my natural ability in leadership. I also experience a form of the alternate pattern: took over a Sunday School Superintendents job. Learned I dd not have administrative abilities or skills or governments or helps.

SUMMARY

In this chapter, we have introduced you to some of the basic concepts which shape our understanding of giftedness. We have defined each element of the giftedness set and looked at the basic process of discovery and development.

In the next few chapters we will look specifically at the God-given resources which we are responsible to develop. In chapter 4 we will look at natural abilities and acquired skills. In chapter 5 and 6 we will look at the issue of spiritual gifts. The overall ideas on giftedness of this chapter should provide a framework for examining these detailed concepts.

CHAPTER TEST

Use the following test as an indicator of what has impressed you and what you have retained from the major concepts of this chapter.

1. What do you think has been the most important single concept to you from this chapter. Check the one that most fits this description for you.
___a. The general notion of the giftedness set.
___b. The importance of natural abilities as part of one's resources.
___c. The importance of acquired skills as part of one's resources.
___d. The concept of beingness tied to all three elements of the giftedness set.
___e. The concept of ministry flowing out of beingness.
___f. The general notion of the giftedness awareness continuum.
___g. The concept of overlap between all three elements of the giftedness set—a given instance an influence act may involve natural abilities and spiritual gifts and acquired skills. All are important.
___h. The emphasis of seeing God in all that we have and are and by faith trusting Him to empower no matter what the giftedness element.
___i. The notion that I don't always have to know exactly whether something is a natural ability, acquired skill, or spiritual gift. Use, by faith, not identification is the Biblical emphasis .
___j. The general notion of the focal element.
___k. That it's o.k. to have a focal element that is natural abilities.
___l. That it's o.k. to have a focal element that is acquired skills.
___m. That it's o.k. to have a focal element that is spiritual gifts.
___n. That a focal element, once solidly identified, usually remains unchanged throughout a lifetime of ministry.
___o. The notion that leaders are multi-gifted.
___p. The concept of a gift-mix.
___q. The concept of a gift cluster.
___r. The concept of a dominant gift in a mix or cluster.
___s. The notion of discovery of gifting and processing God uses to do that.
___t. The fact that experience is dominant in discovering giftedness.
___u. The identification of stages as portrayed in the giftedness development pattern and the notion of pinpointing where one is in the process.
___v. The use of the giftedness time-line to display one's giftedness development.
___x. Insights from the like-attracts-like gift indicator pattern.
___y. Insights from the complementary giftedness-need indicator pattern.
___z. Insights from the giftedness drift pattern.
___aa. Insights from the forced role/gift enablement pattern.
___bb. Other. You name it specifically:

Chapter Test Continued

2. Show that you know the basic definitions by matching the labels with the descriptive explanations which follow. Place the capital letter in the appropriate blank.

A. Giftedness set   D. Spiritual gift   F. Focal Element   I. dominant gift
B. Natural Ability   E. Giftedness   G. gift-mix   J. Giftedness Discovery
C. Acquired Skill   Awareness   H. gift cluster   Process Item
                         Continuum

___ 1. a display along a linear line of spiritual gifts, natural abilities, and acquired skills which enables a person to identify God's involvement all along the line; the display shows that there is overlap between the three.

___ 2. the dominant element in the giftedness set around which a person centralizes effort.

___ 3. the descriptive label for a set of gifts which has matured and which is relatively permanent.

___ 4. a God-given unique capacity empowered by the Holy Spirit for use in ministry.

___ 5. a collection of three elements which include natural abilities, acquired skills , and spiritual gifts.

___ 6. an innate talent in a person, one even possibly observed in childhood.

___ 7. the means whereby God leads a person in to understanding and using giftedness.

___ 8. that spiritual gift which is more central to the gift-mix or gift cluster.

___ 9. a set of spiritual gifts being used at any one time.

___10. a learned resource.

3. Show that you know the basic patterns and processes for identification and use of gifting by matching the labels with the descriptive explanations which follow. Place the capital letter in the appropriate blank.

A. Giftedness development Pattern   D. Complementary Giftedness-Need
B. Giftedness Time-Line   E. Giftedness Drift Pattern
C. Like-Attracts-Like Pattern   F. Forced Role/ Enablement Pattern

___1.   Describes the tendency for emerging leaders to be drawn to other leaders because the emerging leader see needs missing in the leader and to which the younger leader intuitively feels he/she can meet.

___2.   Describes the tendency for emerging leaders to be drawn to other leaders on the basis of similar giftings.

___3.   Describes the tendency to move along lines of least resistance in terms of intuitively using gifting one has.

___4.   12 stages describing when most leaders appropriate various aspects of gifting.

___5.   Describes a situation in which a leader must operate in a ministry for which he/she has no evidently needed gifts for the situation.

___6.   A method of displaying along a linear line, with points along the line identified by dates and various giftings that were appropriated at the various points in time.

ANSWERS————

1. Your choice. But I hope as you reviewed the concepts you realized that some one or more of them was important to you. It may be a new insight or an old one clarified or one which brought release for you.

2. _E_ 1. _F_ 2. _H_ 3. _D_ 4. _A_ 5. _B_ 6. _J_ 7. _I_ 8. _G_ 9. _C_ 10.

3. _D_ 1. _C_ 2. _E_ 3. _A_ 4. _F_ 5. _B_ 6.

CHAPTER 4:
NATURAL ABILITIES AND ACQUIRED SKILLS

INTRODUCTION

Most of the books and material on spiritual gifts only deal with a person's spiritual gifts and don't take into account the natural abilities and acquired skills. Identifying your natural abilities and acquired skills is an important part of identifying who you are in terms of giftedness. And let us remind you again of one of our important presuppositions:

MINISTRY FLOWS OUT OF BEING.

God has made us and is shaping us in terms of our uniqueness and toward our contribution to His purposes.

In this chapter, we will look at several categories of natural abilities and acquired skills. The lists that will be given in this chapter are a compilation taken from various papers of leaders who have studied giftedness with us. There are two important process items which are helpful in learning to identify skills that God has led you to acquire. Many times skills are acquired without a specific plan or understanding of how God will want to use those skills in the future. The basic skills process item and the ministry skills process items describe how God uses skills in developing leaders. The feedback sections of these two process items are helpful in doing reflection and evaluation of your acquired skills.

By the time you finish this chapter you should have:

- compiled a list of your natural abilities,
- grouped this list into a smaller number of major natural abilities,
- placed this list of items along your giftedness time-line,
- compiled a list of acquired skills,
- grouped this list into a smaller number of major acquired skills,
- placed this list of items along your giftedness time-line,
- identified your basic skills processing,
- identified your ministry skills processing.
- selected some items or potential areas that you want to add skills in the future.

This is a simple chapter to read. Basically you read some lists and from those lists identify those items that are appropriate to you. By the time you complete this chapter you will have identified two thirds of your present giftedness set.

NATURAL ABILITIES

introduction   Our understanding of God's sovereignty recognizes that God gives each person a set of natural abilities. Below is a start toward a typology for categorizing natural abilities.

definition   *Natural abilities* refer to those capacities, skills, talents or aptitudes which come naturally to a person and allow him/her to accomplish something.

example   analytical ability—a natural tendency to mentally sift through situations or information and break it into parts and logically see relationships between parts and to order findings.

comment   Many natural abilities have counterparts in acquired skills. The major difference is the notion of it being innate versus a learned thing. Natural abilities can be seen in seed form early on in a life. It of course can be enhanced by analytical skills which build on the tendency.

comment   There are many different kinds of natural abilities. Natural abilities may involve things like mental abilities, social skills, physical dexterity, etc.

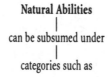

Natural Abilities
|
can be subsumed under
|
categories such as

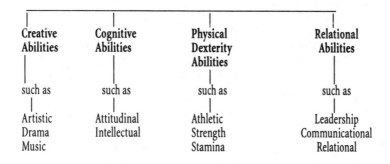

Creative Abilities	Cognitive Abilities	Physical Dexterity Abilities	Relational Abilities
such as	such as	such as	such as
Artistic	Attitudinal	Athletic	Leadership
Drama	Intellectual	Strength	Communicational
Music		Stamina	Relational

comment   When you are identifying your natural abilities for the giftedness set, there will be many natural abilities that you may have. For the giftedness set diagram, focus on the two or three most important natural abilities which are an important part of who you are. You will want to identify general categories of natural abilities.

IDENTIFICATION OF NATURAL ABILITIES—CREATIVE ABILITIES

introduction   In our attempts to identify various natural abilities, we have developed several general categories. The following list is not meant to be exhaustive but is rather a representative list of natural abilities which have been revealed through the leadership research. We will group creative abilities into the following four categories: artistic, drama, musical, and other (a catch-all, after all creativity can't be boxed in). Remember, these lists are only suggestive—you can add more like things to them, things that fit your experience.[1] I suggest that as you go through this list you put a check beside the number of any item that fits you and jot down a word or two to the right that explains or identifies more specifically how it fits you.

CREATIVE ABILITIES

Artistic abilities   *Added Comments*

___1. creative design for art projects such as drawings,
        painting, costumes, dancing, set designs, etc.
___2. implementing creative ideas in artistic projects
___3. painting, sculpture, drawing
___4. strategizing or visualizing in art projects

Drama Related Abilities   *Added Comments*

___1. acting
___2. creating character personalities, etc
___3. communicating messages through drama
___4. ability to memorize
___5. very few inhibitions around people
___6. good stamina
___7. good interpersonal abilities

Musical Related Abilities   *Added Comments*

___1. a musical ear
___2. a good voice
___3. song writing or creating music
___4. playing instruments
___5. organizing music
___6. ability to spot emerging musical talent

Other—You Name It   *Added Comments*
___1.
___2.

---

[1] These lists of items were compiled from comparative studies of a number of leaders who listed these items as part of their natural abilities. The more information we get the more likely it is that other categories will arise. Hence, you should feel free to use the *Other* if you have something that doesn't quite fit one of these categories. Later, after more comparative study we will be able to broaden the number of categories. However, you may want to wait until you have been through all the natural abilities since your new category might fit better under one of the other lists: cognitive, physical dexterity, relational.

Identification Of Natural Abilities—Cognitive Abilities

introduction   Remember, the following list of cognitive abilities is suggestive. It is not meant to be exhaustive but is rather a representative list of cognitive abilities which have been revealed through the leadership research. We group cognitive abilities under three categories: attitudinal and intellectual.   Since these lists are suggestive—you should feel free to add more like things to them, things that fit your experience. For example, you could go further under intellectual such as analysis, synthesis.

Cognitive Abilities

Attitudinal Related Abilities   *Added Comments*

___ 1. achievement oriented
___ 2. an appreciation for diversity
___ 3. competitiveness
___ 4. desire for excellence
___ 5. a disciplined approach to life
___ 6. endurance, perseverance, determination or patience
___ 7. entrepreneurial or pioneering mindset
___ 8. value towards faithfulness
___ 9. a high commitment level or loyalty
___10. isolationist tendencies
___11. self motivated
___12. sense of optimism
___13. a task orientation
___14. a tolerant view towards others

Intellectual Related Abilities   *Added Comments*

___ 1. creativity in thinking and problem solving
___ 2. formal academic tasks were easy
___ 3. able to do self-directed learning
___ 4. good judgment
___ 5. an inquisitive nature
___ 6. good intuition
___ 7. good memory for facts and statistics
___ 8. able to grasp overall perspective in situations
___ 9. perceptive in an analytical or conceptual way
___10. good at evaluating and reflective thinking
___11. good at strategic thinking and planning
___12. able to understand and create systems,
        structures or models

Other—You Name It   *Added Comments*
___1.
___2.

IDENTIFICATION OF NATURAL ABILITIES—PHYSICAL DEXTERITY

introduction   Remember, the following list of physical abilities is suggestive. It is not meant to be exhaustive but is rather a representative list of abilities which have been revealed through the leadership research. We group physical abilities under three categories: athletics, physical and other. Since these lists are suggestive—you should feel free to add more like things to them, things that fit your experience. We have not yet probed the depth of this category—especially as it applies to leadership.[2] We know that it might correlate with other learned behaviors, e.g. athletics may teach teamwork, goal setting, etc. But at this point we are still very much open to learning both how to categorize these natural abilities and recognizing their worth in ministry. I have left space under categories for you to add like items as well as the standard Other Category for new ones.

PHYSICAL DEXTERITY ABILITIES

Athletics   *Added Comments*

___1. good at individualistic sports
___2. good in group sports
___3. good in dance, movement, etc
___4.
___5.

Physical dexterity   *Added Comments*

___1. good with hands
___2. size, stamina, strength
___3.
___4.
___5.

Other—You Name It   *Added Comments*
___1.
___2.

---

[2] For example, there may be some correlation between good athletic ability and charisma. Various cultures view what a charismatic person is in terms of physical traits (size, handsome or beautiful, ability to excel in sports, etc.). This would relate to Wrong's (1979) power form of personal power.

IDENTIFICATION OF NATURAL ABILITIES—RELATIONAL ABILITIES

introduction   We group relational abilities under four categories: leadership/motivational, communication, socially sensitive, and other. Since these lists are suggestive—you should
feel free to add more like things to them, things that fit your experience. We are still in
the earliest stages of this one but feel it relates in a significant way to leadership—
since leadership at its very heart if working with people. Again, remember you can
add to these representative lists. I have left space under categories for you to add like
items as well as the standard Other Category for new ones.

RELATIONAL ABILITIES

Leadership/Motivational   *Added Comments*
___ 1. a high sense of responsibility
___ 2. implementing and creating ministry
___ 3. organizing and planning office systems
___ 4. organizing and planning events (retreats, meetings, etc)
___ 5. a persuasive nature
___ 6. good at completing tasks
___ 7. good at vision setting, goal setting, program development
___ 8. good at building teamwork
___ 9. able to inspire and motivate others
___10.
___11.

Communication abilities   *Added Comments*
___1. Verbal abilities: able to speak to groups, one on one, public speaking
___2. good at teaching
___3. good with visual communication
___4. good with written communication
___5.
___6.

Socially Sensitive abilities   *Added Comments*
___1. compassionate, empathetic, caring, gentle personality
___2. good with children
___3. able to be diplomatic
___4. good listener
___5. able to make friends easily
___6. sensitive to others
___7. able to mix with other groups or kinds of people
___8.
___9.

Other—You Name It   *Added Comments*
___1.
___2.

FEEDBACK ON NATURAL ABILITIES

1. Hopefully you have been checking your items and noting comments as you go. Now it is time to summarize your findings.[3]

    a. Glance back over the Natural Abilities—Creative Abilities list. Note the items you have checked. See if you can group the items you noted under several major categories (with specific names that fit your own groupings of them) which relate to potential leadership usage. Put your final categories here—probably three or four categories.

    b. Glance back over the Natural Abilities—Cognitive Abilities list. Note the items you have checked. See if you can group the items you noted under several major categories (with specific names that fit your own groupings of them) which relate to potential leadership usage. Put your final categories here—probably three or four categories.

    c. Glance back over the Natural Abilities—Physical Dexterity list. Note the items you have checked. See if you can group the items you noted under several major categories (with specific names that fit your own groupings of them) which relate to potential leadership usage. Put your final categories here—probably three or four categories.

    d. Glance back over the Natural Abilities—Relational Abilities list. Note the items you have checked. See if you can group the items you noted under several major categories (with specific names that fit your own groupings of them) which relate to potential leadership usage. Put your final categories here—probably three or four categories.

2. Now finally choose from all of your answers to parts a, b, c, d the most important natural abilities that relate to your leadership. Here you should come up with a list of four or five.

ANSWERS————————-

1. Sorry, your choice I can't help you on this one.
2. Sorry, your choice I can't help you on this one.

---

[3] The idea of looking at a group of items and from that list grouping or synthesizing labels to form new categories is in itself a natural ability or skill that many may not have. Just do the best you can. The idea is to get a smaller workable list of items even though the items themselves may be broader. For further help on this see the Venn Diagrams of Giftedness sets which are given in a later chapter. There you will see the results of leaders' efforts to reduce natural abilities to a manageable number which help them assess their leadership.

ACQUIRED SKILLS

introduction
: Having worked on natural abilities we are one third the way through identifying our giftedness set. Lets work on the second element of the set—acquired skills.

definition
: *Acquired skills* refer to those capacities, skills, talents or aptitudes which have been learned by a person in order to allow him/her to accomplish something.

example
: analytical reading facility—the wherewithal to assess a book as to its overall message, structure for accomplishing that overall message, and seeing how/what each of the parts contribute to the whole.

example
: writing skill—the ability to write an integrated paragraph which takes a topic sentence (either implicit in the paragraph or explicitly stated) and develops that topic by various techniques.

comment
: Acquired skills are closely related to natural abilities. Most people acquire skills which serve to enhance their natural abilities. Because of this, we use the same categories that we used for the natural abilities.

comment
: Though acquired skills do often relate to natural abilities sometimes it is the acquisition of the skill which first prompts the discovery of some natural ability not previously explicitly known.

comment
: Then too, there are acquired skills which do not necessarily relate to any natural ability. They may build on some basic skills or they may be entirely new.

comment
: Usually when you are trying to identify the acquired skills section of your giftedness set, you will want to pick the two or three specific skills that are the most important. Pick the skills which obviously enhance either your spiritual gifts or natural abilities.

comment
: At the end of this list are a grouping of special leadership skills that are acquired in the context of doing ministry. These may help prompt you to see like items in your own personal inventory.

comment
: It is easy to see that God is involved in spiritual gifts and hence to exercise them by faith with expectations of His power in them. You had little to do with getting the gifts in the first place. It is relatively easy to recognize that you also had very little to do with getting natural abilities—so you have to believe that God gave them to you for His purposes. Again you can by faith expect Him to use them. But it is less easy to see that God is involved in acquired skills. After all didn't you choose to get them? But the sensitive leader who recognizes the sovereignty of God in superintending the development of a leader will soon see that there are divine purposes even in acquired skills. A deliberate recognition of this and the related using them too by faith and with expectancy will insure confident use and soon release even more power in a ministry.

IDENTIFICATION OF ACQUIRED SKILLS-CREATIVE SUPPORT

introduction   Acquired skills may involve mental skills, social skills or physical skills. Acquired skills may enhance a person's natural abilities and operated in a supportive way. We have grouped the acquired skills in the same categories that we used for the natural abilities. Again I suggest that you check off the items that fit you or are close and add comments to explain.

CREATIVE SUPPORT SKILLS

Artistic skills   *Added Comments*
- ___ 1. calligraphy
- ___ 2. art design
- ___ 3. drawing
- ___ 4. painting
- ___ 5. paste-up/layout
- ___ 6. organize composition or design
- ___ 7. learning color relationships
- ___ 8. esthetic evaluation
- ___ 9. computer (graphic designs, layout, etc)
- ___10. a sense of responsibility (integrity) to the project
- ___11. learn to deal with criticism
- ___12.
- ___13.

Drama   *Added Comments*
- ___ 1. designing dramatic concepts
- ___ 2. speech (articulation, projection, accents)
- ___ 3. improvise in situations
- ___ 4. learn to present a public presence
- ___ 5. learn to follow direction
- ___ 6. learn to deal with criticism
- ___ 7.
- ___ 8.

Musical Skills   *Added Comments*
- ___ 1. Playing an instrument
- ___ 2. voice training
- ___ 3. develop a musical ear
- ___ 4. develop worship leading
- ___ 5. creative music or song writing skills
- ___ 6. sight-read music
- ___ 7. write musical notation
- ___ 8.
- ___ 9.

Other—You Name it:
- ___ 1.
- ___ 2.

IDENTIFICATION OF ACQUIRED SKILLS-COGNITIVE SUPPORT

introduction   Of all the acquired skills cognitive support skills are probably the most important as far as leadership skills go. We have previously mentioned that all leaders have at least one word gift in their gift-mix (we'll explain word gifts more completely in later chapters). The ability to use word skills rests quite heavily on cognitive skills and their related natural abilities. So examine this list carefully. Again I suggest that you check off the items that fit you or are close and add comments to explain.

COGNITIVE SUPPORT SKILLS

Attitudinal Skills   *Added Comments*

___ 1. self discipline (control of tongue, personal habits, etc)
___ 2. time management
___ 3. personal goal setting
___ 4. ability to perceive, receive, and obey orders from those in charge
___ 5. ability to persevere through an assignment
___ 6. generosity
___ 7. hospitality
___ 8.
___ 9.

Educational Support Skills   *Added Comments*

1. Bible skills
___a. how to study the Scriptures
___b. how to prepare oral presentations
       from the Bible
___c. how to use the Bible devotionally
___d. how to use concordances and original language tools
___e. how to prepare Bible studies for small groups
___f. how to do exegesis
___g. how to do inductive Bible study
___h. how to do topical studies
___i.
___j.

___ 2. learning to read books and other material
       along a continuum for information
       (scan, ransack, browse,
       pre-read, read, study)
___ 3. speed reading skills
___ 4. analytical reasoning skills
___ 5. critical thinking skills
___ 6.
___ 7.

IDENTIFICATION OF ACQUIRED SKILLS-COGNITIVE SUPPORT CONT.

Analytical Skills

Added Comments

___ 1. biblical study perspectives
___ 2. evaluation perspectives
___ 3. logical thinking
___ 4. mathematical thinking
___ 5. objective self-evaluation
___ 6. observation skills
___ 7. studying habits
___ 8.
___ 9.

Technical Skills in Cognition

Added Comments

___ 1. accounting skills
___ 2. archival and experimental research
___ 3. computer literacy
___ 4. curriculum development
___ 5. training designs
___ 6.

Other—You Name it:

Added Comments

___ 1.
___ 2.

IDENTIFICATION OF ACQUIRED SKILLS-PHYSICAL SUPPORT

introduction   Remember that we are yet unsure of how physical skills relate to leadership. Your careful attention to this section may help us see more how these items relate to leadership.

PHYSICAL DEXTERITY SUPPORT SKILLS

Athletic Skills

1. in any given individual sport
2. in any given group sport
3. concentration
4. strategizing
5. adaptation and creativity
6. perseverance
7. goal setting and finishing

Technical Skills

1. building things (construction)
2. carpentry
3. sewing
4. weaving
5. fixing things (repairs)

Other—You Name it: *Added Comments*
___ 1.
___ 2.

IDENTIFICATION OF ACQUIRED SKILLS-RELATIONAL SUPPORT

introduction   This is a scattered categorical list of items that include relational but go somewhat beyond them. Later analysis may break this category into finer tuned ones. Again this is an important area in terms of leadership expertise.

RELATIONAL SUPPORT SKILLS

General Leadership Skills   *Added Comments*

___ 1. budgeting
___ 2. decision making
___ 3. delegating responsibility
___ 4. financial management
___ 5. group dynamics
___ 6. motivating others
___ 7. organizational skills
___ 8. organizing committees
___ 9. writing proposals
___10. designing brochures and other publicity materials
___11. organizing church bulletins
___12. assessing jobs and prioritizing them
___13. assigning people to various responsibilities
___14. designing structure in an organization
___15. setting goals for a group
___16. persuasion skills
___17. flexibility with others while making decisions
___18. communicating new ideas
___19. moving people towards consensus in groups
___20. getting people to take ownership for a decision
___21. leading small groups (Bible study, prayer, evangelistic)
___22. planning (short term and long term)
___23. supervisory skills
___24. vision casting and pace setting
___25.
___26.

Special Leadership Skills: Mentoring   *Added Comments*

___ 1. coaching
___ 2. counseling
___ 3. discipling
___ 4. modeling
___ 5. sponsoring
___ 6. teaching
___ 7. spiritual guidance

IDENTIFICATION OF ACQUIRED SKILLS-RELATIONAL SUPPORT CONT.

Special Leadership Skills: Ministry   *Added Comments*

___ 1. Bringing closure with commitment (altar calls, etc)
___ 2. counseling skills (dreams, active listening, conflict resolution)
___ 3. developing and articulating a ministry philosophy
___ 4. evangelism skills
___ 5. identifying, selecting and developing leaders
___ 6. preaching in various settings
___ 7. teaching (various settings, kinds of groups, sizes of group, etc.)
___ 8. training others
___ 9.

Special Leadership Skills: Prayer   *Added Comments*

___ 1. how to fast
___ 2. how to use the Bible in prayer
___ 3. how to spend extended times in prayer
___ 4. how to lead conversational prayer in a group
___ 5. learning to hear the voice of God as He initiates your prayer
___ 6. developing intercessory aids (notebooks, journals, etc)
___ 7. laying on of hands for a release of power
___ 8. laying on of hands for impartation of gifts
___ 9. disciplined perseverance in prayer
___ 10.

Technical Support Skills   *Added Comments*

___ 1. management of office machines
___ 2. basic business management
___ 3. fund-raising
___ 4. real estate and property management
___ 5. tax or legal specialist
___ 6.

Communication Skills   *Added Comments*

___ 1. active listening
___ 2. correspondence/letter writing
___ 3. desktop publishing capabilities
___ 4. editorial skills
___ 5. international perspective
___ 6. lecturing
___ 7. polemical abilities
___ 8. proof reading

IDENTIFICATION OF ACQUIRED SKILLS-RELATIONAL SUPPORT CONT.

Communication Skills	*Added Comments*

____ 9. public speech writing and delivering
____10. use of humor
____11. use of visual graphics
____12. writing skills

Linguistic Skills	*Added Comments*

____ 1. linguistic abilities (learning other
     languages—verbal)
____ 2. linguistic abilities (learning other
       languages—reading)
____ 3. linguistic abilities: other

Relational Skills	*Added Comments*

____ 1.within an organization
    ____a.relating to superiors
    ____b. relating to peers
    ____c.relating to subordinates
____ 2. public relations
____ 3.

Technical Skills in a Relational Arena	*Added Comments*

____ 1. Nursing
____ 2. marketing and sales
____ 3. consulting (problem solving,
    conflict resolution, etc)
____ 4.

Other — You Name it.	*Added Comments*

____ 1.
____ 2.

FEEDBACK ON ACQUIRED SKILLS

1.   Hopefully you have been checking your items and noting comments as you go. Now it is time to summarize your findings. This will be a little bit more difficult for you to do than for natural abilities since the skills list is not as tightly grouped in categories and contains numerous items. Still give it your best attempt.

      a.   Glance back over the Acquired Skills—Physical Support list. Note the items you have checked. See if you can group the items you noted under several major categories (with specific names that fit your own groupings of them) which relate to potential leadership usage. Put your final categories here—probably three or four categories.

      b.   Glance back over the Acquired Skills—Relational Support list. Note the items you have checked. See if you can group the items you noted under several major categories (with specific names that fit your own groupings of them) which relate to potential leadership usage. Put your final categories here—probably three or four categories.

2.   Now finally choose from all of your answers to parts a, b, c, d the most important natural abilities that relate to your leadership. Here you should come up with a list of four or five.

ANSWERS———————-

1. Sorry, your choice I can't help you on this one.
2. Sorry, your choice I can't help you on this one.

BASIC SKILLS PROCESS ITEM[4]

introduction   During the foundational phase, the early growing up years, the potential leader will participate in various life experiences through which he/she will learn skills and values which will inevitably affect later leadership influence capacities. Examples of such experiences include educational programs, various kinds of social activities including athletics, and kinds of activities for earning money.

definition   The *basic skills process item* refers to actual skills acquired and/or values learned in picking up those skills, during the foundational phase, which will later affect leadership skills, leadership attitudes, and leadership styles.

example   Doug McConnell's leadership development study (1984) is filled with entrepreneurial-like instances of developing businesses which financed his way through school. Creativity, management of financial affairs, supervisory skills, and self-reliance were skills learned by McConnell through these foundations.

example   Michael Senyimba's leadership development study (1986) reveals that from an early age he was forced to fend for himself. He learned perseverance, ingenuity, the value of hard work, the value of money, self-reliance, and the value of an education.

example   Richard Loving (1986) grew up on a farm. He was given responsibility for basic tasks. In these he learned self-reliance, management of money, skills in repairing various equipment and a bent towards working with and repairing equipment.

example   Robert Edwards (1986) was highly involved with athletics during his time in high school and college. Many valuable lessons concerning discipline, fairness, perseverance, teamwork, and the desire to do one's best came out of this focus on athletics.

comment   Any skills or attitudes associated with skill acquisition which later will have a bearing on the exercise of leadership should be analyzed in conjunction with this process item.

---

[4] This concept, the basic skills process item, and the next, the ministry skills process item, are concepts which come from leadership emergence theory and which deal with God's indirect shaping of a leader toward ministerial formation (i.e. the acquisition of leadership skills).

FEEDBACK EXERCISE ON BASIC SKILLS PROCESS ITEM

1. From your general knowledge of the Apostle Paul's life what early skills or attitudes associated with those skills can you see that were gained during his foundational period? How did these relate to his later exercise of leadership?

2. From your general knowledge of King David in the Old Testament, what early skills or attitudes associated with skills can you see that were gained during his foundational period? How did these relate to his later exercise of leadership?

3. In examining basic skills processing from your own foundational phase identify any attitudes associated with skills that you learned which you feel have been foundational to your present leadership or future leadership.

___ a. teamwork   ___ i. ingenuity
___ b. perseverance   ___ j. value of hard physical work
___ c. desire to do the best
___ d. innovativeness   ___ k. the value of sacrifice
___ e. self-reliance   in developing skills
___ f. discipline   ___ l. value of money
___ g. creativity   ___ m. value of an education
___ h. dependability   ___ n. other values—name them.

4. Check any of the following skills you gained through basic skills processing during the foundational phase.

___ a. critical/analytical thinking   ___ f. repair skills
___ b. management of finances   ___ g. a trade
___ c. entrepreneurial-like thinking   ___ h. music skills—identify
___ d. supervisory skills   specifically:
___ e. relational skills   ___ i. other: name them:

5. Give a major skills process item from your foundational phase. Then list skills and skill attitudes learned through it.

ANSWERS————

1. The vocational skills associated with the tentmaking trade. This was greatly used by Paul especially when doing apostolic church planting. This allowed him to teach on giving with great power. Paul also learned analytical skills from Gamaliel which included the skill attitude of broad mindedness which Gamaliel showed toward all kinds of learning. These skills stood Paul in great stead as he began to formulate his theology.

2. David's shepherd experiences prepared him in many ways. Courage, the ability to believe in himself, and the ability to meditate came out of skills learned as a shepherd.

3. For me: a., b., c., d. These were mostly learned through sports.

4. For me: a., b., e. Learned through paper route, athletics, and military training.

5. For me: Major skills process item: Sports. Skills learned through sports: How to win. How to lose. Skill attitudes learned through sports: Perseverance, relationship skills.

MINISTRY SKILLS PROCESS ITEM

introduction   A major thrust of development during the growth ministry phase is the acquisition of skills which aid a leader in accomplishing ministry. Most skills are acquired in the early and middle portions of this phase. Important skills usually gained include disciplinary, relational, group, organizational, word, persuasive and prayer skills. These skills may be knowledge focused (gaining perspectives on leadership) or influence focused (learning how to exercise leadership). These skills may or may not be directly supportive of spiritual gifts the leader has already been using.

definition   *Ministry skills* refers to a definite acquisition of one or more identifiable skills which aids one in a ministry assignment.

example   how to lead various kinds of small groups: prayer groups, kinship groups, bible study groups, committees.

example   how to prepare bible study materials for small groups

example   how to organize committees, write proposals, persuade people of the importance of new ideas

example   how to persuade people so as to implement change

example   how to relate to various people in organizational structures including superiors, co-equals, and subordinates

example   conflict management

example   Bible study methods, Bible communication skills

plateau
problem   A commonly observed pattern is the **plateau pattern.** Often, initially a person will learn new skills until he/she can operate with a reasonable amount of comfort. After this point, if a person does not deliberately and habitually seek new skills but rather chooses to coast on prior experience and a minimum skills level, their development will plateau. There will be a leveling off.

FEEDBACK ON MINISTRY SKILLS

introduction   You may find the following listing of items helpful to you not only in identifying what
has happened in the past but also suggestive for skills you need in the future. Use the
lists in two ways: check off the ones already acquired; place an "F" by those you would
like to work on in the future.

1. Check any of the following disciplinary skills that you acquired early in your ministry:
___a. self-discipline (control of tongue, other personal habits)
___b. time management
___c. personal goal setting
___d. management of personal finances
___e. ability to perceive, receive, and obey orders from those in authority (in a submissive spirit, even if in
   disagreement)
___f. ability to persevere through on an assignment
___g. devotional habit
___h. Other—

2. Check any of the following relational skills that you learned early in your ministry:
___a. how to or not to relate to superiors in your organization
___b. how to or not to relate to peers in your organization
___c. how to or not to relate to subordinates
___d. beginning strategy for how to or how not to handle conflict
___e. Other—

3. Check any of the following group skills that you learned early in your ministry:
___a. how to lead prayer groups
___b. how to lead growth groups
___c. how to lead evangelistic groups
___d. how to lead Bible study groups
___e. how to lead committees
___f. how to start any of the above groups/ specify which ones:
___g. Other—

4.Check any of the following organizational skills that you acquired early in your ministry:
___a. how to organize committees
___b.how to write proposals
___c. how to design brochures and other publicity materials
___d.how to organize a church bulletin
___e. how to assess jobs which need to be done
___f. how to assign people to jobs in order to accomplish a task
___g.how to recognize structure in an organization
___h.how to prioritize
___i. how to set goals for a group
___j. Other—

5. Check any of the following word skills that you learned early in your growth ministry:
___a. how to study the scriptures
___b. how to prepare oral presentations from the word
___c. how to use the Bible devotionally to feed one's soul
___d. how to use Bible study aids like concordances and original language tools
___e. how to prepare Bible study materials for small groups
___f. how to study the Bible topically for theological findings
___g. Other—

FEEDBACK ON MINISTRY SKILLS CONTINUED

6. Check any of the following prayer skills that you acquired early in your ministry:

___a. prayer discipline

___b. learning to hear God give initiative on what to pray for

___c. intercessory aids (how to use a prayer notebook, how to journal in praying, etc.)

___d. how to fast (different kinds of fasts: isolation, working, group fasting, etc.)

___e. how to use the Bible in praying

___f. how to have a day of prayer

___g. conversational praying

___h. laying hands on a person for special release of power (physical healing, inner healing, commissioning, empowerment, gifting, etc.)

___i. Other—

7. Check any of the following persuasion skills that you learned early in your growth ministry:

___a. how to convince individuals and motivate them without overriding their own desires

___b. how to be flexible while verbally interacting with followers and peers in regards to decision-making issues,

___c. how to communicate a new idea so as to excite followers

___d. motivation techniques (use of scriptural case studies, review of God's past working, demonstration of power, use of gifting)

___e. how to gain consensus in a group

___f. Other—

8. What was the most important practical ministry skill you acquired in your early growth ministry?

9. Give an example of an important practical ministry skill you have learned recently? What was the processing that God used to bring about your acquisition of that skill?

ANSWERS————

These are my answers, yours may differ greatly.

1. a., b., c., g.
2. how not to's in all categories—vicariously some; some via negative processing in my own life.
3. a., b., d., e., f.
4. d.
5. a., b., c., d., e., f.
6. a., c., e., f., g.
7. c.
8. How to hold the attention of a small group Bible study for up to two hours.
9. Writing skills—programmed instruction and information mapping. The challenge came initially through a ministry assignment to create a theological education by extension program in Jamaica. This necessitated preparation of materials forcing me to pick up programmed instruction writing skills. Information mapping followed as an attempt to improve on programmed instruction. Both of these forced me to learn more about the nature of the teaching/learning dyad. They led to pursuit of communication skills as well. All along the way there was the divine touch in getting information, books, workshops, and financing.

CHAPTER FEEDBACK

At this point in your study you have worked with two/thirds of your giftedness set. You have identified items in your Natural Abilities and Acquired Skills. But you need to integrate your findings. That is the purpose of this chapter feedback. Do this work carefully as you will build upon it later after doing your personal spiritual gifts assessment to come up with your whole analysis of your giftedness set.

1. At this point you have identified the what of many items involved in both your natural abilities and your acquired skills. But you haven't identified when these were discovered, realized or learned. You need to place these items along a time-line like the Whitworth time-line given on page 55. Perhaps you may want to glance at that example again. If you have too many items to fit comfortably on a composite time-line you may want to break your time-line up into natural phases and put each phase on a separate sheet of paper. Review all the list for natural abilities and all the list for acquired skills. Transfer the most important of this information over to your time-line.

2. Now go back over your summary of natural abilities and your summary of acquired skills. Assess which of these, natural abilities or acquired skills, is more important to you in terms of exercising your ministry. That is, if there were only two elements in the gifted set (natural abilities and acquired skills) which would be focal. List here the major items from both natural abilities and acquired skills. Underline those which are dominant. Put a double underline under the element which is more focal.

Natural Abilities: Acquired Skills:

SUMMARY

Ultimately, we minister out of our beingness. Giftedness is one of the most important elements that shapes our beingness. Reflecting back over your life and learning to identify the natural abilities and skills that you have acquired is an important exercise. These elements make up two thirds of your giftedness set.

Natural abilities and acquired skills are closely related. For every natural ability that you identify, you will most likely be able to identify skills that you have acquired that enhance those natural abilities. The key to identifying natural abilities and acquired skills in terms of your giftedness set is to focus in on the most important ones that reflect how you operate in your ministry context.

We made some claims at the beginning of the chapter. Have you met these chapter goals? Read again our claims. Check off the ones you have done.

By the time you finish this chapter you should have:

- compiled a list of your natural abilities,
- grouped this list into a smaller number of major natural abilities,
- placed this list of items along your giftedness time-line,
- compiled a list of acquired skills,
- grouped this list into a smaller number of major acquired skills,
- placed this list of items along your giftedness time-line,
- identified your basic skills processing,
- identified your ministry skills processing.
- selected some items or potential areas that you want to add skills in the future.

CHAPTER 5:
SPIRITUAL GIFTS PART I

INTRODUCTION

Thus far we have talked about part of the giftedness set—natural abilities and acquired skills. Now we will turn our attention to the third element—spiritual gifts. Before we look specifically at each gift (chapter 6), we need to lay some foundational concepts that affect our interpretations. We will give you our opinion on the number of spiritual gifts and compare it to other positions on gifts. We will look at the Biblical data on spiritual gifts and see the passages involved—both the major passages and minor ones. You will be surprised at how much information is available.

We will also introduce more terms and concepts to enable us to view giftedness and development. We will touch on the issue of spiritual gifts and Christian roles. We will talk about the corporate functions of gifts. This leads us to the notion of balance. We will describe how a person receives spiritual gifts. We'll talk about primary, secondary and tertiary gifts as well as vested and non-vested gifts. These latter notions relate to development.

By the time you finish this chapter you,
- should be familiar with a number of general definitions, helpful categories and descriptions about spiritual gifts issues including:
    - the basic definition of a spiritual gift (p. 100),
    - The gifts Identification Continuum (p. 100),
    - the notion of Clusters of gifts passages: unique and common items (p. 110) ,
    - the distinction between Christian roles and spiritual gifts (p. 123),
    - the three corporate functions of spiritual gifts: love, power, word (p. 125,126)
    - the seven ways people receive spiritual gifts (p. 128),
    - the notion of vested and non-vested gifts (p. 130),
    - primary, secondary, and tertiary gifts (p. 132).
- should recognize a variety of comparable lists of spiritual gifts (p. 92-96),
- should be familiar with the 9 presuppositions underlying the author's view for identifying spiritual gifts (p. 101),
- will be introduced to various Biblical data on spiritual gifts including a number of major and minor passages (this will forma a data base that you will build upon throughout your own ministry experience) (p. 103-108),
- will recognize the importance of comparative study of the major passages for commonalities, distinctions, and diverse contributions along with the problems that come from over-emphasizing or neglecting each major passage (p. 110, 112-122),
- will recognize the place of Christian roles yet differentiate between them and spiritual gifts (especially the items common to both categories) (p. 123),
- will identify the 3 major corporate functions of gifts and associated clusters of gifts (p. 125,126),
- will be able to profile a given parachurch or church ministry in terms of the three corporate functions (p. 125-127),
- will be understand and use the notion of balance concerning the three functions and clusters so as to describe what is and what is needed in a situation (p. 125),
- will differentiate between vested and non-vested gifts (p. 130),
- will differentiate between primary, secondary, and tertiary gifts (p. 132).

How Many Spiritual Gifts? 7 Representative Lists

introduction | **How many spiritual gifts are there?** Different authors come up with different numbers. And that is particularly confusing to a person just beginning to study spiritual gifts. So this is a good question. The answer to this question varies depending on the interpreter's rationale.

7 Rationale factors | The following are some of the factors that we have identified which cause interpreters to see things differently as they view spiritual gifts. There are probably more factors but at least we know that these do cause differences. 1. where you draw your data from concerning spiritual gifts, 2. your theological bias for or against certain gifts, 3. your experience with the whole range of possible gifts, 4. your view of the work of the Holy Spirit today, 5. your view of the functions that spiritual gifts are supposed to accomplish for a body, 6. your experiences with the use and abuse of gifts. 7. denominational issues.

Need for tolerance | If you are a beginning student of spiritual gifts you will probably not be satisfied with our answer. We are not saying that there is only one answer to this question. To be honest, in our opinion, the Bible is not clear on this point.[1] There is no text in the Bible which outlines a complete teaching on spiritual gifts and how they operate. Because of this, we need to allow some freedom and latitude on how we interpret the data on spiritual gifts. Let us show you seven representative lists, from varying theological positions. Our own will be included. Notice the variance in numbers of gifts as well as the wording used to describe them. But also notice how much common ground there is.

Explanation of choices of representative authors | We could have chosen a number of authors as representative of various perspectives. In general we have a continuum in mind with the far right being fundamentalist, the middle being evangelical and the left being more liberal theologically. We do not use any of the words describing these camps in a pejorative sense. By evangelical we mean a middle of the road theological stance which is not highly separatistic holding core views about the person and work of Christ and usually tolerant on eschatology and other issues. We chose a denomination fairly typical of denominations. In general, a given denomination will publish at least one spiritual gifts book which gives its position and is in harmony with its distinctives. The one chosen is slightly to the right of the evangelical position but to the left of the findamentalistic position. By anti-charismatic we mean a view which does not see or allow the charismatic gifts as valid today. By pro-charismatic we mean a view which not only accepts the charismatics but promotes them. By Pentecostal we mean those mainline Pentecostal denominations which promote strongly the 9 sign gifts of 1 Corinthians—the classical Pentecostal position.

Representative Lists for Comparative Study

List	Basic Position	Representative Author
1.	Evangelical	Hummel
2.	Evangelical	Wagner
3.	Denominational (Baptist)	Blanchard
4.	Anti-Charismatic	McRae
5.	Pro-Charismatic	Wimber
6.	Pentecostal	Gee
7.	Evangelical	Clinton and Clinton

---

[1] One of our philosophical biases is that we as Bible expositors should seek to be as clear as the Bible is clear: nothing less, nothing more, nothing else. That means, if the Bible is ambiguous and unclear on some issue we must be too. We can have our opinions on such topics which we can follow but we must allow tolerance for differences.

7 Representative Lists—2 Evangelical Positions

introduction   Below are given two middle of the road evangelical positions on spiritual gifts.

List 1. Charles Hummel

Basic Theological Position: Middle of Road Evangelical.

Source: Charles E. Hummel's book, **Fire in the Fireplace: Contemporary Charismatic Renewal**
Number Given: 21
Number Extant: All

1. apostle	8. contributing	16. discerning of spirits
2. prophet, (prophesying, prophecy, revelation)	9. leading	17. speaking in tongues (different kinds of
3. evangelist	10. showing mercy	tongues)
4. pastor	11. wisdom	18. interpretation of
5. teacher (teaching, instruction)	12. knowledge	tongues
	13. faith	19. helpful deeds
6. serving	14. healings (gifts of healing)	20. administrations
7. encouraging	15. miracles	21. hospitality

Note: It is difficult to compile a list of gifts from Hummel since he does not give any lists. But he talks about each of the gifts listed above either in the text or his Appendix. His purpose in writing is not to give exhaustive teaching on the doctrine of gifts but to show how evangelicals can view the charismatic renewal. But the book has much excellent information on spiritual gifts.

List 2. C. Peter Wagner

Basic Theological Position: Middle of Road Evangelical.

Source: C. Peter Wagner's, **Your Spiritual Gifts Can Help Your Church Grow**
Number Given: 27
Number Extant: All

1. prophecy	10. faith	19. evangelist
2. service	11. healing	20. pastor
3. teaching	12. miracles	21. celibacy
4. exhortation	13. discerning of spirits	22. voluntary poverty
5. giving	14. tongues	23. martyrdom
6. leadership	15. interpretation of tongues	24. hospitality
7. mercy	16. apostle	25. missionary
8. wisdom	17. helps	26. intercession
9. knowledge	18. administration	27. exorcism

7 Representative Lists: Two Views On Charismatic Gifts

List 3 . John Wimber

Basic Theological Position: Middle of Road Evangelical, Pro-Charismatic

Source: Spiritual Gifts Seminars from the early 1980s.
Number Given: 20 (with possibility of 10 more)
Number Extant: All

1. word of wisdom	9. interpretation	16. exhortation
2. word of knowledge	of tongues	17. giving
3. discernings of spirits	10. apostles	18. helps
4. faith	11. prophet	19. mercy
5. gifts of healings	12. evangelist	20. service
6. effects of miracles	13. pastor-teacher	
7. prophecy	14. administration	
8. kinds of tongues	15. teaching	

He also lists the following gifts as possibilities:

1. celibacy	5. craftmanship	8. music
2. philanthropy	6. judge	9. intercession
3. hospitality	7. worship leading	10. missionary
4. interpretation of dreams		

List 4 . William McRae

Basic Theological Position: Dispensational, anti-charismatic (or at least non-charismatic)

Source: William McRae's book, **Dynamics of Spiritual Gifts**
Number Given: 18
Number Extant: 9 for today

1. serving or helping	4. giving	7. evangelism
2. teaching	5. administration (ruling)	8. pastor-teacher
3. exhortation	6. showing mercy	9. faith

Note: Though he gives a listing for and defines 18 spiritual gifts in the New Testament, he only gives 9 spiritual gifts that are available for today. The reasoning for excluding some[2] is a philosophical view concerning the closing of the canon and thus no longer a need for those gifts which were for the transition era until the Word of God was finalized. This would be a typical viewpoint of a dispensational position in the 60s and 70s. This position is changing slowly toward a less closed one.

---

[2] Particularly revelatory ones like word of knowledge, word of wisdom, prophecy and faith (a revelatory sense), tongues and interpretation of tongues.

7 REPRESENTATIVE LISTS: TWO DENOMINATIONAL VIEWS

LIST 5. TIM BLANCHARD

Basic Theological Position: Baptistic, Denominational, somewhat non-charismatic

Source: Blanchard's book, **Finding Your Spiritual Gifts**
Number Given: 13
Number Extant: All

1. prophecy (preaching)	6. faith	11. ruling
2. teaching	7. discernment	12. giving
3. knowledge	8. helps	13. mercy
4. wisdom	9. serving (ministry)	
5. exhortation	10. administration (governments)	

Note: Blanchard simply omits the controversial charismatic gifts (healing, miracles, tongues, interpretation of tongues) but does include some—knowledge, wisdom, faith, and prophecy (as preaching only), and the analytical view of discernment . He makes a disclaimer concerning the Ephesians list (offices verses gifts problem) as being beyond the scope of his book. But he conveniently picks and chooses (I think to line up with denominational pressures).

LIST 6. DONALD GEE

Basic Theological Position: Classical Pentecostal

Source: Donald Gee's book, **Concerning Spiritual Gifts.** First published in 1949.
Number Given: 9
Number Extant: 9

1. word of wisdom
2. word of knowledge
3. faith
4. kinds of healings
5. working of power
6. prophecy
7. discernings of spirits
8. kinds of tongues
9. interpreting of tongues

Note: Gee is typical of early Pentecostal writers. Until the late 60s or 70s few non-pentecostal writers dealt with spiritual gifts. That is, the only writers dealing with spiritual gifts were Pentecostals. And they usually were not academic in their treatment of spiritual gifts but were dominated by their experiences. After the spate of writings which issued in the late 70s and early 80s from non-pentecostal writers, even Pentecostal writers now write viewing more than the 9 sign gifts from Corinthians. But the classical Pentecostal approach was that given above of which Gee is typical.

7 Representative Lists: Our Viewpoint

List 7. Clinton and Clinton

Basic Theological Position: Evangelical/ Toward Fundamental but pro charismatic

Source: J. Robert Clinton's book, **Spiritual Gifts**
Clinton and Clinton book, **Unlocking Your Giftedness**.
Number Given: 19
Number Extant: All

1. word of wisdom
2. word of knowledge
3. faith
4. kinds of healings
5. working of power
6. prophecy
7. discernings of spirits
8. kinds of tongues
9. interpreting of tongues
10. apostleship
11. teaching
12. helps
13. governments
14. giving
15. exhortation
16. ruling
17. mercy
18. evangelism
19. pastoring

Note: There is variation in Clinton's listing. In **Spiritual Gifts** 18 gifts are actually defined. In **Developing Leadership Giftedness** 19 are given. There has been some waffling on what to do with ministering, leading (ruling), governments. Presently we are viewing ministry as a generic label (indicated as such in 1 Peter 4), ruling as a local leadership gift, and governments as a local leadership supportive gift (like helps).

FEEDBACK ON REPRESENTATIVE LISTS

1. Examine list 4, McRae's list. Though McRae believes that the charismatic gifts, the so called sign gifts of 1 Corinthians 12, are not extant today, he includes one of them on his list? Check the one he includes.

___a. service or helping   ___d. giving   ___g. evangelism
___b. teaching   ___e. administration (ruling)   ___h. pastor-teacher
___c. exhortation   ___f. showing mercy   ___i. faith

2. Why do you suppose McRae includes this one sign gift on his list but omits the others?

3. McRae chooses some gifts from the Ephesians 4 list but omits others. **a.** What does he choose? **b.** What does he omit? **c.** Why do you think he has this inconsistency?

    a.   **b.**
    c.

4. Examine list 4, McRae's list again. Which of the gifts listed by him occur on all of the other lists (though they may not have exactly the same name)? Check the ones that have the same or similar names.

	List 1 Hummel	List 2 Wagner	List 3 Wimber	List 5 Blanchard	List 6 Gee	List 7 Clinton
___a. service or helping						
___b. teaching						
___c. exhortation						
___d. giving						
___e. administration (ruling)						
___f. showing mercy						
___g evangelism						
___h. pastor-teacher						
___i. faith						

5. What gift(s) occur uniquely to Wagner's list 2 and on no other list?

6. What gift(s) occur on Wagner's and Wimber's lists and on no others.

7. Examine Wimber's List 3. The 20 gifts are taken from New Testament lists and he states them with a certainty not given for the second 10 possible gifts. Several of these gifts, the 10 possible list, are taken from the Old Testament. **a.** What gifts are listed that occur only on Wimber's list and no others? **b.** From our perspective of giftedness set, which of these might be really natural abilities or acquired skills and not really spiritual gifts at all? **c.** Why would you think Wimber would include these apparent natural abilities and/or acquired skills?

    a.   **b.**
    c.

8. What one gift occurs on every list except McRae's and Blanchard's?

9. What is the most important insight you have gained from a comparative study of these lists

FEEDBACK ON REPRESENTATIVE LISTS CONTINUED

ANSWERS———————

1. _√_ i. faith

2. Most likely because he recognizes that Christians must have faith today (a Christian Role) and doesn't see the distinction between gifts and roles. Further, he most likely does not associate the same supernatural enabling behind the other sign gifts with this faith gift. That is, he does not associate a supernatural revelation which engenders the faith. Therefore, it is hard to abuse the faith gift, especially if it does not involve revelation (which I think the 1 Corinthian 12 use of faith does).

3. a. evangelism, pastor-teacher (teaching from Romans), **b.** apostleship, prophecy **c.** presuppositions— Apostleship is an office for him, prophecy is a revelatory gift which he does away with.

4.

	List 1 Hummel	List 2 Wagner	List 3 Wimber	List 5 Blanchard	List 6 Gee	List 7 Clinton
___ a. service or helping	√	√	√	√		√
___ b. teaching	√	√	√	√		√
___ c. exhortation	√	√	√	√		√
___ d. giving	√	√	√	√		√
___ e. administration (ruling)	√	√	√	√√		√√
___ f. showing mercy	√	√	√	√		√
___ g evangelism	√	√	√			√
___ h. pastor-teacher			√			
_√_ i. faith	√	√	√	√	√	√

The faith gift occurs on everybody's list though they do not see it the same. Gee, Clinton, Wimber, Wagner and Clinton most likely see the faith gift as part of the sign gifts and hence carries with it the supernatural revelation from God of what to believe. The others simply use faith as exercising trust and belief in God—what we will later call a Christian role (required of all Christians).

5. Voluntary poverty, exorcism, martyrdom

6. Including Wimber's possibility list: celibacy, intercession, missionary occur on both Wagner's and Wimber's and nowhere else.

7. **a.** philanthropy, interpretation of dreams, craftsmanship, judge, worship leading, music **b.** craftmanship, judge, worship leading, music (maybe philanthropy) **c.** Wimber has a strong natural ability in music; he has functioned as a strong worship leader, he is a craftsman in music—having composed and used a number of songs which have proliferated throughout his movement.

8. prophecy (Prophecy occurs on all the major New Testament gifts lists, even the Roman's list—but McRae omits it because of the philosophical view about revelation; Blanchard most likely omits it because of controversy and because it occurs on the Ephesians 4 list (which may be offices). He defines the Roman's use of it as preaching.

9. Your choice. I see three major values coming out of this comparative study. (1) A person teaching on gifts must be well read and know the various positions of others and why they hold what they do. (2) A person teaching on gifts must not exclude any data base on gifts in the Scripture. (3) When some gifts occur only on one or two persons list and not on any others, they are probably suspect. A fourth value which will become clearer later is the problem of gift projection. Those who omit some gifts given in the New Testament lists, are by default projecting their listed gifts upon people who may in fact not have them but have the missing gifts. Such people will not only be frustrated but may well end up never developing gifts and using them for the good of the body of Christ. Also the elimination of charismatic gifts depletes the church of the power cluster and its testimony to the world of the unseen God's reality.

COMMENTARY ON NUMBERS OF GIFTS/ REPRESENTATIVE LISTS

numbers: 9-30 19-21	If you compare these representative authors on numbers of gifts for today you'l see they range from a low of 9 or 13 up to a high of 27 or 30. Usually differences in interpretation indicate two things: 1. there are some philosophical or theological biases going in which affect the interpretation (our opinion of the two low numbers and the one high one), 2. the Scriptures are not clear enough to resolve the differences. But apart from the extremes the middle ground interpreters are fairly close (19-21).
philosophical bias	In our opinion the New Testament does not exclude the possibility of any gift that it mentions as being extant today. That is, there is no exegetical reason why some gifts should cease and others not. Some groups, particularly the classical dispensationals, hold a philosophical position which says that after the canon of Scripture was closed there was no more need for the miraculous kinds of gifts to exist. Hence they philosophically omit them. The pragmatic reasons for this view point, that is, the apparent abuses of these giftings, probably have as much to do with this position, as the philosophical.
denominational bias	Some denominational groups (especialy those that have a large conservative following—between evangelical and fundamentalistic) for various reasons, usually not exegetical, don't permit the spread of charismatic gifts. They simply ignore those gifts. Such is the case with the Baptistic position.
what is clear	There is no comprehensive list or teaching in the New Testament which exhaustively treats the doctrine of spiritual gifts. Each listing of gifts occurs in special contexts which were treating special issues. Each covers areas of doctrine which have some things common with other lists but also some things different. Listings of gifts flow with the purposes of the author in the context. So the compilation of a list of gifts have to be made comparatively. Some gifts occur repeatedly on several lists. Others do not. If there were more lists there may well be more gifts. But we can probably assume that the most important gifts are covered. So there will be differences. We do not believe that any list should be excluded or any list given any more prominence that any other.
How rationale affects views	We mentioned 7 factors: 1. where you draw your data from concerning spiritual gifts (Wimber draws from Old and New Testaments, Wagner from all New Testament—they will have larger numbers—others from all lists, the middle positions; still others from limited lioto, Coo), 2. your theological or philosophical bias will affect gifts you allow (McRae illustrates this—low numbers of gifts, the inclusiveness of evangelicals—Hummel, McRae, Clinton and Clinton—higher numbers of gifts), 3. your experience with the whole range of possible gifts (a charismatic experience will tend to make you open to the whole range of charismatic gifts), 4. your view of the work of the Holy Spirit today (if only to illunine the written Word and not to lead us into all truth as well, you will stress maily teaching, pastoring, etc), 5. your view of the functions that spiritual gifts are supposed to accomplish for a body (more will be said on this when we talk about power, love and word clusters), 6. your experiences with the use and abuse of gifts (negative experiences with charismatics will tend to make you omit those gifts,. 7. denominational biases and issues (Blanchard illustrates this).

Gifts Identification Continuum

introduction   We often introduce our workshops on giftedness with this continuum. We ask each of the participants to locate themselves in terms of their original position on the continuum when you first became aware of spiritual gifts and in terms of where they are now on the continuum. This usually gets there attention and cues us in to the kinds of issues we will be facing as we teach on gifts to that particular group. So then, here is another way to look at this issue. You could spread out the various positions along a continuum in terms of how many gifts people believe are operating today. It would look something like this.

definition   A *spiritual gift* is a God-given unique capacity which is given to each believer for the purpose of releasing a Holy Spirit empowered ministry in a situation or to be repeated again and again.

definition   A *gift* is said to be extant if it is available to today's church and can be seen in operation today.

description   The *gifts identification continuum* is a linear line, pictorial display, along which a given Bible interpreter can be located based on his/her believe in how many spiritual gifts are available today—higher numbers go to the left; lesser numbers to the right.

Gifts Identification Continuum

```
ALL  <———————————       Many gifts      Fewer gifts ————————> NO
|————————————x———————————x———————————x———————————x—————|
A              B            C            D            E            F
```

Position A =   All the gifts are available to any believer. Gift lists are drawn from both the Old Testament and the New Testament. (Wimber) [Extreme position of this is that one has the Holy Spirit and hence has all the gifts.] 30+ gifts

Position B =   Gift lists are drawn from entire New Testament. (Wagner) [Charismatic people will usually fit here.] 21-27 gifts allowed.

Position C =   Gift lists are drawn from the church era. Epistles but not Gospels. (Clinton) [Some charismatics would fit here] 19-21 gifts are seen.

Position D =   Gift lists are drawn from the 1 Corinthians 12 text. 9 Gifts are listed. [This is a common Pentecostal focus.]

Position E =   Limited use of lists from N.T. For example, gift lists are drawn from the Romans 12 text. 7 gifts are listed. (This is the so-called Motivational Gifts Viewpoint—one prominent widespread view given by a popular strong seminar teacher) [Fundamentalist would be in this area in terms of numbers of gifts but would differ on which ones they are.] Any position which picks and chooses from lists or focuses on a given list to the exclusion of another is here.

Position F =   There are no spiritual gifts. [a liberal position]

9 REASONS UNDERLYING OUR POSITION

introduction   As you can see from this material, there are a wide range of positions on how many spiritual gifts there are. Because the Scriptures don't address the issue of how many spiritual gifts there are directly, we don't believe that anyone can dogmatically say "these are the exact number of spiritual gifts and there are no others." Each position has a rationale behind it. We want to offer you the rationale behind our position. Our position says that the listing of spiritual gifts should be limited to the church era which means the epistles in the New Testament. Further, we limit a gift label to one which is actually drawn from a passage clearly talking about gifts. From these passages, we list 19 different spiritual gifts.

1.   **INDWELLING HOLY SPIRIT PHENOMENA.** Spiritual gifts are associated with the coming of the Holy Spirit. The Holy Spirit is the giver of the gifts. John 7:37-39 shows us that the Spirit was not given until after Jesus was glorified. The Ephesians 4:7 passage confirms this and shows that gifts were given then. The Holy Spirit was released at the initiation of the church era for empowerment of each believer to be a functioning part of the New Testament church.

2.   **NEW TESTAMENT CHURCH PHENOMENA.** Spiritual gifts are a New Testament church phenomena. They are given to the members of the church (the body of Christ) for the common good of its members as well as building up the body. (1 Corinthians 12:7; Ephesians 4:12)

3.   **SPIRITUAL GIFTS ONLY AFTER RELEASE OF SPIRIT.** Because of these first two points, we do not define spiritual gifts prior to the release of the Holy Spirit and the initiation of the church. Before that time there were anointings by the Spirit (which is what we assert for natural abilities and acquired skills even today). This eliminates data from the Old Testament and the Gospels in terms of defining and listing of spiritual gifts.

4.   **MAJOR CONTEXTUAL PASSAGES ON GIFTS.** Our listing of spiritual gifts comes primarily from a comparative study of the major gifts passages: 1 Corinthians 12-14 (several listings in this large context); Romans 12; Ephesians 4.

5.   **COMPARATIVE STUDY.** Because we believe in a balanced perspective on the Scriptures as a whole, we do not believe that one passage should be emphasized more than any other. We want each passage to contribute to our understanding of spiritual gifts.

6.   **VARIANCE IN INFORMATION FOR DEFINING.** We recognize that the Biblical data allows for a range of certainty on defining the spiritual gifts. Some gifts can be defined with more certainty than others because there is more information on them. Some gifts have very little information. Because of this, we recognize and allow a range of definitions on some of the gifts.

7.   **STRESS ON USE NOT IDENTIFICATION.** For the average person, we stress using gifts in ministry. Because of the difficulties involved in defining and identifying spiritual gifts, we don't want people to get bogged down in the process of identifying the gifts. Simply use what God has given you and the process of identification will become clearer as you move along.

8.   **LEADERS RESPONSIBLE FOR IDENTIFICATION AND USE.** For leaders, we stress identification as well as use. Because giftedness is such an integral part of moving toward maturity, it is necessary to have a clear understanding of your giftedness so that you can move toward development and growth with some deliberateness. And we feel you must facilitate the use of gifts among those to whom you minister. Therefore, we believe that leaders should be thoroughly familiar with the doctrine on gifts.

9.   **STEWARDSHIP MODEL.** Because of the stewardship model and its stress on accountability, we emphasize the giftedness set which includes natural abilities, acquired skills, and spiritual gifts.

FEEDBACK ON GIFTEDNESS CONTINUUM AND RATIONALE

1. To be sure you understand the 9 reasons given in our rationale statement answer the following questions.

    a. What position(s) on the Gifts Identification Continuum would automatically be excluded if one held strictly to Rationale statement #1. Check any which apply:

    ___A.   ___B.   ___C.   ___D.   ___E.   ___F.

    b. How does Rationale statements #2 (taken along with #1 and #3) affect position B?

    c. Which positions on the continuum are particularly affected by Rationale statement #4 and #5? Check any which apply. How affected?

    ___A.   ___B.   ___C.   ___D.   ___E.   ___F.

2. What rationale statements do not relate directly to the Gifts Identification Continuum which stresses numbers of gifts? What do they related to?

ANSWERS— — — — — —

1. a. √ A.   √ B.   ___C.   ___D.   ___E.   √ F.

   b. Gifts identified and defined from the Gospels would have to be omitted.

   c.   ___A.   ___B.   ___C.   √ D.   √ E.   √ F.

   They would have to allow each passage to contribute its emphasis to gifts not just the one they focus on.

2. Statements 6-9 do not refer to numbers of gifts. They refer to how one stresses definitions and use of gifts. They will come in to play in chapter 6 Spiritual Gifts, Part II.

THE BIBLICAL DATA ON SPIRITUAL GIFTS: 8 MAJOR PASSAGES

introduction   There is much more data in the New Testament on spiritual gifts than is usually reckoned with by spiritual gifts writers. There are both major and minor passages which deal with spiritual gifts. We identify a spiritual gifts passage as a passage in which two or more gifts are given by name or the text speaks about the use or abuse of spiritual gifts. Major passages are differentiated from minor ones in that they are a specific context which deals with spiritual gifts. Minor passages do not list gifts but incidentally discuss them along with some other contextual focus. These passages shed light on how some gift was used or what it meant or some other miscellaneous information about it.

description   A *major passage* refers to any context in the New Testament epistles in which two or more gifts are listed either specifically or by a generic label and/or the passage deals with the use or abuse of a gift or gifts.

comment   The gifts are numbered in order that they occur in the passages listed below. When certain gifts are repeated in a subsequent passage, the duplications are indicated by parenthesis and the number given to them when they first appeared. Where gifts are given via metonymy[3], that is, the possessor of the gift indicates the gift that is given, it will be noted.

MAJOR PASSAGES

List	Text		Gift(s)Listed
List A.	1 Corinthians 12:8-10	1.	word of wisdom
		2.	word of knowledge
		3.	faith
		4.	kinds of healings
		5.	working of power
		6.	prophecy
		7.	discernings of spirits
		8.	kinds of tongues
		9.	interpreting of tongues
List B.	1 Corinthians 12:28	10.	apostles (metonymy for apostleship)
		(6)	prophets (metonymy for prophecy)
		11.	teachers (metonymy for teaching)
		(5)	working of powers
		(4)	kinds of healings
		12.	helps
		13.	governments
		(8)	kinds of tongues

---

[3] A metonymy is a figure of speech in which one thing stands for another to which it has some relationship. The Ephesisan passage on gifts is treated this way. Those possessing the gifts are substituted for the gifts they demonstrate: Apostle for Apostleship, Prophet for prophecy, Evangelist for evangelism, pastor for pastoring, teacher for teaching. See Clinton, **Interpreting the Scriptures: Figures and Idioms**, available through Barnabas Publishers, P.O. Box 6006, Altadena, Ca, 91001.

THE BIBLICAL DATA ON SPIRITUAL GIFTS: 8 MAJOR PASSAGES CONT.

<u>List</u>	<u>Text</u>	<u>Gift(s) Listed</u>
List C.	1 Corinthians 13:1-3	(8) kinds of tongues (6) prophecy (1) word of wisdom (2) word of knowledge (3) faith 14. giving (martyrdom is a supreme act of giving)
List D.	1 Corinthians 13:8	(6) prophecy (8) kinds of tongues (2) word of knowledge
List E.	1 Corinthians 14:6	(8) kinds of tongues (revelation, word of knowledge, prophecy, teaching)
List F. 1	Corinthians 14:26,27	15. exhortation (a psalm is a means of using the gift) (11) teaching (8) kind of tongues (6) prophecy (9) interpreting of tongues (7) discernings of spirits
List G.	Romans 12:6-8	(6) prophecy ministry (occurs as a generic gift; it also occurs like this in 1 Corinthians. 12:4 and 1 Peter 4:11)[4] (11) teaching (15) exhortation (14) giving 16. ruling 17. mercy
List H.	Ephesians 4:11	(10) apostle (metonymy for apostleship) (6) prophet (metonymy for prophecy) 18. evangelist (metonymy for evangelism) 19. pastor (metonymy for pastoring) (11) teacher (metonymy for teaching)

---

[4] The notion of a generic label refers to a category of gifts under which several may fit. The notion of ministry could subsume helps, governments, or other supportive gifts). Both the gift labels in 1 Peter 4 are used this way, in my opinion (speak could be any of the basic word gifts).

BIBLICAL DATA ON SPIRITUAL GIFTS: NUMEROUS MINOR PASSAGES

introduction   There is much more data in the New Testament on spiritual gifts than is usually reckoned with by spiritual gifts writers. Most spiritual gifts writers deal only with 1 Corinthians 12, Romans 12 and maybe Ephesians 4. But there are many passages which mention gifts frequently incidentally and not as the major focus. Much can be derived from these minor passages. Major passages are differentiated from minor ones not only in the number of gifts being talked about but also in that they are a specific context which deals with spiritual gifts. Minor passages do not list gifts but incidentally discuss them along with some other contextual focus. These passages shed light on how some gift was used or what it meant or some other miscellaneous information about it. Particularly important are the non-Pauline passages which give added confirmation from other New Testament writers (John, Peter, author of Hebrews) of gifts information. This shows that the concept of gifts in the New Testament church was indeed widespread.

description   A *minor passage* refers to any context in the New Testament epistles in which one or more gifts are mentioned either specifically or by a generic label or by implication.

comment   I use here a continuation of the numbering system given in the major passages. Where a gift is not stated but implied, I give it in parenthesis, e.g. see 1 Thessalonians 5:21,22.

MINOR PASSAGES

List	Text	Contributes to Understanding of Gifts
Minor 1.	1 Thessalonians 5:12-22	(17) ruling (6) prophecy (7) (discernings of spirits)

Note: These contain a number of exhortations which are helpful regarding the use of these three gifts. The ruling gift seems to be a local church leadership gift in this use. Note the respect indicated for followers and also the relational admonition. Evidently there should be a closeness between followers and leaders. See also the 1 Timothy passages which seem to confirm this usage. This is the first mention of gifts (time-wise) in the New Testament. To refuse prophecy is to quench the work of the Spirit. But also note that prophecy is to be tested. That means that the prophetic gift is not expected to be always perfect. It must be confirmed. That which is true is to be held onto. And prophecy must not be denied as a valid New Testament church gift. The implication is that the gifts must be tried by discernings of spirits (see parallel passage in 1 John 4:1-3 for a like use).

Minor 2.	Hebrews 2:1-4	signs and wonders (generic label) (5) miracles

Note: Signs and wonders is best understood either as parallel to miracles or as a generic category of gifts that could involve healing, miracles, or other power gifting; miracles (5) are listed as a specific gift. This is an important passage, for it shows the place of the power gifts—to confirm the reality of the unseen God and give authority to His workers and the message they bring. It also gives another indication of the widespread happening of gifts in the New Testament church confirming Pauline doctrine.

Biblical Data On Spiritual Gifts: Minor Passages Continued

List	Text	Contributes to Understanding of Gifts
Minor 3.	1 Corinthians 7:7	celibacy (not a spiritual gift)

Note: This passage identifies celibacy as a special gift from God but it is not in connection with a spiritual gifts passage. I would interpret this to be a natural ability or acquired skill (a disciplined decision). In Matthew 19:1,2, Jesus describes celibacy in this way before the coming of the Spirit. Wagner probably uses this to indicate this as a spiritual gift. The problem being dealt with here is not one dealing with spiritual gifts but with sexual issues.

| Minor 4. | Romans 16:1,2 | minister (servant—generic label) |

Note: Minister (diakonon—same root of word as in Romans 12 and 1 Peter 4) is listed in a generic way. It could be that this is a leadership gift and describes Phoebe as one who operated in it.

| Minor 5. | 1 Timothy 1:18 | (6) prophecy is mentioned. |

Note: This use of prophecy was a leadership committal for Timothy and destiny preparation for the future. Now Paul encourages him to look back, remember it and be encouraged by it to recommit himself to the task—one that he is tempted to draw back from.

| Minor 6. | 1 Timothy 3:1-7, 8-13 | (17) ruling |

Note: insights are given on the ruling (leadership) function

| Minor 7. | 1 Timothy 4:1 | (6) prophecy. |

Note: There can be good and false prophecy.

| Minor 8. | 1 Timothy 4:14-16 | no gift listed but important information is given |

Note: This passage mentions the issue of impartation as well as the development of gifts. Paul exhorts Timothy to keep learning and growing in his gifts which were imparted through the laying on of hands.

| Minor 9. | 1 Timothy 5:17 | (17) ruling (leadership) |

Note: Ruling is tied to a local church position. There is a qualitative expectation concerning those operating in this capacity. It mentions the possibility of leaders being multi-gifted. Evidently the ruling gift could be alone or in conjunction with teaching or other word gifts.

| Minor 10. | 1 Timothy 6:20 | no gift mentioned directly |

Note: The idea that God has entrusted something to Timothy implies the values brought out in the stewardship model (responsibility and accountability). It also confirms the notion of vested gifts. Also, see 2 Timothy 1:12,14.

BIBLICAL DATA ON SPIRITUAL GIFTS: MINOR PASSAGES CONTINUED

List	Text	Contributes to Understanding of Gifts
Minor 11.	Titus 3:8,14	maintain (root word for ruling)

Note: The root word for ruling is translated maintain here and implies the idea of maintaining and practicing diligently the things that are good—evidently a modeling function of local leadership.

Minor 12.	2 Timothy 1:6	no gift mentioned directly

Note: Though no gift is mentioned directly important information is given. It is possible to neglect gifts that were imparted through the laying of hands. This confirms both the idea of vested gifts and accountability and developmental ideas from the stewardship model.

Minor 13.	2 Timothy 1:12-14	similar passage to 1 Timothy 6;20
Minor 14.	2 Timothy 4:5	ministry (generic label) (18) evangelism

Note: Here, the word used for ministry implies that ministry is a generic title not a specific spiritual gift. This seems to indicate that Timothy needs to do evangelism as a forced role/ gift enablement type of pattern. Paul does not say use your gift of evangelism.

Minor 15.	1 Peter 4:10-11	speaking and serving (ministry) are given as generic categories of gifts.

Note: The speaking most likely is a generic label for all word gifts. The emphasis here is not on identity but use. They must be used with power. The ministry label, used here (probably a generic label for any service type gift), must also be used with expectancy—here to show the glory of God.

Minor 16.	1 John 4:1-4	(6) prophecy (7) (discernings of spirits)

Note: Prophecy is mentioned. The emphasis is on discerning what spirit is behind the prophecy. Prophecy is to be tested. The implication is that discernings of spirits is used to test the spirits (the origin behind the prophecy);

BIBLICAL DATA ON SPIRITUAL GIFTS: POSSIBLE EXAMPLES

introduction   In addition to major passages and minor passages one can do studies of words or
                  phrases used to describe gifts in both major and minor passages. This not only pro-
                  vides additional helpful information in defining the gifts but also leads to possible
                  illustrations of gifts in passages. These may contain words or phrases from the gifts
                  passages. Or they may simply seem to illustrate what we may think a particular item
                  on a gift list means. The book of Acts has numerous possible examples of people
                  operating with spiritual gifts. This listing will only attempt to give a sampling of what
                  is in the book.

Gift	Text
kinds of tongues[5]	Acts 2:1-40
	Acts 10:46
	Acts 19:1-7
working of miracles	Acts 2:43
	Acts 4:33
	Acts 19:11-12
kinds of healings	Acts 3:1-10
	Acts 5:15
	Acts 9:32-34
exhortation	Acts 4:36
	Acts 7 (the whole thing)
	Acts 11:23-24
discernings of spirits	Acts 5:1-10
	Acts 13:9-11
	Acts 16:16-18
	Acts 19:11-12
word of knowledge	Acts 5:1-10
	Acts 9:10-19
prophecy	Acts 13:1
	Acts 16:9,10
	Acts 18:9,10
	Acts 21:9-12
word of wisdom	Acts 6:8
	Acts 15:13-21
evangelism	Acts 8:26-39
	numerous examples on the three
	missionary journeys
apostleship	throughout the entire book

---

[5] Some Pentecostal writers assume the confusing passage 1 Corinthians 12:1-3 (speaking by or in the Spirit) to refer to an instance of
kinds of tongues. The implication is that no person can use the gift of tongues to blaspheme, i.e. say that Jesus is accursed. This is
supposedly in answer to a query about tongues and their use with perhaps a suspected abuse in the Corinthian church.

FEEDBACK ON BIBLICAL DATA ON SPIRITUAL GIFTS

1. There is one thing common to all the major lists. See if you can select that one item that is common to all lists:
   ___ a. All the lists are ordered; the gifts appearing at the top of the list are more important than the ones further down the list.
   ___ b. Each of the lists simply gives the names of the gifts on the list; they do not define what the gift is.
   ___ c. Each of the lists carefully defines each of the gifts it has listed; note the context immediately following the list of gifts.
   ___ d. No list is ordered; that is, there is no priority of items on any of the lists.

2. Which of the following gifts contexts define the actual notion of what a spiritual gift is in an explicit statement?
   ___ a. 1 Corinthians 12
   ___ b. Romans 12
   ___ c. Ephesians 4
   ___ d. all of the above
   ___ e. none of the above

3. What is the most important insight you have received by studying The Biblical Data on Spiritual Gifts: 8 Major Passages?

4. What is the most important insight you have received by studying the Biblical Data on Spiritual Gifts: Numerous Minor Passages?

5. What is the most important insight you have received by studying the Biblical Data on Spiritual Gifts: Possible Examples?

ANSWERS—————-

1. √ b. And herein lies a problem. It is difficult to define each of the spiritual gifts—some moreso than others. None of the spiritual gifts passages bother to define the gifts; they just list them or talk about them. They assume the people reading the letters are familiar already with these gifts. Only one context, List B, indicates in the context that ordering of gifts are important. The 1 Corinthian List B indicates that there is a priority—apostleship, prophecy, and teaching are important. Note these are word gifts and hence carry strong influence implications. None of the other lists give any contextual warrant for saying they are prioritized. We can not assume that.

2. √ e. The Corinthian passage gives more general information about a spiritual gift as it describes how the Holy Spirit operates. The Romans passage gives a few qualifiers on its small list. But none define either the notion of a spiritual gift in general or any of the gifts in particular. Now you see why there are differences on definitions.

3. Your choice. For me, I am impressed with the necessity of comparative study. I am also overwhelmed with how little definitive information is given—meaning that interpreters will supply a lot of ideas heavily conditioned by their own understandings of many of these concepts.

4. Again, your choice. I am impressed that there is much more in the Scriptures about gifts than I had ever thought. I have a lot of work ahead of me doing detailed study of the many passages and drawing out implications.

5. Again, your choice. There is much more here than I have seen. I have not even pointed out the illustrations of spiritual gifts in Jesus life.

CLUSTERS OF SPIRITUAL GIFTS—VENN DIAGRAM

introduction   We have been mentioning the comparison of gifts passages. Sometimes a picture is better than a thousand words. It is helpful to use a Venn diagram to portray the various gifts passages in relationship with one another so as to identify the common items and the distinct differences. In reading the Venn diagram below if a gift occurs inside an oval-like enclosure it belongs to that group (i.e. occurs on that list). In fact, a given gift occurs on any list represented by enclosures that surround it. For example, the helps gift occurs in the 1 Corinthians oval and the Romans oval but not the Hebrews 2, Ephesians 4 or 1 Peter 4 ovals. Prophecy occurs inside all ovals but the Hebrews 2 and 1 Peter 4, indicating it a solid gift, indeed.

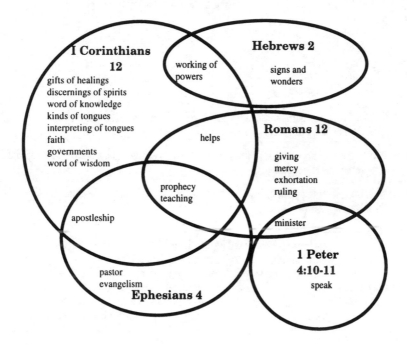

    This Venn diagram helps one identify the concept of generic labels. It is clear that 1 Peter and Hebrews contain names not commonly found among a majority of the other passages and hence are probably indicating generic function-like labels.

FEEDBACK ON VENN DIAGRAM OF BIBLICAL DATA

1. Glance again at the Venn diagram picturing the five gifts passages. According to this diagram, which passage has the most information on spiritual gifts. Check your choice.

___a. 1 Corinthians ___ b. Hebrews 2 ___c. Romans 12 ___d. Ephesians 4 ___e. 1 Peter 4

2. What two gifts occur only in the Ephesisans passage and not any other lists?
___a. signs and wonders, working of powers
___b. minister, speak
___c. prophecy, teaching
___d. pastor, evangelism
___e. none of the above

3. What two gifts occur commonly on all of the following lists: 1 Corinthians, Ephesians 4, and Romans 12 lists.

___a. helps, minister
___b. prophecy, teaching
___c. pastor, evangelism
___d. signs and wonders, working of powers

4. List the gifts that occur exclusively (only) for each of the passages.
a. 1 Corinthians 12:
b. Hebrews 2:
c. Romans 12:
d. Ephesians 4:
e. 1 Peter 4:

ANSWERS————————

1. __√__ a. 1 Corinthians. This is a normal feature of Venn diagrams. Something is larger when it is more important or has more prominence or in this case a longer list of gifts.

2. __√__ d. pastor, evangelism

3   __√__ b. prophecy, teaching

4. a. 1 Corinthians 12: word of wisdom, word of knowledge, faith, gifts of healings, discernings of spirits, kinds of tongues, interpreting of tongues, governments,
b. Hebrews 2: signs and wonders
c. Romans 12: giving, mercy, exhortation, ruling
d. Ephesians 4: pastor, evangelism
e. 1 Peter 4: speak

Perspectives On Gift Passages—The Corinthian Passage

introduction   In the next chapter we shall define each of the basic spiritual gifts that we have compiled from each of the major passages. Before doing that we will list how different
groups view each of these passage. Glance at the chart given below which gives some
common viewpoints.

NO GIFTS	GIFTS ARE OPERATIVE			
liberals some dispensa- tional groups	Some gifts but no sign gifts	All gifts exist but we don't permit the use of sign gifts	All gifts are to be used. especially the sign gifts; 2 views of sign gifts	
	teaching helps govenments faith (as a Christian Role)	Certain Mission boards certain churchs issue of tongues is especially sensitive	sign gifts are valid as gifts but not as signs	certain gifts such as tongues are seen as signs of the Holy Spirit

overview   There are nine gifts given on List A, the sign gifts.[6] These are kinds of healings,
discernings of spirits, word of knowledge, word of wisdom, kinds of tongues, interpreting of tongues, faith, work of powers (miracles), and prophecy. List B gives another 8, some by metonymy. All in all this list repeats 4 of the ones on List A and
introduces 4 new gifts: teaching, apostleship, helps and governments. List C repeats 5
already introduced and adds giving. Since there is question about the added gift I
don't cover it here but do so in Romans where it is clearly give. List D repeats 3 already
give. List E repeats one already given. List F gives 6 of which 5 are repeated and one
new one is incidentlly given. Again I don't give it here but include it in the Romans
group where it is explicitly given. For different reasons not all approach the Corinthian
gifts passages the same way. As you can see from the above chart not all groups believe that all the Corinthian gifts are available today. And some give special meaning
to the sign gifts. The problems primarily are with the sign gifts. Some don't believe
they exist. Others view them, or at least tongues, as a necessary sign of the presence of
the Holy Spirit.

---

[6] Sometimes we use the term charismatic gifts to mean word of knowledge, kinds of healings, tongues, interpretation of tongues from
among the sign gifts.

FEEDBACK ON CORINTHIAN PERSPECTIVES

For all of the following you will have to examine the diagram on the Corinthian passage.

1. Look at the second column under GIFTS ARE OPERATIVE, All gifts exist but we don't permit the use of sign gifts. Assume that the people holding this position believe in the authority of the Word of God. How would you explain this apparent inconsistent position?

2. Explain the implications of the differences between the two sub-columns (sign gifts are valid as gifts but not as signs, certain gifts such as tongues are seen as special signs of the Holy Spirit).

3. From an examination of the Clinton and Clinton List 7 on page 96 can you tell in which column Clinton and Clinton would be on the Corinthian diagram?

4. From an examination of the McRae List 4 on page 94 can you tell in which column McRae would be on the Corinthian diagram?

5. From an examination of the Blanchard LIST 5 on page 95 can you tell in which column Blanchard would be on the Corinthian diagram?

6. From an examination of the Gee List 6 on page 94 can you tell in which column Gee would be on the Corinthian diagram?

ANSWERS—————-

1. They in effect are saying God gives all these gifts but we are going to override Him in our situation. In effect, they are challenging the authority of the Word. Most groups take this position because of the abuses seen with those gifts. The enthusiasm of groups to push the sign gifts as signs of a more effective relationship with God is an abuse that splits groups. But we must all remember that we can not ignore a truth simply because it is abused. Who knows? The forbidding of use of those gifts may be just as much an abuse as the other in the total strategic picture of what God is wanting to do. The old saying two wrongs don't make a right seems to apply.

2. Recognition of all gifts as valid as gifts means that all the gifts listed are extant. They can be used as gifts in the body for the purposes that the gifts are given. The final column means that some groups believe all believers should have certain sign gifts and are missing out on the blessing of God If they don't seek and obtain those special sign gifts. To them the presence of the gifts in a believer's life is often more important than the use of the gift for the edification of the body.

3. Can't tell exactly but since all the gifts are listed you know that Clinton and Clinton are on the GIFTS ARE OPERATIVE side and at least in the sub-column All gifts exist. In fact, they are in the position that sign gifts do exist but valid as gifts only.

4. He would be in the GIFTS ARE OPERATIVE, Some gifts but no sign gifts.

5. Apparently Blanchard would be in GIFTS ARE OPERATIVE, All gifts exist but we don't permit the use of sign gifts.

6. Gee would be in the GIFTS ARE OPERATIVE, at least the two final columns. From a knowledge of classical Pentecostalism you could identify him as being in the final column but you couldn't tell that just from his list.

COMMENTARY ON 1 CORINTHIAN PASSAGE

introduction
Thus far we have identified some major passages and given labels to list of gifts in them. What we have not done is to say what the passages are actually given in Scripture for. We must always hermeneutically study each passage. Before we can draw out teaching we must study each of the passages in terms of the purposes for which they were given. I have done this fairly thoroughly in a previous book, **Spiritual Gifts**, which you should probably get and use in a complementary fashion with this manual. But I shall at least summarize some of what was given there so you can see that our use of gift information is in harmony with what Paul was teaching. Don't forget that though none of the major passages on gifts has as it primary purpose an exhaustive treatment of the doctrine of spiritual gifts, 1 Corinthians 12-14 probably contributes the most information about spiritual gifts. And we must underline that one must first recognize the major purposes of any passage and interpret teachings drawn out of the passage in the light of the purpose.

purpose of
1 Corinthians
12-14
related to the
book as a
whole
Paul, in 1 Corinthians, is dealing with a series of problems which confronted the church in Corinth. The letter as a whole has as its main purpose the solutions of these problems. The book as a whole teaches that church problems, individual or corporate, can be solved by submitting to God's revealed truth concerning those problems. To the various problems Paul does *not* just give an authoritative command or an arbitrary rule. He states the principles with which the problems are concerned and thus gives solutions which have value for us today. For while specific conditions today may differ from those of the Corinthian church, the problems dealt with are analogous and Paul's principles can often be reapplied to our situation. The problems to which Paul addresses himself are grouped as follows: an ecclesiastical problem—divisions in the church; then three moral questions—about discipline, law suits, impurity in social life; two questions of expediency—marriage, meats; three problems of public worship—conduct of women, practice of the Lord's supper, and orderly exercise of spiritual gifts; and a final doctrinal problem—the resurrection. The purpose of 1 Corinthians 12-14, which contain the gifts passages we have referenced, is aimed at the third and probably most important problem of public worship—the orderly exercise of spiritual gifts.

specific
problem
defined
1 Corinthians
12-14
Certain spiritual gifts (tongues singled out especially) were being regarded almost as ends in themselves rather than means used by God for purposes relating to His church. The use of these gifts for pride and gratification of the user was evident. Further, the particular gift singled out (tongues) was most highly prized though not the most useful by far. The exercise of these gifts was resulting in envy, spiritual pride, and divisions. Further, public worship services were being disrupted and were not accomplishing their God-given purposes because of the emphasis on exercising the gifts.

Paul's basic
answer to the
problem
Paul answers the problems above by showing in,

1 Corinthians 12:1-11,
- That the test of true spirituality involves submission to the Lordship of Christ.
- That all gifts are important because they come as a direct result of the Holy Spirit's sovereign ministry.

1 Corinthians 12:12-27,
- That all gifts are important because of the inderdependent nature of the church.
- That the gifts operating harmoniously together, each contributing its function, should have as its purpose the edification of the church as a whole.

1 Corinthians 12:28-31,
- That the possession of no single gift is a test of one's spiritual maturity. Not all church members can be expected to have any one particular gift.

COMMENTARY: ON THE CORINTHIANS PASSAGE CONTINUED

1 Corinthians 12:28-31 continued

- That God has in fact given an order to the gifts which places what are sometimes called leadership gifts at the forefront and that the particular gifts being prized by the Corinthian church were quite far down the ladder. But even so, Paul's tone indicated that due to the inderdependent nature of all gifts there should be no spiritual pride associated with any of these gifts.
- That, if there is a prizing of gifts, at least seek that which is most useful and beneficial to the whole church.

1 Corinthians 13,

- That a proper attitude behind our exercising our gifts, that of love, is essential more important than the gifts or results of exercising hose gifts.
- That love is an enduring quality while gifts are to be used in time.

1 Corinthians 14,

- That the relative value of spiritual gifts is to be tested by their usefulness to the church as a whole (contrast of prophecy and tongues is the example illustrating this).
- That joint participation of each gift in public worship should be in terms of edifying the whole church.
- That orderliness in public worship is consistent with the way God does things.

caution
in drawing
out teaching

Having recognized what Paul is trying to do in this passage it is well that we give some cautions in drawing out teaching on spiritual gifts. Paul does <u>not</u> purpose to give an exhaustive list of gifts <u>nor</u> to define the various gifts. he does <u>not</u> tell exactly how the gifts are to be used except to show that they are necessary because of the interdependent nature of the church. He does say the gifts should be used to edify and hence there should be an orderly and <u>not</u> confusing use of these gifts in public. He does show that love should be an essential part of our use of our gifts. Keep these limiting factors in mind, then, in observing the list of gifts and implications on these gifts.

principles

From the 1 Corinthians 12-14 discourse we can draw some principles:

- On the one hand, spiritual gifts are sovereignly given by the Holy Spirit, and yet on the other hand, believers are admonished to desire the best gifts.
- The Holy Spirit gives all the gifts necessary to accomplish His work in a local church.
- Every believer has at least one gift and may have more and may seek in God's will for more.
- A believer's gift may differ in degree and effectiveness from another believer having the same gift.
- Each member with his/her gift is necessary to the whole body and therefore if any member is UnotU active the body as a whole is weakened.
- The gifts emphasize servcidc3 to the body of Christ.
- The motivation behind the exercise of a gift is love.

PERSPECTIVES ON GIFT PASSAGES—THE ROMANS PASSAGE

introduction   There are seven gifts that are listed on List G, the Romans passage. The gifts listed are
                prophecy, teaching, exhortation, ruling, serving, mercy, and giving. Pictorially here
                are some common viewpoints on the gifts listed in this text.

NO GIFTS	GIFTS ARE OPERATING		
	Some gifts but not all	All the gifts	These 7 gifts are the only valid gifts
Liberals Some dispensational groups	no prophecy (based on 2 Peter 2:1)	All gifts are valid as gifts	called the motivational gifts all other spiritual gifts are manifestation of these seven gifts

overview   This list with the exception of prophecy contain no controversial gifts hence it is used
                by most teachers, even those with very conservative views on gifts. Some would view
                all but prophecy valid and would rule it out on the basis of 2 Peter 2:1, that teaching
                has replaced the prophetic function. Others would simply define prophecy in this in-
                stance as the preaching gift and not a revelatory gift. One teacher with widespread
                influence sees the Romans passage as *the gifts passage.* He would define these gifts in
                our terms as the only *vested gifts.* All other items we would term gifts from other
                major gifts lists, he would say are manifestations which are rooted in these gifts.

FEEDBACK ON ROMAN PERSPECTIVES

For all of the following questions you will have to examine the Diagram on the Romans perspectives.

1. Where would McRae be on this diagram (see his List 4 page 94)?

2. Where would Blanchard be on this diagram (see his List 5 on page 95)?

3. What valid exegetical reason would there be for someone to hold the position taken by the final column, These 7 gifts are the only valid gifts?

4. What is your opinion concerning the notion held by some in the second column that prophecy is not valid and has been superseded by teaching, based on the 2 Peter 2:1? Is that a valid, exegetical argument?

ANSWERS———————-

1. Some gifts but not all.

2. Some gifts but not all. He probably, personally drifts toward the next column.

3. In my opinion there is no valid exegetical reason for giving more weight to the Romans passage, that is, interpreting all others only in the light of it. Just as it is not valid to interpret only List A on the sign gifts as the most important.

4. In my opinion, this is shaky. The verse is dealing with the recognition that we can expect false teaching. It is not talking about cessation of gifts. Not all who teach the Bible will be giving truth.

COMMENTARY ON ROMANS PASSAGE

introduction   Thus far we have identified some major passages and given labels to list of gifts in
                      them. I have given you a summary of what I think Paul was saying in the 1 Corinthians
                      12-14 passage. Let me now do the same for the Romans 12 passage. Remember I am
                      basically summarizing what I have done in a previous book, **Spiritual Gifts**, which
                      you may want to get and use in a complementary fashion with this manual. Though
                      none of the four major passages on gifts has as its primary purpose an exhaustive
                      treatment of the doctrine of spiritual gifts each contributes in some way to the infor-
                      mation on gifts. Romans 12:1-8 does so by adding several new gifts to the list of gifts
                      and by correlating the use of gifts with determining the will of God for our lives.

purpose of   Romans teaches that God's gracious provision of Christ's righteousness
Romans   (=the Gospel of God) to every believer encompasses mankind's total need,
12:1-8   is consistent with redemptive history, and applies to all of life's
related to   relationships. The passage touching on gifts occurs in the large section (12-
the book as   15) which deals with the application of the Gospel to relationships of life—
a whole   one of the practical outflows of the gospel is service to God. Romans 12 connects
                      service to God and practical everyday living of Christianity back to what God has
                      done in the Gospel. Romans 12:1-8, the gifts passage, shows that true dedication to
                      God involves,

                      •   surrender to Him,
                      •   constant change in our lives which results in maturity,
                      •   a search of God's will which involves service for Him in terms of a proper
                             evaluation of one's gifts and exercising of those gifts interdependently
                             with others.

principles   •   All of us as believers are to evaluate ourselves in terms of our God-given
                             gifts (12:3).
                      •   We should recognize that our gifts will differ and hence we should have
                             liberty to apply ourselves to the particularly gift or gifts that are uniquely ours
                             (12:6).
                      •   We should exercise our gifts in faith according to the depth of faith which God
                             gives each of us (12:6).
                      •   How we exercise our gifts, that is, the motivating spirit behind the use of t h e
                             gift and the attitude prevailing as we exercise the gift, is as important   as the
                             fact that we do exercise it. (Note the qualifying phrases—according to the mea-
                             sure of faith, sharing in simplicity, ruling diligently, showing mercy cheerfully.)
                      •   Each member should have an opportunity to use his/her gifts interdependently
                             with others (12:4-6).

Perspectives On Gift Passages—The Ephesians Passage

introduction   In this passage there are five gifts that are listed. Paul uses a metonymy (in our opinion) in this passage to describe 5 gifts. A metonymy is a figure of speech in which one word is substituted for another word to which it is closely related in order to emphasize something that is indicated in the relationship. In this passage, Paul uses people to describe certain kinds of spiritual gifts that the people demonstrate. There are five that are listed: apostles (apostleship), prophets (prophecy), evangelists (evangelism), pastors (pastoring), and teachers (teaching). Pictorially then here are some common viewpoints on the gifts listed in this text.

NO GIFTS	GIFTS ARE OPERATING		
liberal groups some dispensational groups those who view these as roles, functions, or offices of leaders in the church	Some gifts are operating but not all	All gifts are operating but a couple	All are operating
	only pastor-teacher gift is operating evangelism is not a gift prophecy is not operating	some groups say all are operating except apostleship some groups say all are operating except prophecy	All gifts are operating

overview   The major problem with this is as a gifts passage has to do with the use of Apostles, Prophets, Evangelists, Pastors, Teachers as opposed to the name for the gifts. Some people view these as offices and not gifts. Then the question arises, do these offices still exist, especially the Apostolic office. However, since three of the five do appear on other lists as spiritual gifts and a fourth is on a mixed gift list (List B) in which it is clear that gifts are being talked about, we think it reasonable to interpret these as metonymies (certainly an option) to be the gifts of apostleship, prophecy, evangelism, pastoring, teaching. One prominent Christian leader does not. This means that for him evangelism is not a spiritual gift (it only occurs here). If it is not a gift then all should operate in it—a Christian role. They can not use lack of evangelism as a gift as a cop out for exercising a strong witness with others. There are differences on viewing this passage. We must be tolerate with different views. However, ours is reasonable since we can back up all the gifts on this list except evangelism and pastoring via other passages.

FEEDBACK ON EPHESIANS PERSPECTIVES

For all of the following questions you will have to examine the Diagram on the Ephesians perspectives.

1.   Where would McRae be on this diagram (see his List 4 page 94)?

2.   Where would Blanchard be on this diagram (see his List 5 on page 95)?

3.   Where would Gee be on this diagram (see List 6 page 95)?

4.   From a study of the passage itself what valid reason would there be to exclude Apostleship and Prophecy as not being valid today but choose evangelism and pastor-teacher as being valid?

ANSWERS——————-

1.   Most likely in the third column. He does list evangelism, pastor-teacher.
2.   Some gifts but not all. He probably, personally drifts toward the next column.
3.   You can not tell since he doesn't really deal with this passage per se. However, one of his sign gifts, prophecy does show up here. Some Pentecostal groups hold these as offices (and of course, they would believe those in the offices have the gifts that go with the office).
4.   In my opinion there is no valid exegetical reason for excluding the two based on the Ephesians passage. If one lists evangelism and pastoring-teaching as gifts they have already gotten beyond the office problem. So they are treating these as gifts. Since pastoring and apostleship do occur on other gift lists they can't ignore them and be consistent. If they hold these as offices only there is some validation for excluding pastoring and evangelism as gifts since they don't occur on any other lists.

COMMENTARY ON EPHESIANS PASSAGE

introduction
: Thus far we have identified some major passages and given labels to list of gifts in them. I have given you a summary of what I think Paul was saying in the 1 Corinthians 12-14 and Romans 12 passage. Let me now do the same for the Ephesian 4 passage. Remember I am basically summarizing what I have done in a previous book, **Spiritual Gifts**, which you may want to get and use in a complementary fashion with this manual. We definitely need to see what was happening contextually before we try to draw out giftedness information. This passage contributes less to the actual information on gifts than does 1 Corinthians 12-14 and Romans 12:1-8. However, it is extremely important in that it connects the teaching of gifts to the eternal purpose of God for the church and thus implies that gifts within the church are an essential part of the nature of the church and hence of the eternal purposes.

purpose of Ephesians 4:1-16 to the book as a whole
: Ephesians is primarily a book dealing the high purposes of the church. It teaches us that the revealed wonder of the church demands a holy walk. The revealed wonder of the church relates to a cosmic purpose that God has for the church—to show his power and his ability to integrate into oneness diverse elements in the universe. This wonder of the church was revealed to Paul. Because of its wonder and eternal significance there are demands made upon believers to live out their part of this reveled wonder. The very first demand made upon believers to live out their part of this revealed wonder involves unity (Ephesians 4:1-16). It is in this section of practical application toward unity that the Ephesian passage on gifts is given. Its primary purpose is to show that gifted leadership was given to the church in order that it might progress toward a unified spiritual maturity. It also indicates how these *leadership gifts* are part of an interdependent exercise of gifts of all members of the church. The proper interdependent exercise of leadership gifts and other gifts will bring about a maturity of oneness in believers and continued progress toward Christ-like living.

comment
: The gift of evangelism and pastoring which did not occur in any of the lists in Corinthians or Romans is included in the Ephesian list. By adding it to the apostles, prophets, etc., it would seem to rank in importance with them.

principles
: • People with leadership gifts are to train others so that every member will contribute to the overall growth of the whole body.

: • The church as a whole will not reach a unified maturity unless each of its members is exercising his/her gift in concert with other members.

possible differences
: Some would not interpret the list given in verse 11 as representing (by figure of speech, metonymy) gifts but leaders given to the church. One would assume that the names mean something. That is, a prophet leader would be one who exercises the gift of prophesy; an apostle would be one who exercises an apostlic function; an evangelist would be one who exercises the gift of evangelism; a pastor would be one who would exercise a pastoral gift; a teacher would be one who would exercise a teaching gift. Further, since apostles, prophets, and teachers occurs on List B from Corinthians in a gifts context it seems logical to assume that the other two, pastor and evangelist, are also really representing gifts (by metonymy). As a matter of fact all gifts given to the church are in the form of people.

other possible difference
: Some would say that the leadership gifts listed here belong to the universal church (roving itinerant type ministry). They would thus say that the *saints* they are equipping would have *lesser* gifts. However, again other gifts passages describing local church situations mix these so-called leadership gifts in with the lesser gifts and assume all of them present among the local saints.

: The pastors and teachers could be interpreted as pastors who are teachers. Some analysts so interpret. Here they would then have a pastor-teacher gift. McRae does so.

FINAL COMMENTARY: THE THREE MAJOR PASSAGES COMPARED

introduction

What do we gain if we emphasize one passage to the exclusion of others? Or what do we lose if we emphasize one passage to the exclusion of others? Here I am referring mainly to List A in Corinthians, List G in Romans and List H in Ephesians.

focus on
List A
only

If we only use List A, the so called sign gifts, as the classical Pentecostals do what do we gain. This passage taken in the light of the contexts leading up to it which refer to the ministry of the Holy Spirit indicate that the Spirit manifests (in the context of the body meeting) gifts sovereignly. When the body meets we can expect the Holy Spirit to manifest gifts. That is, the gifts may be a *come and go* type thing. There will be spontaneity meeting needs. There will be power. There will be the sense of God's presence and reality. All of these are the positive effects of majoring on this passage. But what we lose is the on-going continuity seen in vested gifts. While there is spontaneity when the body meets there is also an on-going exercise of gifts on a regular basis by leaders and by others. They repeatedly exercise these gifts. If you take List A alone there is no accountability or even much possibility of developing since no one can count of any gift. Further, there is the lack of directedness implied by List H by responsible leadership. But the use of List G or List H implies vested gifting and on-going development as well as direction of responsible leadership as gifts are used for the body. So then List A is important but needs the other two lists to add stability.

focus on
List G
only

List G shows that God gives not only gifts to individuals but they have a responsibility to know themselves and develop to the measure of potential God has given them. There is an accountability attached to giftedness. There is a seeking of God's will related to giftedness. The body will have stability. These are the positive things. But if we limit ourselves to List G alone we miss the spontaneity of the Holy Spirit—the surprises when the body meets and has its needs met by the dancing hand of God.[7] We also miss the emphasis of the importance of the responsible gifted-leadership of List H.

focus
on List H
only

List H indicates that responsible gifted leadership is given the church by God. This leadership will unify, edify and bring the body to maturity as each grows and contributes to the process. There is a stability which can take the church to its ideals—form which it was created. Those are the positive things. But if this passage alone is used what is missing is the strong contribution of the laity with their giftedness (seen in the context following List A and along with List G). What is missing is the spontaneity of the sign gifts (apart from the prophetical).

flexibility
and balance

So then we need the flexibility to allow the come and go gifts of List A to operate when the body meets as well as the need to recognize on-going responsibility to develop those gifts which are permanently (vested) given to leaders and followers. And we need to recognize gifted leadership and its functions. All the clusters—word, power, and love—will be manifest if we allow the gifts of all the lists to have their place.

---

[7] The *dancing hand of God* is Wimber's phrase referring to the ministry of the Holy Spirit as implied in the List A passage and its surrounding contexts.

The Gift-Role Chart

introduction | In our opinion, some people confuse Christian Roles with spiritual gifts. A Christian role is an activity commanded for every believer. There is much overlap between some expected Christian roles and some of the uses of spiritual gifts. The Bible is clear in articulating that many activities are expected of each believer. Many of the reciprocal commands (the one another commands) reveal that we are to be involved in such activities as giving, having faith,[8] witnessing, exhorting, teaching, showing mercy, being helpful, and caring for one another. These same activities also are seen to be similar to the use of some gifts as seen in the chart given below.

definition | A *Christian role* is an activity that every believer is commanded to be involved in due to being part of the Christian movement.

comment | While all Christians will operate in Christian roles and thus witness to the fact of the impact of Christianity in their lives some will be able to operate in some of these functions with powerful results because they are gifted to do so.

comment | Avoic two extremes on this issue. First, people who do not have certain gifts that overlap with certain roles can not use that as an excuse to not operate in the role. For example, every believer is to be a witness to the world concerning Jesus Christ regardless of a gift of evangelism. Secondly, people with strong gift projection tendencies should not use Christian roles to lay guilt trips on people not having those gifts. Often, people who project certain gifts on others expect and evaluate people on the basis of how they operate in that type of ministry.

Spiritual Gift	Similar Christian Role
1. pastoring	caring for others (1 Corinthians 12:24-25; Galatians 6:9,10)
2. evangelism	being a witness (Acts 1:8)
3. faith	we are all to believe. (Hebrews 11:6)
4. word of knowledge	we are all to gain knowledge (2 Peter 1:5)
5. word of wisdom	we are all to gain wisdom (James 1:5; 3:17-19)
6. discerning of spirits	we are all to be discerning (Hebrews 5:14; 1 John 4:1-3)
7. kinds of healings	Leaders are all expected to pray for the sick. (James 5:13-18)
8. giving	we are all to give to others
9. mercy	compassion for others (parable of the Good Samaritan)
10. exhortation	encourage one another (1 Thessalonians 5:11)
11. teaching	we are to instruct one another (Romans 15:14)

---

[8] See Sue Harville's manual, **Reciprocal Living**, published by Worldteam in 1976. It is now out of print but often available in Seminary and Bible College libraries.

FEEDBACK ON GIFT VERSUS CHRISTIAN ROLES

1. Examine again McRae's List 4 on page 94. Notice that gift 9 is faith. a. From what list in Scripture could he possibly get this gift? b. How can he be consistent with his anti-signs posture and yet use this gift?

2. I have been told that one prominent Christian leader today who has consistently led many people to Christ and has many followers who have also led many to Christ holds that List H, the Ephesians list, does not refer to gifts. He then consistent with his view asserts that there is no gift of evangelism. Why can he do this? How do you explain his effectiveness in evangelism (and his followers)?

3. Look at item 3 on the list. How would you differentiate between faith as a gift and faith as a Christian role?

4. Look at item 8 on the list. How would you differentiate between giving as a gift and giving as a Christian role?

5. Look at item 9 on the list. How would you differentiate between mercy as a gift and mercy as a Christian role?

ANSWERS———————-

1. It only occurs on List A with the sign gifts. He does not take into account the context of gifts surrounding the faith gift. They are all supernatural manifestations. I think he is identifying this gift with the Christian role of faith. We all are to believe.

2. If evangelism does not appear anywhere else and the Ephesians List H is not spiritual gifts then he is consistent. He would assert that evangelism is a Christian role that all are to participate in. He would see it in terms of a skill that can be learned by anyone. And he applies this skill with great enthusiasm and results. He would contend that anyone could also do this. I would assert that he has the gift of evangelism. And he attracts others like himself with that gift. That could be one reason for his success and his followers. But God does bless our attempts to witness to Christ and His saving power. Even if we don't have the gift of evangelism. But those with evangelism as a gift see more fruit and have an inward drive to use that gift. Their ministry would be more natural for it flows out of who they are.

3. This is really an unfair questions since we haven't yet defined faith as a gift. But in my opinion faith is a revelatory gift in which God reveals something to one having that gift. They then can trust God to see it come to pass. Faith as a Christian role includes learning about God and what He says and taking steps to accept that and act upon it.

4. Again this is unfair since we haven't yet defined giving as a gift. All Christians are to give and we do that to promote God's work among ourselves and around the world. But a person with the gift of giving will be supernaturally led as to when to give, who or what to give to and will see God supply or give resources to allow the giving to happen. A person with a giving gift needs no exhortation or pledge cards or elbow twisting to give. He/she will do so with a great sense of freedom and joy.

5. Again as with question 3 and 4 this is unfair. Christians with the gift of mercy will *drift* toward roles and ministries that allow for that God-given empathy to demonstrate His love on a regular basis. The inner drive within them will enable them to engage in outward manifestations of their compassion. They will see needs and be more sensitive to them than a Christian without the gift. All of us are to have compassion and to some extent we will as we learn more of God's truth and apply it to our lives. But the mercy gifted person will not need the encouraging that a non-mercy person would to get involved.

THREE CORPORATE FUNCTIONS OF GIFTS: WORD, POWER, LOVE

introduction   We now recognize three generic functions, i.e. groupings of spiritual gifts. We call these power gifts, word gifts and love gifts.[9] These three categories represent crucial corporate functions.

description   *Power gifts* demonstrate the authenticity, credibility, power and reality of the
power gifts   unseen God.

examples   miracles, kinds of healings, word of knowledge

description   *Love gifts*_are manifestations attributed to God through practical ways that can be
love gifts   recognized by a world around us which needs love. They demonstrate the reality of relating to this God.

example   mercy, helps, pastoring

description   *Word gifts* clarify the nature of this unseen God and what He expects from His
word gifts   followers. People using these gifts both communicate about God and for God.

example   exhortation, teaching, prophecy

description   *Balance* is the term used to describe a proper relationship between manifestations
balance   of love, word, and power clusters operating in a given context so that God's witness in that situation can be adequate.

comment   There are two reasons why this concept of corporate functions of spiritual gifts are important. First, a leader can evaluate his/her situation and look for balance in the groups giftedness. All three of these corporate functions are needed in each ministry situation. One of the things that leaders need to do is to create a context in which there can be balance. Balance does not mean equal representation between the three types of functions. Rather, balance means that the appropriate level of word, love and power gifts are operating as needed in the situation. Some ministry contexts need more of one kind of gifting than another. And frequently there are gift vacuums, that is, a ministry may be missing one or more clusters altogether.

   Secondly, our studies of leaders have revealed that all leaders have at least one word gift in their gift-mix. This can be a helpful piece of knowledge when it comes to leadership identification.

---

[9] These categories originated out of our study of Paul's affirmation to churches (corporate groups) for their impact on their environ-ments. These affirmations occurred in an almost formula-like way in many of his salutations in his epistles. His full affirmation formula included faith. love, and hope. With some churches he would give partial affirmation. And with one church, with which he was extremely displeased he gave no affirmation at all. A study of these affirmations led to the identification of the functions: faith—the ability to believe in the unseen God (the function of the POWER gifts) , love—the manifestation of the reality of the unseen God in the lives of those who know Him (the function of the LOVE gifts), hope—the expectation of what He is doing; that is, the clarification of who He is, what He desires and what He is doing.(the function of the WORD gifts). The identification of clusters of gifts that did those functions followed as did the actual naming of them as WORD, POWER, and LOVE clusters. It was after this identification of clusters that we saw the connection between Word gifts and leadership. *All leaders we had studied always had at least one word gift in their gift-mix; many had more than one.* This idea is a powerful implication for the selection and development of leaders.

THREE CORPORATE FUNCTIONS: WORD, POWER, LOVE CONTINUED

introduction   Below, given in pictorial form are the three clusters, along with the individual gifts
                 that aid these functions. Notice some gifts operate in more than one cluster.

POWER, LOVE AND WORD GIFTS

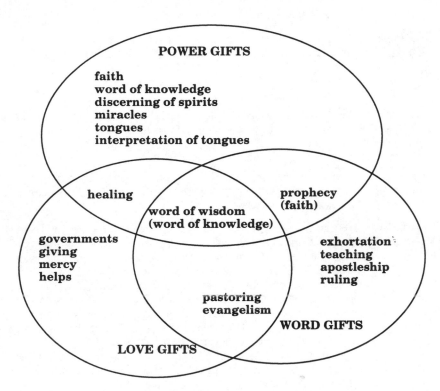

Power gifts =   faith, word of knowledge, discernings of spirits, miracles, tongues, interpretation of
                 tongues, healing, word of wisdom, prophecy. These all help demonstrate the reality of
                 the unseen God.

Love gifts =   governments, giving, mercy, helps, pastoring, evangelism, healing, word of wisdom,
                 word of knowledge. These all demonstrate the beauty of that unseen God's work in
                 lives in such a way as to attract others to want this same kind of relationship.

Word gifts =   exhortation, teaching, apostleship, ruling, prophecy, faith, pastor, evangelism, word of
                 wisdom, word of knowledge. These all help us understand about this God including
                 His nature, His purposes and how we can relate to Him and be a part of His purposes.

FEEDBACK ON CORPORATE FUNCTIONS OF GIFTS

Examine the three profiles shown below then answer the questions which follow. An oval labeled with **A** means a **Word cluster**. An oval with **B** means a **love cluster**. An oval with **C** means a **power cluster**.

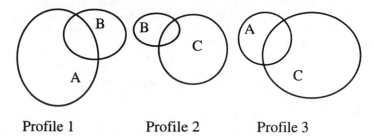

Profile 1   Profile 2   Profile 3

1. In your own words describe a church that would be represented by Profile 1.

2. In your own words describe a church that would be represented by Profile 2.

3. In your own words describe a church that would be represented by Profile 3.

4. How would you assess balance in each of the three profiles.

ANSWERS——————

1. Profile 1 represents a church with a strong word ministry—since there is absolutely no power it means dominantly teaching and exhortation gifts. This would be a typical Bible Church. It has some compassion ministry but it is clear that it is dominantly a classroom type of church. The love cluster is about half within and half without the church. This means that there are probably a number of helps and governments gifts operating in the church doing service ministries and a number of mercy, helps types reaching out of the church. This church could use some power gifts in order to break through and reach new people for Christ. Its leadership gifts are probably pastoral and teaching. There could be some evangelism. No apostolic or prophetic types would probably be welcome here.

2. This church has strong power gifts. Since it has power gifts there will be some word ministry through the prophetical, word of knowledge, word of wisdom gifts. But for the most part there will be no teaching and any exhortation would be in terms of the power gifts. It also has some love gifts working both in and out of the church—more outside than in. But its lack of teaching means probably no Sunday School ministries so it probably doesn't need as many helps and governments inside the church. The question is how to get word gifts in here. The leadership gifts in this church are probably apostolic, maybe evangelistic, maybe prophetic. There is probably a need for pastoral ministry.

3. This is a church dominated with power gifts but one which has some ministry in the word. This means the leadership gifts in the church are probably apostolic and prophetical with possibly some teaching and a little pastoring. What is probably missing is an evangelistic thrust—no love gifts working. This church probably is having a hard time getting people to do ministry jobs in the church.

4. Unfair to ask. We need to know the contextual situations. For example, if Profile A was in the highlands of Papua New Guinea it would extremely out of balance—for power gifts are needed to get a hearing. But, in general, all three profiles are somewhat weak. Whenever a cluster is missing altogether there is a need.

7 Factors Concerning A Person Receiving Spiritual Gifts

introduction   The Scriptures indicate that the bestowal of a spiritual gift is a sovereign act of the Holy Spirit (1 Corinthians 12:11) At the same time, the Bible indicates that believers (perhaps as a corporate body and not as individuals) can desire gifts that are necessary for the ministry of the body. (1 Corinthians 12:31) How does an individual receive spiritual gifts? While one can not dogmatically assert them to come in any specific way at a given instant the following are Scriptural implications drawn from various passages as to how, or when the gifts come.

definition   *Impartation* refers to the giving of spiritual gifts to a believer by the Holy Spirit.

This may occur:

1. by the laying on of hands (2 Timothy 1:6) by leaders,

2. by the sovereign act of the Holy Spirit to confirm someone's words and ministry (Acts 19:6),

3. each believer receives the Holy Spirit when he/she is born again. Gifts are released when the person receives the Spirit. (Romans 8:9),

4. gifts are released when the believer receives the baptism of the Holy Spirit (1 Corinthians. 12:13),[10]

5. the Holy Spirit can release the gifts as they are needed in a specific ministry situation,

6. in answer to a Spirit-led prayer for gifts that are needed in an ongoing ministry situation,

7. by the principle of spiritual contagion. Spiritual gifts are released and caught in an environment where spiritual power and ministry are happening.

comment   Some people would merge items 3 and 4 together saying that when one is born again at that same time he/she is incorporated into the body of Christ.

comment   The Scriptures do not clearly teach when or how the Holy Spirit released the gifts. The means that we have articulated above are some of the ways that gifts have been released. One thing is clear in Scripture, each believer has been given at least one spiritual gift. We are told to assess our gifts "according to our faith" (Romans 12:3) and that we are to operate in them faithfully.

comment   The Corinthian passage indicates the Holy Spirit's involvement. The Ephesian passage indicates the Lord Jesus's involvement. The Roman passage identifies God (presumably the father). Apparently the Godhead is involved in this important means of power in the church.

---

[10] Pentecostals would see items 3 and 4 as separate. That is, they would hold to a second experience in which a believer is baptized into the Holy Ghost. Most non-charismatics and non-Pentecostals will merge 3 and 4 into one item.

Feedback On Impartation

1. As far as you can tell at this point which of the following have you personally experienced or have been taught is legitimate.

___1. I received one or more spiritual gifts by the laying on of hands by leaders. (like 2 Timothy 1:6)

___2. I received gifts by the sovereign act of the Holy Spirit to confirm someone's words and ministry (like Acts 19:6),

___3. I have been taught that I received the Holy Spirit when I was born again. I must have therefore received my spiritual gift(s) then. (Romans 8:9),

___4. I have been taught that the Holy Spirit baptized me into the church—my gifts were released in conjunction with that baptism. (1 Corinthians. 12:13),

___5. I have been taught that the Holy Spirit can release the gifts as they are needed in a specific ministry situation and that has been my experience.

___6. I have been taught that in answer to a Spirit-led prayer for gifts that are needed in an ongoing ministry situation they will be given. I have seen gifts prayed for and given to a body that needed them.

___7. I know that where there are gifts that are active, the principle of spiritual contagion happens. Spiritual gifts are released and caught in an environment where spiritual power and ministry are happening. I have seen this happen.

2. Look back at Profile 1 on the Feedback sheet, page 127. a. If you were a member of that church and were concerned about the profile and wanted to see power gifts come into the church which of the possible impartation idea(s) would be most helpful to you. b. which one(s) would be least helpful. Mark most helpful with an M. Mark least helpful with an L.

___1. I could probably count on the laying on of hands by leaders. (like 2 Timothy 1:6)

___2. I could count on someone with a power ministry coming into the church and imparting gifts (like Acts 19:6),

___3. We would have to see a number of people converted and hope that as they were saved and received the Holy Spirit they would have some power gifts. For everyone in our church now was born again sometime ago and no one has power gifts so if gifts only come when you are born again we are in trouble.

___4. If the Holy Spirit gives gifts in conjunction with baptizing people into our church then we need a new influx. I don't see how this could work.

___5. It is clear that we need power gives hence we can trust the Holy Spirit to release the needed gifts either in us or by bringing them to us.

___6. As a body we will need to agree together that we need these gifts and then pray for them.

___7. I know that where there are gifts that are active, the principle of spiritual contagion happens. Spiritual gifts are released and caught in an environment where spiritual power and ministry are happening. I have seen this happen. But since absolutely no power gifts are in our church it doesn't seem possible that this principle will do us any good.

ANSWERS————————-

1. Your choice. For me √ 3. √ 7. But I am being stretched to see ___1. ___2. ___5. ___6. happen.

2. Your choice. Here is how I would answer it. L 1. L 2. L 7. M 5.

VESTED AND NON-VESTED GIFTS

introduction One of our primary points of emphasis on giftedness and particularly spiritual gifts is on growth and development. However, the use of some of the spiritual gifts are not within the control of the person whom God is using. For example, the gift of miracles is a difficult one to pull out of your pocket if God isn't doing it. Either God releases it through you or He doesn't. Many of the gifts operate in this way. However, there are other gifts that operate within the control of the person. A person can release the gift at any time. In order to describe this issue of development and growth of spiritual gifts, we have developed two concepts: vested and non-vested gifts.

definition *Vested gifts* are spiritual gifts that appear repeatedly in a person's ministry and can be repeated at will by the person.

example G. Campbell Morgan manifested teaching, exhortation, and prophetical gifting from his 30s onward. It was clear that this was a vested gift-mix. Earlier for about a 1-2 year period he had operated with evangelism. And while he was concerned about people knowing Christ throughout his whole ministry (and he saw people come to Christ from time-to-time) it was clear that his major ministry was that of a public Bible expositor with a large face-to-face direct sphere of influence.

definition *Non-vested gifts* are spiritual gifts that appear situationally and can not be repeated at will by the person.

example In a given Vineyard service at Anaheim in the early 80s it was usual for there to be a number of words of knowledge from people in the congregation. They may or may not see this kind of happening again.

comment Vested gifts carry with them the responsibility for development and the realization that you will be held accountable for the use of them in ministry.

comment Vested gifts are related most closely to List G from Romans and List H from Ephesians. List B from Corinthians would also seem to correlate with vested.

comment Non-vested gifts do not carry the same degree of responsibility in terms of development. We will be held accountable for being used by God in ministry situations but will not be held accountable for developing the spiritual gifts. There are other things that can be developed in relationship to gifts like these. Availability, faith, attitudes and expectations can all be worked on in regards to non-vested gifts.

comment Non-vested gifts correlate closely with the List A gifts which manifest with spontaneity when the body.

comment When a leader identifies a gift-mix which is vested then there will be movement toward a gift-cluster. Usually in the earlier stages of ministry the gift-mix can not be identified with certainty. More experience and situations may allow the gift-mix to emerge and be counted on.

FEEDBACK ON VESTED AND NON-VESTED

1. A person like Gee, see List 6, page 95 is most likely to not recognize:

   ___a. the concept of a vested gift   ___b. the concept of a non-vested gift

2. A person like McRae, see List 4, page 94 is most likely to not recognize:

   ___a. the concept of a vested gift   ___b. the concept of a non-vested gift

3. Why is the concept of vested versus non-vested gifts important?

ANSWERS———————

1. √ a.

2. √ b.

3. For several reasons. (1) The stewardship model requires accountability and development of what is entrusted to us. If we do not have gifts that we can exercise on a repeated basis then we most likely will not be able to develop. The notion of vested, that is, having permanent spiritual gifts allows for development, a stewardship model concept. (2) The Spirit sovereignly gives gifts when the body meets as described in the first Corinthian list. At least that is a possible emphasis. The concept of non-vested allows the flexibility to cope with those ideas. If we have only a fixed vested notion, then we are liable to put God in a box and not be open to His working. We may miss out on His blessing.

PRIMARY, SECONDARY, AND TERTIARY GIFTS

introduction | When we first began to interview students regarding their spiritual gifts, we would often get people that would check off that they operate in 5, 8, 10 or more different spiritual gifts. We found this a little difficult to believe. We followed up this brief introductory interview with further questions. What we found was that most people operated in maybe 3 or 4 spiritual gifts in their gift-mix at any given time. The reason that they checked off so many gifts is that God used them in the past in some gift but they don't operate in it any longer. Our question didn't take this into account. We began to develop some language and concepts which help a person understand how this works in ministry.

definition | *Primary gifts* are gifts that are vested gifts and are currently being demonstrated as a significant part of the gift-mix.

example | An older Campus Crusade worker on a large campus is being used in evangelism to win people to Christ—Lets call her **CC Leader A**. This has been a steady pattern for 14 years on three different campuses and two different local church scenes. In addition, this worker has a strong exhortation gift and has been able to relate as a mentor discipler to many of her converts over the years. These two gifts would certainly be primary gifts.

definition | *Secondary gifts* are gifts that were at one time primary gifts but are no longer being demonstrated as part of the current gift-mix.

example | **CC Leader A** in her first ministry assignment was forced almost by necessity to organize the ministry of the worker to whom she was assigned as an apprentice. She did a good job at organizing the ministry and its training program. This forced role/ gift enablement type of phenomena lasted for 4 years until she moved on to a new campus. In later ministries she has never seen this happen. In fact, God has brought to her team people who could do this. The governments manifestation was a secondary gift. It did operate with good effectiveness for a four year period of time but has never been repeated.

comment | Secondary gifts are often gifts that were tied to or needed as a result of a role that the leader had. The role changed and the gifts needed changed.

definition | *Tertiary gifts* are gifts that are non-vested gifts. They are gifts that operate situationally as needed or spontaneously by the Holy Spirit.

example | **CC Leader A** during one summer camp retreat situation was a counselor to 12 girls for a two week period. One of the girls began to cause trouble and not only bring about disunity among the 12 but began to manifest some unusual power (apparently psychic).**CC Leader A has** never faced any kind of demonic situation previously in her ministry. One night, she awoke in the middle of the night from a very vivid dream in which the very situation she was presently in was opened to her via a pictorial scene. It was clear to her what she was to do. She and one other girl went to the troubled girl, laid hands on her and prayed that she would come to know the truth and be freed. And she was. This unusual supernatural kind of power encounter was a one of a kind of thing. It never happened again.

FEEDBACK: PRIMARY, SECONDARY, AND TERTIARY GIFTS

1. A campus worker operated in evangelism with good results until about age 30. From ages 28 on the thrust of the ministry on campus evolved more toward teaching and training. From 40 on the worker moved into a Bible School situation and was a professor on staff. He taught course on strategizing to reach a campus, how to evangelize 3rd world students on campus, how to organize Bible studies, how to disciple. From this information you could say that (check any correct answers),

    ___a. teaching is a primary gift
    ___b. evangelism is a secondary gift
    ___c. both evangelism and teaching are tertiary gifts
    ___d. none of the above

2. Frequently in missionary settings where the surrounding contexts involve the spirit world and power is associated with religious practitioners, when a leader ministers to a group of people in that context, they expect he/she to be able to have power and use it. Several times in these kinds of situations I was expected to lay hands on people and pray for them with power—i.e. demonstrate results that showed my God was real and powerful and can heal. I have done so on 2 or 3 instances though I rarely ever see anything like that in my normal situation at seminary. In view of this little scenario you could say that,

    ___a. it is reasonable to assume that kinds of healings is a primary gift.
    ___b. it is reasonable to assume that kinds of healing is a secondary gift.
    ___c. it is reasonable to assume that kinds of healings is a tertiary gift.
    ___d. can't tell.

3. Chat with some experienced Christian worker having ministry experience of 15 or 20 years who has had a number of varied ministry assignments and roles. Ask that leader if during the past there were any spiritual gift(s) that they used which they do not now see in their present ministry.

ANSWERS——————

1. √ a. teaching is a primary gift
    √ b. evangelism is a secondary gift

2. √ c. it is reasonable to assume that kinds of healings is a tertiary gift.

3. Your choice. Did the experience confirm or disagree with the notion of permanent and transitory gifts as indicated by the concept of primary, secondary, and tertiary gifts.

Chapter Feedback

instructions   Glance again on page 91 at the goals for chapter 5. Go through them carefully to see
how well you have done. You may have to review the appropriate pages if some of the
concepts are vague and don't come readily to mind. After your review do the following
questions and exercises to see how much you have retained.

I. Basic Concepts

Show that you are familiar with the following basic spiritual gifts concepts by placing the capital letter of
a given label in the blank next to its definition or description. Some labels may appear more than one
time.

A. spiritual gift	F. Word Gifts	K. secondary gift
B. Gifts Identification Continuum	G. Impartation	L. tertiary gift
C. Christian role	H. vested gift	M. balance
D. Power Gifts	I. non-vested gift	N. extant gift
E. Love Gifts	J. primary gift	O. not given in this chapter

_____ 1.   refers to the actual skills acquired and/or values learned in picking up those skills, during
the foundational phase, which will later affect leadership skills, leadership attitudes, and
leadership styles.

_____ 2.   gifts that demonstrate the authenticity, credibility, power and reality of the unseen God.

_____ 3.   an activity that every believer is commanded to be involved in due to being part of the Christian movement.

_____ 4.   Acts 19:6, when Paul laid his hands on the followers who knew only John's baptism and they
spoke in kinds of tongues and also prophesied, is an example of this concept.

_____ 5.   a pictorial representation of a persons view on extant gifts.

_____ 6.   describes a proper relationship between love, word, and power clusters in terms of a given
situation.

_____ 7.   refers to the act (maybe process) of the giving of a spiritual gift to a believe by the Holy Spirit.

_____ 8.   those gifts which are manifestations attributed to God through practical ways that can be recognized by a world around us which needs love. They demonstrate the reality of relating to this God.

_____ 9.   a label that refers to the set of spiritual gifts being used by a leader at any given time in his/
her ministry.

_____10.   a gift which was once used regularly for a period of time but is not longer being used would
be this kind.

_____11.   gifts that clarify the nature of this unseen God and what He expects from His followers.
People using these gifts both communicate about God and for God.

_____12.   a gift that may be seen only once or twice over a lifetime would be this kind of gift.

_____13.   a give that comes and goes and can not necessarily be repeated is labeled by this term.

_____14.   Some examples of these would be miracles, kinds of healings, word of knowledge, discernings
of spirits, working of power

_____15.   refers to the idea of a gift being available today

_____16.   a gift that is used regularly throughout a lifetime would be this kind of gift.

_____17.   spiritual gifts that appear repeatedly in a person's ministry and can be repeated at will by
the person is called this type of gift.

_____18.   writing of worship music is an example

_____19.   a God-given unique capacity which is given to each believer for the purpose of releasing a
Holy Spirit empowered ministry in a situation or to be repeated again and again.

_____20.   typical examples of these include mercy, helps, pastoring, governments

CHAPTER FEEDBACK CONTINUED

II. INTERPRETING THE VENN DIAGRAM—CLUSTER OF GIFTS FROM VARIOUS PASSAGES

Examine the Venn diagram on page 110. Use it to answer the following.

1. What two gifts are common to the Romans <u>and</u> Corinthians <u>and</u> Ephesians lists?

    a. _____   b. _____

2. What one gift is common to the Romans and 1 Corinthians list but <u>not</u> on the Ephesians list?_____

3. The gift of faith appears on what list? _____

4. The gifts of pastor and evangelism appear on what list? _____

5. Working of powers appears on what two lists?

    a. _____   b. _____

6. The minister (service or ministry) generic label for service type gifts appears on what two lists?

    a. _____   b. _____

7. The ruling (a local leadership gift) occurs on what list? _____

8. Gifts of healings appears on what list?   _____

9. The leadership gifts of apostleship, pastor, evangelism, prophecy, and teaching all appear together on what one list? _____

10. Governments (local administration gift) appears where? _____

III. SPIRITUAL GIFT DEFINITION (VESTED AND NON-VESTED CONCEPTS)

1. Examine the definition of spiritual gift given below. Then underline the phrase that refers to vested gifts(s) with a single line; Underline the phrase that refers to non-vested gifts with two lines.

    A *spiritual gift* is

    • a God-given unique capacity

    • which is given to each believer

    • for the purpose of releasing a Holy Spirit empowered ministry

    • in a situation or

    • to be repeated again and again.

IV. CONCEPT OF CHURCH PROFILE AND BALANCE

Happy Valley Church is an eight year old church that was planted by Pastor Happy Jones. It has grown to 450 in an area which is not particularly receptive (other churches are not growing). Most of the growth has been conversion growth. There is a strong small groups ministry in the church. In addition, there are various ministries of all kinds generally headed up by lay people but fully supported and sponsored by the church. Read the description of the leadership of Happy Valley Church. Then examine the profile which is given below. Finally in light of this information answer the questions which follow. In order to keep the exercise brief I will not show the giftedness set of each of these. All but Mary Artisan have a focal element of spiritual gifts. She is bi-focal: natural abilities and spiritual gifts.

Senior Pastor—Happy Jones, age 37, male, gift-mix=*faith,* evangelism, pastoring , mercy

Associate Pastor—John Paul Raboni, age 61, male, gift-mix=*teaching,* exhortation, word of wisdom (strong analytical skills), in charge of training ministries.

Associate Pastor—Mary Annette Caringheart, age 43, female, gift-mix=*exhortation,* teaching, pastoring, mercy, (natural abilities: relational skills, intuitive ideational skills, creative bent), in charge of special ministries

Associate Pastor—Andrew Emphathine, age 56, male, gift-mix=exhortation, word of wisdom, discernings of spirits, working of powers (mainly in deliverance), pastoring, (strong acquired skill in counseling, trained with Barry Crabbapple), in charge of pastoral visitation and counseling ministries.

Assistant Pastor—Philip Joyner Goodnews, age 23, male, *word of knowledge,* evangelism, occasional faith, in charge of youth ministries (first full time ministry assignment)

Examine the diagram which follows. Then use it to help you answer the questions which follow.

Chapter Feedback Continued

In the following A = Word Cluster Gifts, B = Love Cluster Gifts, C = Power Cluster Gifts. All caps are gifts exercised by the full time leadership. Lower case are gifts exercised by other church members. Italics means the gifts are dominantly used outside the church toward ministries reaching unbelievers. Underlined means gifts used in church structured groups. Bold faced are gifts exercised in the weekly public gathering service which lasts about 2 hours. There are more gifts operating than I have shown but I have attempted to simplify but leave enough that you could get a feel for it.

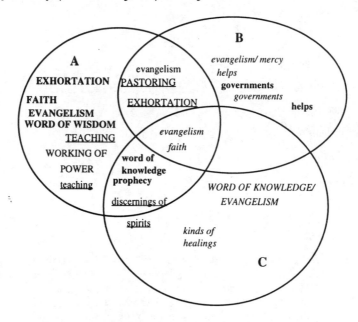

1. What evidence from the diagram can you see of Pastor Happy Jones' ministry?

2. What evidence can you see in the diagram of Phil Joyner's ministry?

3. What evidence can you see in the diagram of Pastor Mary Caringheart's ministry?

4. What gifts are lay people operating in outside the church?

5. What gifts are lay people using in structured goups?

6. What gifts are lay people using in the public service?

7. Examine the 7 impartation methods on page 128. What method seems to be happening in this church? How do you know?

8. How would you assess this church for balance?

9. If you were to give suggestions to improve balance, what would they be?

ANSWERS————————

I. _O_ 1.   _D_ 2.   _C_ 3.__   _G_ 4.   _B_ 5.   _M_ 6.   _G_ 7.   _E_ 8.
   _O_ 9.   _K_ 10.   _F_ 11.   _I,L_ 12.   _L,I_ 13.   _D_ 14.   _N_ 15.   _H,I_ 16.
   _H_ 17.   _O_ 18.   _A_ 19.   _E_ 20.

II. 1. a. prophecy b. teaching

2. helps

3. 1 Corinthians

4. Ephesians

5. a. 1 Corinthians 12 b. Hebrews 2

6. a. Romans 12 b. 1 Peter 4

7. Romans 12

8. 1 Corinthains 12

9. Ephesians 4

10. 1 Corinthians 12

III. 1. in a situation ;   to be repeated again and again.

IV. 1.   Public ministry of faith, evangelism; pastoral ministry in some sort of strucured situation, evangelism/ mercy reaching outside the church (this is actually through one of the ministries led by a lay leader in the inner city)

2.   The word of knowledge/ evangelism in the power cluster is most likely his.

3.   The exhortation in structured setting is most likely hers. The teaching in structured groups is most likely hers. She is most likely involved in the mercy reacing outside the church. She is probably also represented in the structured pastoring.

4.   kinds of healings, governments, evangelism/mercy, helps, evangelism, faith.

5.   discernings of spirits, teaching

6.   word of knowledge, prophecy, governments, helps

7.   The contagion principles seems to be really working. Pastor Jones models evangelism all over the place. It has caught on. The like-attracts-like principle is in effect and contagion is happening.

8.   The church has good balance. It is reaching its community in evangelism and good works. It has growth ministries as well as outreach. Leadership is emerging in the many sponsored/ structured ministries headed by lay people. I would assess balance as good.

9.   I would suggest that the full time leadership become involved in modeling some of the power gifts in the public ministry. Otherwise, looks good.

SUMMARY

We hope you realize that the material you see in this chapter is not the run of the mill stuff on gifts. You will not find these concepts and the various perspectives anywhere else. These concepts are cutting edge ideas that have come out of actual research with gifted leaders over the past 10 years or so. And I hope you see that they are not only conceptual but very practically oriented. They will help you recognize, use, and develop giftedness in your church or parachurch situation.

We have introduced a number of key concepts which shape our understanding of giftedness and giftedness development. First of all, we limit our listing of spiritual gifts to those mentioned after the release of the Holy Spirit in the church age. We have shown that there are a number of various positions regarding how many spiritual gifts there are. And though this may appear confusing to a beginning student of gifts I hope you will come away fairly confident, for there is much agreement on many items even though differences on some key ones. We hope you will understand a bit better why there are differences.

We have listed the various Biblical passages, both major and minor, from which we draw our list of spiritual gifts. The major passages are in 1 Corinthians 12-14, Romans 12, and Ephesians 4.

We have also introduced the concept of corporate functions of gifts. We have identified and defined love, word and power gifts. Thinking about the corporate functions of gifts helps leaders to see their ministry situation in terms of giftedness balance. Each ministry context needs a balance of love, word and power gifts that is appropriate.

We have also introduced the concepts of vested and non-vested gifts as well as primary, secondary and tertiary gifts. The concept of vested gifts and non-vested gifts allow us as leaders to become more responsible for the development of our gifts. Vested gifts are gifts that can be developed and used at will by the person. Non-vested gifts are the gifts that God released on a situational basis. These terms help us describe what is really happening over a lifetime in terms of leaders and gifts they use.

Primary, secondary and tertiary categories of gifts describe the function of the gift-mix in the current ministry context. A person's gift-mix could change over time and with the change of ministry roles. These concepts take the possibility of change into consideration.

In chapter 6, we will take an in-depth look at the spiritual gifts themselves. We are ready for it now.

CHAPTER 6:
SPIRITUAL GIFTS PART II

INTRODUCTION

In this chapter, we will turn our attention to the spiritual gifts themselves. We will look at each of the nineteen gifts that we have listed. We will give a definition along with the central thrust of using each gift. We will also address the certainty of our definitions when we give them. The Biblical data differs greatly concerning source material which is used to form definitions of the various gifts. Some of the gifts have a great deal of information about them and others are only given once in a list. We will list the source of our definitions. Some are based on Biblical evidence while others are based on a combination of Biblical evidence, empirical observation and our own reasoning. We will also list any key observations or insights into the functioning of the gifts.

We will group the gifts in terms of word, power and love clusters.

In the word gifts we include: teaching, exhortation, prophecy, pastoring, apostleship, evangelism, ruling.[1]

In the power gifts we include: word of wisdom, word of knowledge, faith, kinds of healing, working of powers, discernings of spirits, tongues, and interpretation of tongues.[2]

In the love gifts we include: governments, giving, mercy, and helps. We recognize that more than giftedness functions to demonstrate God's love, the major thrust of the love cluster. Many of the Christian roles serve this same function. But the body couldn't operate with harmony and efficiency without the functions of the love gifts. Their supportive functions free up, for example, those with word gifts.[3]

We don't ask you to necessarily agree with our definitions. You may need to modify them to fit your own understanding. But we do ask you to at least understand our definitions and where we are coming from. With that in mind, by the time you complete this chapter you will be able,

- to give the central thrust of each of the 19 definitions,
- to be familiar enough with our definitions to recognize them,[4]
- to recognize a given gift if we give you the symptoms for it.

---

[1] Prophecy is a power cluster gift as well but we include it here since it is grouped with the Ephesian leadership gifts. We place the ruling gift here since it is a local leadership gift and we have already noted that leadership gifts will relate to the word of God. We could have included it in the love cluster because in the final essence it is dominantly a service gift. All leaders in using their giftedness with the body will be responsible to the truth of the word. Some will more directly use the word than others. But for all it will serve as the authority for their ministry.

[2] We recognize that some of these power gifts also do word functions, at least sometimes: word of wisdom, word of knowledge, faith (occasionally), and tongues/ interpretation of tongues. But for the most part it is the demonstration of the reality of God that is usually carried when these gifts are exercised so we have grouped them with the power gifts.

[3] In essence, this is the principle underlying the choice of supportive church leaders in the Acts 6 passage as voiced by Peter.

[4] Again may we refer you to Spiritual Gifts, my first book on the subject. There I list the basic Greek word studies that were done to arrive at definitions. I omit that technical data is this presentation of gifts.

TEACHING	CENTRAL THRUST	TO CLARIFY TRUTH

introduction The gift of teaching is mentioned in three major passages on spiritual gifts. (1 Corinthians 12; Romans 12; Ephesians 4) The gift of teaching is fairly well defined in Scripture. Most people would agree that this gift is in operation today.

definition A person who has the *gift of teaching* is one who has the ability to instruct, explain, or expose Biblical truth in such a way as to cause believers to understand the Biblical truth.

certainty of definition We are fairly certain of this definition. The source of the definition is primarily Biblical illustrations, word studies and some empirical observation into the usage of the gift. Teaching, along with exhortation, and prophecy have the strongest certainty of all the word gifts.

comment Methodology used by a teacher will vary according to cultural expectations for teaching and learning. But the central thrust is always the same—to clarify and explain so people can see. For example, Jesus used a parabolic teaching method in His culture. His methodology in teaching reflects many valuable principles which could be transferred to other methodologies. The apostle Paul evidently used a more formal approach to teaching when he was in Ephesus. (Acts 20:9) He also used the written word to communicate truth as he wrote the various churches that he was involved with.

importance of the gift This gift is extremely important because of its function in the body. In order to live out the practical implications of our faith, we must first understand the truth that we are basing our convictions upon. Teaching provides us with a clarification and an explanation of the Biblical truths.

symptoms Here are some common symptoms of this gift:
- people will constantly understand truth as a result of what you say about the Bible,
- you will have a tremendous drive within you to understand truth and will look for ways to explain that truth to others,
- you will be able to discipline yourself to study the Word of God,
- you will find yourself overly concerned about meaning and will not be satisfied with unclear explanations (either your own or others),
- you will constantly be learning new communication methodologies which will help you become more effective in your teaching,
- you will see people becoming more Christ-like in their actions and thoughts as a result of your helping them understand and Biblical truth,
- people will know God in ever increasing depth because of your ability to practically explain Biblical truth in terms of their context.

caution Teachers, because of their influence over others, will be held accountable at a higher standard than others. This is implied in James 3:1 which says, "Not many of you should presume to be teachers, my brothers, because you know that we who teach will be judged more strictly."

EXHORTATION	CENTRAL THRUST	TO APPLY BIBLICAL TRUTH

introduction   The Bible contains much about the gift of exhortation. It is definitely a distinct gift and not just a part of another gift such as prophecy. It is listed in Romans 12 as a gift. The epistles are full of examples of this gift which imply that it was a very important gift in the life of the church.

definition   The *gift of exhortation* is the capacity to urge people to action in terms of applying Biblical truths, to encourage people generally with Biblical truths, or to comfort people through the application of Biblical truth to their needs.

certainty of definition   We are fairly certain that is a strong definition. The definition comes from good Biblical data—word studies, and illustrations. Exhortation, with teaching and prophecy have the greatest certainty of all of the word gifts.

comment   There is a three-fold expression of this gift: admonition, encouragement, and comfort. There is the admonition aspect in which the person urges others to take action based on Biblical truths. This implies a strong application of truth and can come across as a type of correction. There is the encouragement aspect in which the person tries to lift or build others up by applying Biblical truths. There is the comforting aspect in which the person provides a measure of comfort to a hurting person as a result of applying Biblical truths to the situation.

comment   Generally speaking, most people will start out stronger in one of the three aspects of this gift than the other two. The mature development of this gift will see all three aspects of the gift operating in harmony.

symptoms   Here are some common symptoms of this gift:
- people generally react strongly (sometimes for, sometimes against) what you say,
- you frequently find yourself giving advise to others to do this or that,
- you often find that you have a word to share with someone in need and the person receives it as a comforting word from God,
- people frequently confide their inner thoughts to you because they sense that you have an empathetic ear and they are comforted in the process,
- people like to be around you because you often cheer them up simply by your attitude or demeanor,
- you often sense an urgency to get something done and are willing to communicate that urgency to others,
- you love to share with anyone a truth from a passage of the Bible that means something to you,
- you are not satisfied with a superficial acceptance of truth but you want people to use that truth in their lives,
- you enjoy sharing stories about God's involvement in your life because you know that God can use it to encourage others.

comment   The gift of exhortation is the major way through which God allows the body of Christ to enable each other to live practical Godly lives. Christians encourage one another to face trials by sharing what God has done for them in similar situations. Christians urge one another to take action in terms of applying Biblical truths. Christians encourage one another to have faith and be confident in God and the future. It is a gift that quite a few people in the body can expect to have and operate in.

| PROPHECY | CENTRAL THRUST | TO PROVIDE CORRECTION OR PERSPECTIVE ON A SITUATION |

introduction   A fair amount of information concerning the gift of prophecy occurs in the New Testament. In the early church, there was no finalized form of New Testament teaching as it exists today. God used the gift of prophecy to reveal truth to His people. Sometimes the truth was predictive (concerning something in the future) and sometimes the truth was new ideas for the church to learn about God. Both of these aspects of this gift occur in the New Testament.

        With the completion of the New Testament canon, many believe that the need for new revelational truth ceased to exist. People holding this viewpoint would say that the gift no longer exists or it exists only in its present day corrective function. Many who hold this would say that God is not now revealing future events to people operating in this gift but rather that discerning people can read the Scriptures and understand the times in which we live.

definition   A person operating with the *gift of prophecy* has the capacity to deliver truth (in a public way) either of a predictive nature or as a situational word from God in order to correct by exhorting, edifying or consoling believers and/or to convince non-believers of God's truth.

certainty of   We are fairly certain of this definition. It is based strongly on the Biblical
definition   material including word studies and illustrations of the use of this gift. Prophecy, with teaching and exhortation, have the strongest certainty of the word gifts.

comment   A person operating in this gift is deeply impressed that God has by His Spirit given him/her a message to deliver in the situation. He/she proclaims that message with authority and conviction. The message may result in further insight into God's Word, cause conviction of sin, bring reproof, provide comfort or a new sense of direction to the group. Many times the message may speak to a prominent issue that is facing the group. The person is not one who exposes the Biblical Word of God but rather is one who exposes the will of God.

symptoms   Here are several symptoms of this gift:
- you are not afraid to speak out publicly or take strong stands on issues,
- you tend to see the needs of the group as a whole and are willing to take stands on Biblical standards,
- when you speak publicly, people are convicted by the truth that you give,
- you demonstrate an inner sensitivity to God and have a variety of experiences in which the Holy Spirit speaks to you.

comment   Those holding the view that the gift of prophecy ceased after the completion of the canon of Scripture but feel that the situational word aspect has been transferred to the gift of teaching base it on the text in 2 Peter 2:1. In this text, Old Testament false prophets are compared with New Testament false teachers. The point of this text is not to show that in the New Testament times teachers have taken the roles of Old Testament prophets but rather that there are teachers who are teaching false truths just as there were false prophets in the Old Testament.

| **APOSTLESHIP** | **CENTRAL THRUST** | **CREATING NEW MINISTRY** |

introduction

Some would not classify apostleship as a gift but would confine it to an office which was filled by those who were hand-picked by Jesus to function in the founding of the church. One who holds this view would say that with the passing away of the twelve (plus Paul) this office ceased. Others would say that there was an apostolic office which continued beyond the twelve and Paul. There is ample evidence that there was a functional apostolic role which was filled by a number of named individuals beyond Paul and the twelve. We believe that there was a special office established by Jesus and would call the twelve and Paul, the Apostles. However, we believe that the gift of apostleship exists and functions today.

definition

The *gift of apostleship* refers to a special leadership capacity to move with authority from God to create new ministry structures (churches and para-church) to meet needs and to develop and appoint leadership in these structures.

certainty of definition

This definition has fair certainty. Its certainty is not as good as prophecy, teaching and exhortation, but better than pastoring, evangelism, and ruling. There is ample Biblical evidence which supports this definition. Refer to our comments on figurative language and metonymy for seeing apostleship as the gift. There were New Testament apostles apart from original 11 and Paul. Their functions were founding works and itinerant work stimulating, evaluating, and correcting works (like Titus, Timothy, John).

comment

The capacity to establish new ministry structures requires a special kind of authority from God. A person who has this kind of special authority is usually recognized by a local church and released to this new pioneering work. The gift can be operated within ones own culture or in a cross-cultural setting. Traditionally, the apostolic gift has been associated with missionary work because the pioneering aspect was easy to see. However, all who go as missionaries certainly don't have this gift.

comment

There have been two normal settings for the release of this gift: founding new church structures and founding new mission structures. As with missionaries, not all church planters operate with this gift. Historically, the individuals that God has used to raise up new mission structures have operated in this capacity.

symptoms

Here are several symptoms of this gift:
- a strong sense of a call by God for establishing new works,
- a strong confirmation on the part of the leadership of the local church of which you are a part,
- a forceful personality which can be trust God to do what is necessary in unusual ways so that the work can be founded,
- an ability to face new situations sensitively,
- a clear understanding of the nature of the church and its purpose,
- a personality which attracts people to follow your leadership,
- a person who can sense what God wants to do and is not afraid to try,
- a drive within you which can't be satisfied apart from seeing people being reached and enfolded into the community of God who were unreached before.

PASTORING	CENTRAL THRUST	CARING FOR THE GROWTH OF FOLLOWERS

introduction The Ephesians passage lists apostles, prophets, evangelists, pastors and teachers. Each of these types of leaders are to equip the church to do ministry. If this list is taken by metonymy (which we believe it is), then each of these types of leaders represents a spiritual gift. The leader who is known by the name pastor is synonymously called *elder* and *bishop.* Most likely the person who exercises the pastoral gift is a multi-gifted person as seen in the qualifying phrase.

definition The *pastoral gift* is the capacity to exercise concern and care for members of a group so as to encourage them in their growth in Christ which involves modeling maturity, protecting them from error and disseminating truth.

certainty of definition There is not a strong certainty on this definition. There are a number of sources that have been drawn from in order to formulate this definition. The *shepherd* concept in New Testament leadership passages sheds some light on what pastoring is. The role of the *elder* and the *bishop* also provide some understanding. The definition is stronger than ruling but definitely not as strong as teaching, exhortation, and prophecy.

comment Some would classify what we have called the pastoral gift as an office only. The person filling the office is picked from his/her spiritual qualifications apart from any so called *pastoral gift.* 1 Timothy 3 and Titus 1 provide lists of qualifications for this office. Anyone meeting those qualifications could function in the office of pastor. In any case, the people operating from this point of view still need to exercise the various functions listed above.

symptoms • people usually look to you to make decisions,
- people feel you have authority in things concerning the church and spiritual matters,
- you are usually picked as the leader in committees, organizations and group meetings,
- you seem to influence the actions of groups by what you do and what you say,
- you have the ability to maintain order or discipline among people,
- you easily see the problems of the group that you are relating to and accept responsibility to help them,
- you are concerned that groups of Christians that you relate to grow in Christlikeness and unity and are willing to do something about it.
- you would be considered by most (if they were asked) that you are a leader,
- you exert influence over people so as to instill loyalty to you and your way of thinking and doing things.

comment If you operate in this gift, your overriding concern is with the health and the growth of the believers that God has put under your care. It is possible to operate in this gift without an *official* role in an organized group or church. There are many people operating in this gift who do not have an official job description that says pastor at the top. In small group ministry often there are men and women who have this concern and exercise it even if they are not *full time paid Christian pastors.*

| EVANGELISM | CENTRAL THRUST | INTRODUCING OTHERS TO THE GOSPEL |

introduction
: The church expands numerically by seeing people converted to Christianity. New people primarily become believers through the operation of this gift.

definition
: The *gift of evangelism* in general refers to the capacity to challenge people through various communicative methods (persuasion) to receive the Gospel of salvation in Christ so as to see them respond by taking initial steps in Christian discipleship.

certainty of definition
: The definition is fair. Evangelism is only listed once, like pastor. There is good illustrations in Acts of concerning evangelism both individual and public. But they presume you already have a basic definition. The definition is roughly equivalent to that of pastoring and apostleship in its certainty.

comment
: There are three aspects to the operation of this gift. First, a person operating with this gift is to proclaim in an authoritative way (publicly or privately) the message of Christ concerning salvation. Secondly, this is a leadership gift and a person operating in this gift is to influence and lead other Christians in the work of evangelization. Thirdly, the gift is to operate through the daily lives and testimonies of the believer's who are to live exemplary lives as a witness to the world. Their example often causes unbelievers to ask questions about their lives and creates opening to share the Gospel.

uses
: The gift of evangelism is the primary means of God's reconciling men and women to Himself. It causes numeric growth in the Church and initiates people in the discipleship process.

symptoms
: Here are some common symptoms of this gift:
  - the ability to talk before groups of people and easily converse with strangers,
  - the ability to persuade or influence people,
  - an intense sense of unrest with the thought of people being unsaved and eternally unreconciled to God,
  - the ability to insert spiritual truth in normal conversation with the unsaved,
  - a freedom and joy in talking about Christian things naturally in an unforced way,
  - the fact that unsaved people with whom you have contact often end up pursuing and asking what Christianity is all about,
  - the fact that unsaved people actually make discipleship commitments as a direct or indirect result of your influence,
  - the fact that you feel led to pray often for unsaved people by name,
  - the fact that your intercessory prayer time focuses in on unsaved groups of people,
  - the ability to make friends easily.

RULING   CENTRAL THRUST   INFLUENCING OTHERS TOWARD VISION

introduction   This gift is only listed once in the Romans 12 passage. It is sometimes called the
                leadership gift. Usually, this gift operates in tandem with other *leadership* oriented
                gifts such as apostleship, pastor, teacher, prophecy, and exhortation. See the reference
                in Timothy which shows this tandem operation (1 Timothy 5:17). Because of this it
                can be difficult to isolate this gift as one that operates on its own. What is clear is that
                it is a local leadership gift—not listed with the Ephesians cluster of leadership gifts.

definition   A person operating with a *ruling gift* demonstrates the capacity to exercise influence
                over a group so as to lead it toward a goal or purpose with a particular emphasis on
                the capacity to make decisions and keep the group operating together.

certainty of   Because this gift is only listed once, there is not a lot of Biblical data from
definition   which to define the gift. This definition comes from a study of the root word for ruling
                and the isolated references to ruling in 1 Thessalonians and 1 Timothy. Of course our
                own empirical observations and reasoning were used. So then, there is lack of cer-
                tainty on this definition.

comment   Because this gift is only listed once, it is not clear from the Biblical data whether or not
                the gift of ruling is a distinct gift or whether it is part of another leadership gift such
                as pastoring. Arguments could be made for both sides.

symptoms   Here are several symptoms:

                •   an ability to get direction or vision from God for a group,
                •   an ability to influence others to follow that direction,
                •   an ability to organize and build structures that allow for ministry to happen
                     efficiently.

comment   This gift, if it is perceived as a distinct gift, operates in conjunction with other gifts.
                For example, all of the leadership gifts have some aspect of this gift in operation.
                Also, a person operating in this gift will more than likely have one or more of the word
                gifts in operation in order to flow in this gift.

FEEDBACK ON WORD GIFTS

1. Match each word gift with its central thrust by placing the capital letter in the blank next to the descriptive statement.

A Teaching   C. Prophecy   E. Apostleship   G. Ruling

B. Exhortation   D. Evangelism   F. Pastoring

___(1)   to provide correction or perspective on a situation
___(2)   caring for the growth of followers
___(3)   to clarify truth
___(4)   creating new ministry
___(5)   influencing others toward vision
___(6)   to apply Biblical truth
___(7)   introducing others to the gospel

2. Examine the following composite profiles of two churches in terms of their leadership gifts. Church A represents about 9 leaders including 1 full time and 8 lay. Church B represents 4 full time and about 32 lay leaders.

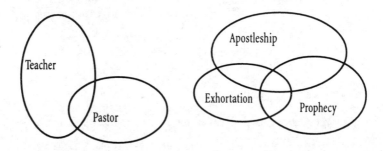

Church A   Church B
size = 189 (trend slowly downward size = 460 (trend upward, but big back door)
        over last 8 years)

a. Describe what you think the situation would be like in each church and discuss what kind of leadership gifts might be needed to balance the situation in each.

Church A

Church B

GIVING	**CENTRAL THRUST**	A SENSITIVITY TO GOD TO CHANNEL HIS RESOURCES TO OTHERS

introduction Because giving and sharing are so much a part of every Christian's responsibility, it is hard to recognize that there is a gift called giving which uniquely operates in certain individuals. But we know that this is true because Paul lists the gift of giving in his list in Romans 12. His qualifying descriptive phrase in Romans 12:8 forms the basis for the definition given below.

definition The gift of giving refers to the capacity to give liberally to meet the needs of others and yet to do so with a purity of motive which senses that the giving is a simple sharing of what God has given.

certainty of definition There is limited Biblical data from which to draw a definition. Our definition is drawn from a combination of Biblical data, empirical observation and our own reasoning and is on a par with mercy, governments, and helps in terms of certainty of definition

example Acts 4:34-37 describes a church context of many individuals sharing and giving to one another. Barnabas is one that is commended for his generosity.

uses The gift of giving can operate in order to:

- meet the needs of believers in your own assembly (Ephesians 4:28; Galatians 6:10; 1 John 3:17; 1 Timothy 5:33ff),
- meet the needs of believers in other assemblies (2 Corinthians 8,9; Romans 15:25,26),
- meet the needs of persons operating in leadership on a full time basis (Philippians 4:10; Galatians 6:9; 1 Corinthians 9:1-11; 1 Timothy 6:16),
- meet the needs of non-believers (Galatians 6:10).

symptoms Here are several symptoms of this gift:

- a sensitivity to recognize the needs of others,
- a quickness to assume some burden for meeting the needs of others when you sense that they have a need,
- a relative freedom from a self-serving attitude,
- a capacity that provides the means to give to others,
- the abilities to amass financial resources,
- a carefulness in handling finances with a bent toward living a simple lifestyle,
- a conviction that all of what you have belongs to God and you are a steward of it. You look for ways to channel His resources to others.

comment Don't think that this gift is limited to rich people. The Macedonian Christians were poor people but God gave this gift to them as a group. Paul notes that they gave beyond their means and were supplied again and again by God. George Mueller is another case in point. He was not a rich businessman but a full-time worker who was totally dependent on God to meet his own needs. Mueller gave liberally out of what God gave to him.

comment Some, perhaps rightly so, extend the notion of giving as a spiritual gift beyond the giving of material resources. They would say it is an inner ability to give of one's self which includes material things but goes beyond.

COMMENTARY ON WORD GIFTS

introduction
The following are miscellaneous remarks concerning the word gift cluster. In the next chapter we shall return to some of this when we talk about leadership gifts. These remarks are not integrated. They have come to mind as we wrote the definitions and designed the feedback section for the word gifts. That is, they are items of information that we have seen and shared in our oral teaching but are not covered specifically in the definitions. We feel they are worth noting.

leaders—
word gifted
One of the important insights that has come out of our research on leaders is that all leaders have at least one word gift in his/her gift-mix. This is an important finding which has implication for selection and development of leaders in churches and parachurches. One of our values that we have identified concerning effective leaders is, **EFFECTIVE LEADERS RECOGNIZE LEADERSHIP SELECTION AND DEVELOPMENT AS A PRIORITY FUNCTION.** This insight relating leadership and word gifts is very helpful in early selection and hence a more proactive development of emerging leaders. We will return to this idea in the next chapter.

certitude
By certitude I mean how certain can we assert something with confidence in its correctness. Lay Christians have a tendency to think that if something is published and put in print and sells it must be solid. But this is not the case. I have read many, many books on spiritual gifts. Very few authors say anything about certitude. They give their definitions, almost without even saying how they arrived at them. They give them as finished products. By implication they assert them as having solid certitude. Because I hold a presupposition that the Bible is authoritative and I must be as clear as it is clear (in my own opinion—granted), nothing more, nothing less, nothing else I have to be as honest about my interpretations as I can. To add things that aren't there to apparently clear up things not so clear in the Bible may be opening oneself up to introducing error, orthodoxic or orthopraxic. My information on certitude of definitions of gifts should be helpful information for you as you read in the literature on giftedness.

word
cluster
vacuum
One of the feedback questions dealt with a church profile in which the word cluster was missing altogether. When that is so, the central thrust of the word cluster is most likely missing. That is, there is a lack of understanding about God including His nature, His purposes, how we can relate to Him, His resources for us as believer to be and grow and do and to be a part of His purposes. When this vacuum is there then all of these missing elements are supplied generally by what the current views on them are in the culture and society. Eventually there is a loss of whatever truth there was and possibly even a movement to apostasy as described in 2 Peter and Jude and 1 Timothy 4.

leadership
gift
vacuums
From my concept of central thrusts, balance, and profiles you are probably becoming aware of the possibility of assessing churches and parachurches in order to pinpoint overemphasis of certain gifts and the flip side, lack of certain emphases. I believe leadership in churches should be thoroughly familiar with giftedness and its ramifications for their situations. What happens when certain leadership gifts are missing. Let me give some suggestions which are my opinions based on observation of leaders and

`their ministries over the past 30 years. Of course, some of these gift vacuums can be made up for by leaders with strong natural abilities or acquired skills in the similar areas. Column one suggests the gift that is missing. Column 2 suggests some possible lacks if the gift is missing.

Gift Vacuum   What Might Be Missing—Possible Lack

APOSTLESHIP   1. need for, insights as to how, ability to inspire, and creativity to start new ministries to meet needs.
               2. lack of an authoritative sense of God's hand on the ministry.
               3. a sense of sameness, traditions prevail, forms more than functions dominate.

PROPHECY   1. no application of Christian truth to environment.
               2. frequent plateauing.
               3. no sense of where God wants to take the group
               4. no sense of the big picture in the world and what God is doing

EVANGELISM   1. no conversion growth
               2. lack of excitement and sense of vitality
               3. lack of responsibility for the lost

PASTOR   1. believers not growing
               2. believers not seeing truth being helpful for their lives
               3. believers led astray by teaching that is heretical or at least not healthy

TEACHER   1. lack of stability
               2. immature, ignorant believers
               3. believers who can be swayed by worldly influences
               4. untrained, non-equipped body
               5. lack of interdependency in body

RULING   1. lack of follow through on ideas
               2. lack of organizational drive to accomplish
               3. sense of loss of direction
               4. a leadership which may be indecisive

danger of gift projection

Leaders are people who influence. Generally, they are strong people who have evident leadership gifts. Strong gifted leaders tend to project (i.e. lay expectations, maybe even produce guilt trips) on followers in terms of their own strong gifts. Evangelists tend to think everybody ought to have evangelistic gifts. They exhort toward evangelism and sometime make people feel guilty because they are not seeing fruit. Teachers want everybody to study the Bible like they do. They expect everyone to want to study and teach and to see truth like they do. If you don't have a marked up Bible or a well worn Bible you must be immature. Prophets are impatient with those who can't see the need for the correction they are forcefully asserting. Pastors don't want the boat rocked. They want to maintain harmony. Apostles tend to overpower people. In short, strong gifted people tend to project their own gifts on others. This means that people who don't have those gifts feel like second class citizens, like they don't measure up as Christians. They become frustrated. They can't do what is expected. They may become inoculated after repeated beatings. Or they may simply drop out. In any, case all strong leaders need to be aware of this projection tendency. This should cause them to recognize the other kinds of gifts in the body and to affirm those gifted people as well.

WORD OF WISDOM   CENTRAL THRUST   APPLYING REVELATORY INFORMATION

introduction

The gifts called *word of wisdom* and *word of knowledge* appear only in the 1 Corinthians passage. Because of this, there is some difficulty in understanding and identifying these two gifts. There are several possible illustrations of these gifts in operation in the Bible but there is no *hard evidence* that these examples are these gifts in operation. The definitions are formulated primarily from the phraseology that is involved.

definition

The *word of wisdom* gift refers to the capacity to know the mind of the Spirit in a given situation and to communicate clearly the situation, facts, truth or application of the facts and truth to meet the need of the situation.

certainty of definition

There is limited Biblical data from which to draw a definition. Our definition is drawn from a combination of Biblical data, empirical observation and our own reasoning. While our definition is not based on hard data, the very fact, that this is a word of wisdom and not wisdom and occurs in the power gifts cluster gives strong backing to the idea of a revelatory word for a situation and not an accumulation of wisdom.

some assumptions

There is limited Biblical data within the gifts passages to give us a clear picture of word of wisdom and word of knowledge. There are several ways to interpret the data regarding these gifts. We will list several different possibilities. In our opinion, the last two assumptions that are listed carry the most weight and are what we believe about these gifts.

- The two descriptions (wisdom and knowledge) are really one. That is, knowledge and wisdom are being used synonymously. The phrases are repeated for emphasis.
- The two gifts are really not distinct gifts but are simply ways in which some of the other gifts are released such as prophecy and exhortation.
- These two gifts are distinct gifts in their own right though there may not be enough evidence to finely distinguish between the two. One can certainly offer tentative definitions which are backed by possible illustrations from the Scriptures.
- The use of logos prefacing both wisdom and knowledge suggests that these gifts are situational communications given by the Holy Spirit for that moment. Thus, we are not just talking about people who are knowledgeable about the Bible or God but are talking about a word which comes from God as wisdom or knowledge for a certain specific situation.

use

It would seem entirely feasible that this gift could be operated in conjunction with any of the speaking gifts either by the speaker or by some hearer who is led to see the value of what is being said in terms of his/her specific situation.

possible example

In Acts 15:19-21, we see James operating as the leader of the church in dealing with the complex issue of Gentile believers. It is highly likely that James was able to see the value of what was being said from both sides and having grasped the bigger picture was able to give a word of wisdom for the group.

WORD OF WISDOM CONTINUED

James 3:13-18	This passage gives the Biblical guidelines for the kinds of words of wisdom that are given.

symptoms   Here are several symptoms of this gift.

- the ability to be sensitive to the prompting of the Holy Spirit which allows for the recognition of ideas and concepts that God is speaking into the situation,
- the quickness to transfer concepts into application for a situation,
- a good understanding of spiritual truth in the Bible,
- an ability to see principles of truth,
- the ability to grasp situations by intuition and see solutions for the situation almost simultaneously—further analysis and evaluation will often confirm the intuitive solution,
- when a word of wisdom comes in the intuitive way and is given in a group setting, it is usually authenticated by those who hear it by a consensus approval.

source of wisdom   When a person operates in this gift, they report that the source of the wisdom comes in a variety of different ways. The following continuum helps to diagram this. Ultimately, all wisdom comes from God but the person's awareness of God's involvement varies depending on how the word comes.

High Awareness of   Low Awareness of
Sovereign Intervention   Sovereign Intervention

Word of Wisdom   Wisdom

|——-

<————spontaneous;   deliberately repeated ————>
          situationally specific;   general or specific;
          could be non-vested;   vested;
          less or non-developable   developable (accumulated)

Word Of Knowledge Central Thrust   Getting Revelatory Information

introduction	The gifts called word of wisdom and word of knowledge appear only in the 1 Corinthians passage. Because of this, there is some difficulty in understanding and identifying these two gifts. There are several possible illustrations of these gifts in operation in the Bible but there is no hard evidence that these examples are these gifts in operation. The definitions are formulated primarily from the phraseology that is involved.
definition	The *word of knowledge* gift refers to the capacity or sensitivity of a person to supernaturally perceive revealed knowledge from God which otherwise could not or would not be known and apply it to a situation.
certainty of definition	Like word of wisdom there is limited Biblical data from which to draw a definition. Our definition is drawn from a combination of Biblical data, empirical observation and our own reasoning.

possible
examples

- Acts 5:3ff Peter's knowledge of God's supernatural judgment.
- Acts 16:28 Paul's knowledge of the jailer's suicide thoughts.
- Acts 18:9 Paul's confirmation to stay at Corinth.
- Acts 20:25 Paul avers that he would not see the Ephesian elders again.
- Acts 21:10 knowledge in conjunction with prophecy.
- Acts 27:22-26 knowledge of the shipwreck with loss of life.

symptoms

Here are several symptoms of this gift:

- sensitivity to the Holy Spirit's prompting which allows for the recognition that certain thoughts or impressions are from God,
- a recognition that in certain situations the Holy Spirit wants to do something and gives you knowledge that could not have originated with you. This knowledge helps release the activity of God in the situation.
- an awareness that God releases knowledge and information in a variety of ways.

current use
of this gift

John Wimber, of the Vineyard Christian Fellowship of Anaheim, has modeled and taught people how to operate in this gift. In his ministry, the word of knowledge gift is used in a complimentary fashion with healing ministry as well as for other purposes. In his teaching, he identifies 5 ways that a person receives supernatural information from God.

- in the mind's eye, a person could see words written like newspaper headlines or ticker tape,
- a person could hears God speak in an inner voice,
- in the mind's eye, a person could see pictures or visions,
- in healing situations, a person might actually feel pain or other symptoms of a condition that God wants to heal. The person feeling the symptoms does not have the condition.
- Rarely, a person opens his/her mouth an utters information without a prior consciousness of the information.

source of
knowledge

When a person operates in this gift, they report that the source of the knowledge comes in a variety of different ways. The following continuum helps to diagram this. Ultimately, all knowledge comes from God but the person's awareness of God's involvement varies depending on how the *word* comes.

WORD OF KNOWLEDGE CONTINUED

High Awareness of   Low Awareness of
Sovereign Intervention   Sovereign Intervention
Word of Knowledge   Knowledge

|—————————————————————————————————————|

<——————— spontaneous;   deliberately repeated ————>
             situationally specific;   general or specific;
             could be non-vested;   vested;
             less or non-developable   developable (accumulated)

comment   Over the past several years as we have done empirical studies both with Pentecostal and charismatic groups we have seen this gift in operation. Typically the group will be meeting to worship and praise the Lord and someone will receive a word of knowledge (or promptings which they think may be that). In the context of a ministry time which encourages listening to God these words of knowledge (we have seen word of wisdom, prophecy, and discernings of spirits all happen in this same kind of context) are shared. Sometimes the information is pinpoint and precise and the moment it is given the person to whom the information responds and some sort of appropriate action is taken (like a group of people gathering around and praying toward the thrust of the word). Sometimes the word progresses and doesn't come all at once. It is very general, then gets more detailed, then very precise. As detailed fact after fact is revealed it builds a dramatic kind of effect. The fact that it happens, and frequently that only God and the person to whom it refers knows the information, lends credibility, authenticity, and authority to the word. It also heightens faith in God and stimulates worship of God.

FAITH	CENTRAL THRUST	A TRUSTING RESPONSE TO A CHALLENGE BY GOD

introduction

Concerning the gift of faith, very little is mentioned in the Scriptures. If it were not for its inclusion in the list of gifts in 1 Corinthians 12, one would probably not identify it as a gift. However, it is included as a special gift given to some people in order to edify the church. Therefore, it is distinct from faith which each of us must have to be saved and to walk with God. Such faith is seen as a fruit of the Spirit and should be a growing part of every believer's walk with God. Since there is little or no reference to this gift in terms of illustration or a command to exercise it, the definition which follows is simply a logical extension of a word study on the word faith and the fact that it is included in the list of sign gifts, all illustrations of how the Spirit manifests Himself and dispenses gifts.

definition

The *gift of faith* refers to the unusual capacity of a person to recognize in a given situation that God intends to do something and to trust God for it until He brings it to pass.

certainty of definition

Because this definition comes from a word study on faith and does not have any illustrations explicitly identified or background data, this definition should not be presented dogmatically as the only way to define this gift. This definition is certainly in harmony with Biblical truth but there is no hard data, other than word studies and implications of inclusion on this special list, for giving this definition.

uses of this gift

The gift of faith is used by God:
- to bring glory to Himself,
- to reveal who and how He really is to people,
- to exhort the church to pray and believe,
- to meet the crisis needs in the life of the individual and the church,
- to fulfill the inspirational function of leadership.

example

Paul over the course of his life and ministry demonstrated on several occasions what could be called the gift of faith. He received in his unusual call experience a vision of what he was to do with his life. He clung to this vision in the face of adversity and trusted God to bring His purposes about. Also, there are specific instances when he demonstrated a trusting response to God's challenge. Note the following:
- the Macedonian call (Acts 16),
- he was to speak before rulers and kings (Acts 21: 9-14),
- in Corinth, God encouraged him to stay strong (Acts 18:10,11),
- the shipwreck incident (Acts 27:22-26).

comment

I believe that this one of the unseemly parts of the body (1 Corinthians 1222-24) that God will show more abundant honor.

symptoms

Here are a number of possible symptoms of this gift:
- an unusual desire to accept God's promises at face value and to apply them to given situations until God fulfills them.
- receiving what you believe to be a vision of some future work of God and trusting God for it until it comes to pass.

FAITH CONTINUED

symptoms continued

- the recurring experience in the midst of situations to sense that God is going to do something unusual even though most of the people around you don't have this kind of assurance,
- an unusual desire to know God in His fullness and to be cast on Him and Him alone for solutions to problems.
- the thrill of knowing time and time again that God is real because He and He alone has specifically in a detailed way intervened on your behalf.
- an attitude that says that: not only that God can do something but that He will do something in the situation, in fact, in many cases to know that God has already done it.

comment   It is this gift that puts teeth into use of the Future Perfect paradigm[5] in leadership, the essential thrust of vision casing, a necessary ingredient in inspirational leadership.

comment   You will remember that Wagner, List 2 on page 93 and that Wimber, List 3 on page 94 both included intercession as a spiritual gift. Because of my presupposition to use only gifts actually mentioned in Biblical data I do not list intercession as a spiritual gift. I sympathize with them in identifying this gift because the function is so needed in churches, parachurches and for leaders.[6] I think they were more influenced by need, desire, and experience than by Biblical data. Nevertheless I believe that what they call intercession has strong overlap with my view of the faith gift. That is, my own experience and empirical observations frequently have identified the faith gift with intercessor type people. As they intercede they began to seek God for His disposition, His desires, His will for a given situation. As it is revealed they respond by believing God for it.[7] It is the gift of faith that often engenders this response. And the effect of that faith stance can be widespread among a local group. It can literally turn around a dead situation. It can fulfill the inspirational function so desperately needed by leadership. But I see the faith gift as broader than just intercession. It can provide guidance for a group. It will demonstrate the presence of God in a situation, the necessary ingredient of all leadership.[8]

---

[5] See Davis' work in this regard. I summarize it in Handbook I. Leaders, Leadership, and the Bible—An Overview, available through Barnabas Publishers, 2175 N. Holliston Ave, Altadena, Ca, 91001.

[6] Wagner is very strong on the need of intercessors for leaders. In fact he has written a series of books on prayer. One of those treats very strongly this important need and protective screen for leaders.

[7] J.O. Fraser, in Behind the Ranges, Mountain Rain, illustrates the gift of faith mixed with intercession. His bite-sized approach to faith and his finalization of his transaction with God which led to the major breakthrough with the Lisu are inspiring. This is a powerful illustration of what I am saying here.

[8] This is one of the important macro-lessons emerging from our study of leadership values in the Scriptures. The necessary and sufficient condition of leadership, the essential ingredient, is the powerful presence of God in the life and ministry of a leader.

GIFTS OF HEALINGS   CENTRAL THRUST   RELEASING GOD'S POWER TO HEAL

introduction   The gifts of healings, one of the so-called miraculous gifts, is a gift over which there is disagreement. Some would say that the gift does not operate any longer. God released this gift in order to establish the church by giving its messengers power and authority. Once the church was established it was no longer needed. Others would say that it could exist today but that they do not believe that it does. Others would say that the gift does in fact exist today. Still others document its existence throughout the history of the church.[9] And others study, document, and evaluate the contemporary scene. There is ample evidence in Scripture from which to draw a definition and to give illustrations of the gift in action. One should note the double plurality of the words in the phrase—gifts of healings. It is not clear exactly what this means but most likely variety, at the least, is involved. We will usually refer to this gift by the single word, healing, but keep in mind the double plurality in the phrase.

definition   *Gifts of healings* refer to the supernatural releasing of healing power for curing all types of illnesses.

certainty of   There is limited Biblical data from which to draw a definition. Ourdefinition is drawn
definition   from a combination of Biblical data, empirical observation and our own reasoning.

uses   There were several uses of this gift in the New Testament. In addition, to the humanitarian element, showing God's love and compassion to people in need, there was also,

   • releasing healing power gave authority to the message and the messenger who brought God's word to the people,
   • it was a way of demonstrating the love and compassion of God to people.

examples   There are numerous examples of healing in the book of Acts.

   • Acts 3 the lame man
   • Acts 14 the lame man in Lystra
   • Acts 28:8 the people on the island

symptoms   Here are several symptoms.

   • a deep desire to see God alleviate physical problems in people and the willingness to be used by God to do so,
   • an unusual ability to sense the power of God when it is present for healing,
   • the ability to trust God and believe that He wants to heal.
   • the willingness to take risks for God,
   • the principle of contagion probably applies here. People who are around people operating in this type of healing ministry are likely to be drawn into it and be open to God releasing this gift to them so that they can release the healing to others.

---

[9]See Hummel's book for this. See also Chris DeWette's thesis. DeWette was a student of Wagner during the heyday of the MC 510 Signs and Wonders course. He did historical research on this topic.

GIFTS OF HEALINGS CONTINUED

comment   It seems that in the exercise of this gift that faith plays a crucial role. However, faith to be healed does not always originate with the person needing healing although this is often the case in the New Testament. Sometimes the faith originates with the person doing the healing. Other times it appears as if it depends totally upon God and not upon the healer or the person receiving the healing. The phrase, the power of the Lord was present for healing, occurs several times in the New Testament. When the power of the Lord is present for healing the quality of faith in the one being healed and the quality of faith in the healer seemed to be overshadowed by the sovereign work of God.

comment   Abuses of this gift by so-called public evangelists, that is, blaming the failure to heal on the recipient's faith and using this gift as a source of finances—extravagant living, etc., has done much to turn off many Christians to the whole notion of gifts of healings. While empathizing with this feeling I must again assert that we can not afford to neglect a truth from God because of its abuses.

comment   Some Pentecostals hold that the notion of healing is in the atonement, that is, that it is always the will of God to heal. This puts tremendous pressure on those involved when there is failure to heal as there is in many cases. The usual reaction is someone's failure to believe God enough. This kind of dogmatism which is not a theological position of many others also turns many Christians off to the whole notion of gifts of healings.

comment   This gift is frequently the stimulation for a paradigm shift{10} for those who do not believe in God's power and reality. In our empirical studies we have observed situations that to us, in a thrilling manner, attest to the power of God to heal. You only have to experience one of these kinds of things and have that inner confirmation from the Spirit that it is true and of God to change your thinking about God's reality and intervening power today. And the results of this paradigm shift spill over to other gifts. One is able by faith to believe God and see Him release power in other gifts—the so called non-miraculous gifts—in a new way.

caution   Whether or not this gift exists today is a question of its own apart from the definition of the gift. There does not seem to be exegetical evidence showing cessation of the gift. It would seem that the authenticity function where God releases healing power in order to give His messengers authority to proclaim the good news is still needed today. Also, God's compassion and love needs to be demonstrated as well.

comment   This gift certainly carries with it the main thrust of the power cluster. It in a spectacular way demonstrates the reality of God in a powerful way. It often breaks open things in ministry. It often spurs evangelistic outreach. It gets people's attention. Such was surely the case in the Acts. And so it is today.

WORKINGS OF POWERS   CENTRAL THRUST   THE RELEASING OF GOD'S POWER TO GIVE AUTHENTICITY

introduction   This gift is popularly called miracles. 1 Corinthians 12:10 gives the only direct information about it. The words describing this gift are words which usually mean powerful workings. Often these works are attributed to God. Paul in referring to his own
powerful workings says that what he did was used as a sign that his work was of God
(see 2 Corinthians. 12:12). Primarily then the gift of miracles was an authenticity gift
used by God to give credence to the message of the early witnesses of the gospel. The
question of this gifts existence today is disputed. Those claiming that it does not exist
today say that it was only needed in the first century to establish authority for the
message of the Gospel but is not needed today. Others, especially those associated
with missionary work among animistic tribes, feel this gift exists today and provides
the same function in their setting that it did in the early church. God uses it to provide
authenticity, credibility and authority for the gospel message. Again note the double
plural which probably means that there is a variety of miracles. That is, this is a generic label under which many kinds of miraculous activities of God could be attributed.

definition   The *workings of powers*, gift of miracles, refers to the releasing of God's supernatural
power so that the miraculous intervention of God is perceived and God receives recognition for the supernatural intervention.

certainty of   There is limited Biblical data from which to draw a definition. Our definition is
definition   drawn from a combination of Biblical data, empirical observation and our own reasoning. Though limited data, the definition is sound. The real issue is, is the gift valid
today.

use   The gift of miracles seems to be used to validate claims and give authenticity to the
Gospel message and its messengers. The missiological concept of a *power encounter*
involves the use of this gift. The Hebrews 2 gifts passage seems to confirm this function of authenticity. There a synonym is used for powers.

examples   There are several references to this gift operating in the New Testament, the majority
of them from the book of Acts:
   •   Acts 4:33 a reference to God releasing miracles through the apostles
   •   Acts 5:12 Peter's judgment of Ananias
   •   Acts 6:8 Stephen's unnamed miracles
   •   Acts 8:5-7 Philip's miracles
   •   Acts 13:9-12 Paul's encounter with Elymas the sorcerer
   •   Acts 16:16-18 Paul's encounter with the demonized girl
   •   Hebrews 2:3-4 a summary passage concerning the use of miracles

symptoms   Here are several symptoms of this gift.
   •   God will put you in positions in which you must see the power of God demon-
        strated in order to vindicate God's character.
   •   an ability and sensitivity to discern what God wants to do in a given situation,
   •   a willingness to risk your reputation and trust God in unusual situations,
   •   a deep trust and faith in God,

- an ability to see the spiritual realities of a situation and discern the power encounter that is happening.

comment   Many of those who deny the existence of this gift today do so from an ivory tower perspective. That is, they do it from a theoretical base and not from a research base. They do not examine what is happening in the contemporary use of these gifts from a learning posture bias. Usually philosophical considerations sway what they see.

comment   Again, like the gifts of healings this gift certainly carries with it the main thrust of the power cluster. It in a spectacular way demonstrates the reality of God in a powerful way. It often breaks open things in ministry. It often spurs evangelistic outreach. It gets people's attention. Such was surely the case in the Acts. And so it is today.

comment   The double plurality probably indicates that there are probably diverse miracles that are manifestations of this gift in action. The key note as to whether or not a given manifestation is a valid demonstration of the gift would be to see, Does it fulfill the central use of the gift: Does it validate claims and give authenticity to the Gospel message and its messengers. Is God recognized for who He is. Does He receive honor and glory from it? Are His purposes forwarded through it?

DISCERNINGS OF SPIRITS   CENTRAL THRUST   A SENSITIVITY TO TRUTH

introduction
In the early church, there was no finalized form of the New Testament. God used prophets, teachers and other leadership gifts to reveal, explain and apply truth to the early believers. New Testament texts show that there were false apostles and teachers along with others who claimed to have authority from God (see 2 Corinthians 11:13; 2 Peter 2:1; 1 John 4:1-3 and Jude 4). God used this gift to the church to protect the church from these false prophets, false teachers and false apostles. Users of this gift were able to test the spirits, that is, attest to truth or error, by identifying the source from which the information originated—from God or from other spirits. This allowed the church to distinguish between truth and error. Peter warns in 2 Peter that this ability to discern error, particularly from teachers, will be a growing need in the church. Hebrews 5:14 amplifies the function of discernment more broadly to good and evil and indicates that such discernment is the mark of maturity. Again, note the double plural—discernings of spirits, which probably indicates many varied uses of and expressions of this gifting.

definition
The *discernings of spirits* gift refers to the ability given by God to perceive issues in terms of spiritual truth, to know the fundamental source of the issues and to give judgment concerning those issues; this includes the recognition of the spiritual forces operating in the issue.

certainty of definition
There is limited Biblical data from which to draw a definition. Our definition is drawn from a combination of Biblical data, empirical observation and our own reasoning. The definition is more certain than others in the power cluster (except prophecy).

uses
Here are several uses of this gift:
- in the early church, it was used to distinguish truth from non-truth in terms of verbal utterances,
- in the church today, with the entire canon of Scripture, this gift can be used to discern whether teaching is on target or consistent with the revealed truth of the Word,
- to protect the church from heretical tendencies in either teaching or in practice,
- to discern whether the source of a particular activity is generated by the Holy Spirit, the person, or the demonic realm.

example
Hebrews 5:14 says, "But solid food is for the mature, who by constant use have trained themselves to distinguish good from evil."

example
1 John 4:1 says, "Dear friends, do not believe every spirit, but test the spirits to see whether they are from God, because many false prophets have gone out into the world." Spirit, by metonymy, indicates the teachings being prompted by the spirit. The idea being, that you must judge the teaching as to its source. Is it being generated by the Holy Spirit or other spirits? This example could also be expanded to include more than just oral information but ministry situations in general.

symptoms
Here are several symptoms of this gift:
- a keen sense for recognizing inconsistencies,

DISCERNINGS OF SPIRITS CONTINUED

- the tendency to always be figuring out what is wrong with a situation and how it can be improved,
- the ability to categorize and think in logical ways,
- a good grasp of Scriptural truth in general,
- a deep underlying sense of conviction which will not allow you to rest when you know people are being given half-truth, misapplied truth, or false teaching, and are asked to act upon it,
- an unusual sensitivity or intuitive grasp of people and situations,
- you often and usually quickly notice when public speakers give wrong interpretations or misapply the Scriptures,
- on some occasions, you will get a glimpse of the behind the scenes supernatural reality in a situation, either by mental picture or in reality,
- you see physical symptoms that lead you to know something is wrong (like auras about people, colors around them, etc.).

comment   By reading this list of symptoms, it would be difficult to distinguish a person who is operating in discernment and a person who is critical by nature and constantly tears things apart. One major difference is the posture that the person takes when he/she is discerning the situation. Is the person critical negative or is the person critical positive? A critical negative person when looking at a situation or person operating in ministry says...what's wrong with this! A critical positive person says...what's right with this and what's wrong with this? What can we do to improve it? God what are you doing here? What is of you and what isn't?

comment   Discernment is also a natural ability. In its natural expression it is an analytical capacity to distinguish consistency or inconsistency, truth from non-truth, by judging the truth or non-truth in terms of revealed truth or principles taken from that truth. Frequently, the initial judgment is intuitive—but can later shown to be logically consistent. In its widest sense it is the judgment between right and wrong. There are skills like the study of logic and rhetoric that aid one in discernment.

comment   We have done some studies to correlate this gift with the Meyers-Briggs personality profiles. The -N— types seem to relate to those with this gift. That is, apparently all who have shown this gift in their gift-mix have also had a strong N or at least a dominant N in their Meyers-Briggs profile.[11]

source of   This gift, like word of wisdom and word of knowledge has strong overlap with
discernment   natural abilities and analytical skills as seen in the diagram.

High Awareness of Sovereign Awareness   Low Awareness of Sovereign Intervention

Discernings of Spirits   Discernment
|———|
    <————————— spontaneous;   deliberately repeated ————>
                 situationally specific;   general or specific;
                 could be non-vested;   vested;
                 less or non-developable   developable (accumulated)

_____

[11]See Kiersey and Bates book, **Please Understand Me**, for a good popular treatment of Meyers-Briggs concepts including a simple test that will give you a resonably accurate profile.

KINDS OF TONGUES
INTERPRETATION OF TONGUES

CENTRAL THRUSTS
TONGUES — SPEAKING A SPONTANEOUS MESSAGE IN AN UNKNOWN LANGUAGE

INTERPRETATION OF TONGUES — INTERPRETING A MESSAGE GIVEN IN TONGUES

introduction The gift of tongues was one that caused problems at Corinth. It was divisive and was a strong factor in nurturing of spiritual pride. The abuse of the gift brought about ill-desired effects. The Apostle Paul was prompted to write a lengthy section of his letter to deal specifically with this abuse. Most of what we know about tongues is written in this passage. In Acts the gift of tongues was given several different times. In one case, Acts 2, the men who received the gift of tongues spoke in other recognizable dialects. In Acts 10:46, either the gift was in other recognizable dialects or Peter and his friends received the interpretation because they heard them glorifying God. In Acts 19:6, it is unclear whether the tongues were understood or not. In each of the above incidents concerning tongues, the primary purpose of the gift was to authenticate that new segments of people were being added to the church and that God was endorsing them by releasing this gift. Note the double plural again, which probably denotes variety of forms and uses.

definition The *gift of tongues* refers to a spontaneous utterance of a word from God in unknown words (to the individual giving the word) to a group of people.

definition The *gift of interpretation of tongues* refers to the ability to spontaneously respond to a giving of an authoritative message in tongues by interpreting this word and clearly communicating the message given.

certainty of definition There is limited Biblical data from which to draw a definition. Our definition is drawn from a combination of Biblical data, empirical observation and our own reasoning. It is less certain than prophecy and discerning of spirits but more so that word of knowledge and wisdom.

word study When Paul mentions the gift of tongues he calls it kinds of tongues. The word kinds (*genos*) can mean offspring, family, stock, race, sort or species. The word tongues (*glossa*) is used to describe the common tongue in the mouth and by metonymy can mean anything that is spoken by that tongue. It is used by way of metonymy when describing the gift of tongues. It is not clear whether the utterances are always a known dialect or not. It is clear however that the utterances are not known to the one doing the speaking, unless he/she also has the gift of interpreting the tongue. In the Acts 2 passage, the word *dialektos* which indicates a recognizable language is used synonymously with the word *glossa*. In the other Acts passages, the word dialektos is not used. The word interpretation is the word *hermeneuo*. This word is used to describe the process of explaining something to someone who does not understand what is being said and also is a word that describes the process of translating from one language to the other.

KINDS OF TONGUES CONTINUED
INTERPRETATION OF TONGUES

uses   Here are several uses of these gifts:
                •   tongues were used to authenticate the addition of non-Jewish people into God's
                     church (Acts 2,10,19 and thus to show that God's church was to be universal,
                •   tongues were primarily used as a sign to unbelievers rather than to believers (1
                     Corinthians 14:22),
                •   tongues are secondarily used for edification in the gathered church. (1
                     Corinthians 14:22, 26,27),
                •   to worship God, singing in tongues (could be private or corporate, 1 Corinthians
                     14:15),
                •   to intercede, a form of prayer (1 Corinthians 14:14),
                •   to give inner assurance of communion with God, an affirmation of personal
                     presence of God in a life.

order   In public meetings there is to be order when the gift of tongues is operating to give a
                spontaneous message to the congregation. Only a few messages were to be given and
                these were to be given one at a time. There should be time planned for the interpreta-
                tion of the tongue so that all may be edified. (1 Corinthians 14:26,27) Tongues as a
                special spontaneous message should not be given unless there is someone present to
                interpret the message.

symptoms   It is unclear whether these gifts are developable or not. In terms of development they
                are probably like word of knowledge and word of wisdom.

caution   Whether or not these gifts exist today is a question all its own apart from trying to
                define the gifts. There does not seem to be exegetical evidence showing that these
                gifts have ceased. Paul makes a passing comment that forbids people to keep people
                from speaking in tongues. People argue on both sides of the issue.

FEEDBACK ON POWER CLUSTER

1. Match each word gift with its central thrust by placing the capital letter in the blank next to the descriptive statement.

A Word of Wisdom   D. Gifts of Healings   G. kinds of tongues
B. Word of Knowledge   E. Workings of Powers   H. interpretation of tongues
C. Faith   F. Discernings of Spirits

   ___(1)   getting revelatory information
   ___(2)   release God's power to heal
   ___(3)   a sensitivity to truth
   ___(4)   the release of God's power to give authenticity
   ___(5)   interpreting a message given in tongues
   ___(6)   applying revelatory information
   ___(7)   a trusting response to a challenge by God
   ___(8)   speaking a spontaneous message in an unknown language

2. Suppose you were in a church in the independent Bible church movement, most of which hold essentially McRae's views on spiritual gifts, listed below.

(1) serving or helping (4) giving   (7) evangelism
(2) teaching   (5) administration (ruling) (8) pastor-teacher
(3) exhortation   (6) showing mercy   (9) faith

Which of the three clusters of gifts is missing? Check the one right answer?
___a. Word Cluster   ___b. Power Cluster   ___c. Love Cluster   ___d. all are there

3. Essentially a church with the view given in question 3 is evidencing a power cluster vacuum. Draw a Venn diagram to represent this situation.

FEEDBACK ON POWER CLUSTER CONTINUED

4.   In general, what is the effect of a power vacuum as suggested in question 3?

ANSWERS————————
1.   B_(1) _D_(2) _F_(3) _E_(4) _H_(5) _A_(6) _C_(7) _G_(8)

2.   _√_b. Power Cluster. Don't be misled by faith that is listed there. It is not defined as the faith gift from the power cluster.

3.   I'll use an oval labeled with A to mean Word cluster. An oval with B means a love cluster. There is no power cluster.

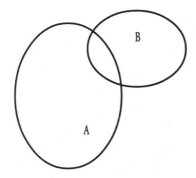

4.   Most likely this would be a church with a strong word ministry—since there is absolutely no power it means dominantly teaching and exhortation gifts. Essentially then this is a cognitive church a church in which what you believe is the most important thing. This would be a typical Bible Church. While it theoretically holds to evangelism, there is usually little evident in reality. It has some compassion ministry but it is clear that it is dominantly a classroom type of church. The love cluster is about half within and half without the church. This means that there are probably a number of helps and governments gifts operating in the church doing service ministries and a number of mercy, helps types reaching out of the church. This church could use some power gifts in order to break through and reach new people for Christ. Its leadership gifts are probably pastoral and teaching. The Christianity is cerebral and ideation centered. There would be little evidence, experientially, of God and His power. But a lot of knowledge about Him.

COMMENTARY ON POWER CLUSTER

introduction

In learning theory, educational technologists describe 4 learning domains that must be addressed for learning to become habitual. There is cognition, that is ideas, knowledge and the like. There is affective learning, that is feelings which become associated with values. Then there must be conative learning, that is willful decisions to enter in and use the truth. Finally there is experiential learning—learning which integrates cognitive, affect, and conative all into daily life. The three clusters of gifts, word, power, and love, focus on different aspects of these learning domains. The word cluster primarily addresses the cognitive domain, with some attention to the will, and a minimum to the affective domain. The power cluster focuses on the experiential and volitional domains. The love cluster dominantly affects the experiential and affect domains. Taken together these clusters affect all the domains of learning and help us to integrate our experience with God.

power
vacuum

If the power cluster is absent what is missed? The central thrust of the power gift cluster—to know firsthand the reality of God. We can know cognitively (a theoretical belief). But the power cluster pushes us to an experientially reality of God. People who experience God's working via the power cluster have radically different paradigms for viewing reality than people who deny them. In leadership emergence theory, we have noted the concept of a paradigm shift, one of God's breakthrough processes for transforming a leader and infusing new life into his/her ministry. Power experiences stimulate such paradigm shifts.

risk
and
power gifts

Normally when we exercise word gifts (prophecy excluded) and love gifts there is no threat, no risk, or no assessment of how we did. But with every one of the power gifts it is always a risky venture. Awareness of the supernatural involvement is high, on the part of all, the one exercising the gift and the ones receiving the ministry. And there is always the fear that what we do may not be genuine, may not be of God. Will God work? Your belief in God, view of God, convictions, and reputation are on the line when you exercise these gifts. It would be safer not to exercise these gifts or to allow them to be used in our situations. But each time we do and we sense again the fresh touch and reality of God we know that we must take the risks. We should not think that our exercise of the gifts must be ideal. We should not expect any more perfect use of these gifts than we do of any other—say teaching. We allow teachers to be less than perfect in their insights and interpretations. We can do no less for the power gifts.

faith
the unsung
gift

I (Bobby) love to watch professional football, especially the Monday night games. If I have heard it once I have heard it a 100 times. *Such and such is one of the most underrated players around.* Usually it's some interior lineman or defensive back. And its true. Everyone knows the star quarterback or running back— the franchise player. Teams in contention always have a franchise player—that is, the success of the club hinges on this player. Well I like to think that the gift of faith is one of the most underrated gifts. Everybody knows the word gifts. There is a phrase in the body metaphor in 1 Corinthians 12 which says, the more unseemly parts, will be honored the more by God. I believe the gift of faith is that way. And when all is said and done we will find out that some unsung interior linemen in our church was the real reason things really happened. May God give us more with the gift of faith.

GIFTS OF GOVERNMENTS   CENTRAL THRUST   SUPPORTIVE ORGANIZATIONAL ABILITIES

introduction   The word translated as governments occurs only once in the entire New Testament. (1 Corinthians 12:28) A study of this word and its cognates which were used in classic Greek of the New Testament times indicated that the word has to do with guiding of affairs. It would seem natural to then say that it is one of the leadership gifts of the local church. However, it is listed in the Corinthian passage not with the leadership gifts, but with the supportive gifts. For this reason (there is no other exegetical reason), we have chosen to identify this gift as an administrative support gift operating at local church level. Since the ruling gift more properly carries the inspiration function at local church level it is likely that this gift carries the administrative support level.

definition   The *gifts of governments* involves a capacity to manage details of service functions so as to support and free other leaders to prioritize their efforts.

certainty of   There is limited Biblical data from which to draw a definition. Our definition is drawn
definition   from a combination of Biblical data, empirical observation and our own reasoning. It carries less certainty than the helps gift and is about on par with the ruling definition.

explanation   This supportive gift when exercised helps the church to run smoothly.

example   Acts 6:1-4 In this passage, people were chosen in order to oversee the details of operating the church and to support the widows in need. This freed up the Apostles to prioritize their time and use it for teaching and prayer. These positions of service were obviously considered to have spiritual importance because of the high spiritual standards that were placed on those who were considered for this role.

comment   The 1 Peter 4 gifts passage indicates that service gifts (like helps) are a special way to bring honor and glory to God. And they must so be exercised to do that. Most likely, this is another one of the unseemly parts of the body (1 Corinthians 12) that God will show more abundant honor. It is probably more recognized as important than are helps or mercy.

symptoms   Here are a few symptoms of this gift:

•   you have a knack for organizing things,
•   you like to standardize methods for doing things,
•   you think in terms of helping people reach their goals,
•   you have a concern for the good of the whole group when you are in charge of that group,
•   you like to do things that help other people,
•   you don't mind managing things or carrying out the details involved in some plan that has been made by others.

FEEDBACK ON WORD GIFTS CONTINUED

3. The following is the list of word gifts arranged in order of certainty. I will use as F=very firm, S=somewhat firm, or 0=open for further insights, in order to judge how sure I am about my definitions. In addition I will use a scale of 1-10 with the extremes of 1 being less certain and 10 being more certain with a category so you can get a feel for relative. Glance through this list then answer the following. How would you use this information? What difference does it make, the certainty of a definition?

Gift	Certitude of Definition
(a) Teaching	F(10)
(b) Exhortation	F(10)
(c) Prophecy	I(10)
(d) Evangelism	S(8)
(e) Apostleship	S(7)
(f) Pastoring	S(5)
(g) Ruling	O(5)

Your comments:

ANSWERS————
1. _C_(1) _F_(2) _A_(3) _E_(4) _G_(5) _B_(6) _D_(7)

2. a. One can not be certain from just a diagram. There are so many complex factors. But from a giftedness standpoint it looks as if Church A has plateaued. There is no growth, maybe not much life. Teaching dominates but little application in lives. A minimal pastoring is going on. What is needed is exhortation and ruling gifts to move the church toward some vision. It could probably use some evangelism gifts though right now evangelism would be stifled because new converts would not be attracted to the church and would not stay in it. Apostleship would probably threaten the present leadership which is probably content with the way things are. Prophecy probably wouldn't be allowed.   Church B has lots of life and growth but not much stability. It has overkill on application and little input. From the dominance of Apostleship it would probably be true that they are starting many new creative ministry situations which attract people. But it is also true that without solid ruling and/or love cluster gifts there will not be follow through on many of these creative ventures. After a while folks will not get excited about the next venture (because they know it will not last). What is needed is some teaching for stability and ruling for strategic thinking to incorporate the new ventures.

3. I would take it in two ways. (1) as a warning to remind me that the Bible is not absolutely clear. All but the ruling gift are very usable definitions. I would confidently use them until I got clear evidence to change some portion of any one of them. I would be more careful about the ruling gift and use it with caution. (2) I would use this information as a sort of standard as I evaluated other authors who write on gifts. I know what data is available. I can evaluate their information in light of these standards. When some author is over dogmatic where I don't think the Bible has that kind of information it tends to make me wary of all else that author says.

MERCY	CENTRAL THRUST	THE EMPATHETIC CARE FOR THOSE WHO ARE HURTING

introduction   In general, Christians should be tender-hearted and compassionate to those who are in need around them. But some Christians are endowed by God in a special way to sense and seek out and help those in need. The gift of mercy is qualified with a descriptive phrase by Paul in the Romans 12 passage which points out the attitude that should exist in a person who operates in this gift.

definition   The *gift of mercy* refers to the capacity to both feel sympathy for those in need (especially the suffering) and to manifest this sympathy in some practical helpful way with a cheerful spirit so as to encourage and help those in need.

certainty of   There is limited Biblical data from which to draw a definition. Our definition is drawn
definition   from a combination of Biblical data, empirical observation and our own reasoning.

uses   People who use this gift in ministry are trying:
- to practically express the love of God to people who are in need,
- to help alleviate problems of social concern as a part of the church's responsibility to society.

example   In Acts 9:36, we are told of a certain disciple named Tabitha (Dorcas) who was full of good works and helps people.

symptoms   Here are several symptoms of this gift:

- tears come easily as you hear or see things that sadden you,
- most people think of you as possessing a very empathetic personality,
- you want to reach out and help people who are suffering,
- you are unusually sensitive to hurting people,
- people in need like to have you around because you cheer them up,
- you have an unusual desire to express you love to helpless people,
- when confronted by hurting people, your first thought is "how can I help them?"

GIFTS OF HELPS   CENTRAL THRUST   THE ATTITUDE AND ABILITY TO AID OTHERS IN PRACTICAL WAYS

introduction
Where there are groups of people, there are always practical needs. So it is in the life of a church. God provides people who have the ability and the unselfish attitude to meet those needs. These people willingly serve others in the group. Such is the nature of a person who operates in this gift and thus demonstrates the very loving nature of God in practical ways. No one would naturally want to unselfishly give of himself/herself apart from an inward motivation and ability to do so which honors God. Though all Christians are to unselfishly regard others more highly than themselves (a Christian role) those with this gift will shine in this role. Again note the plurality probably indicating the diverse forms and uses in which the gift is manifested.

definition
The *gifts of helps* refers to the capacity to unselfishly meet the needs of others through very practical means.

certainty of definition
There is limited Biblical data from which to draw a definition. Our definition is drawn from a combination of Biblical data, empirical observation and our own reasoning. It is more certain than the governments gift occurring on the same list, List B, but less so than the leadership gifts on the list or the sign gifts on that list.

comment
The beauty of this gift is the way God takes the commonplace, routine and menial and raises it to a spiritual level. There are individuals who are empowered by God to offer help to others above and beyond the ordinary service of Christians. And God's divine enabling shines through.

comment
The 1 Peter 4 gifts passage indicates that service gifts (like helps) are a special way to bring honor and glory to God. And they must so be exercised to do that. Most likely, this is another one of the unseemly parts of the body (1 Corinthians 12) that God will show more abundant honor.

uses
The gift of helps is used:
- to render practical service in the church to people in need,
- to do menial jobs of a practical nature which will free-up other people to exercise other gifts,
- to help other individuals reach their full potential,
- to enable the body to function more efficiently by doing those things that if undone might hinder the body,
- to demonstrate the love of God.

symptoms
Here are several symptoms of this gift:
- a desire to help others,
- an ability to see ways that other people will be helped,
- an unselfish nature that can do tasks whether they appear menial or not,
- a bent toward enjoying practical service more than theoretical service of a conceptual nature,
- a willingness to do little jobs without any credit. It is done just for the joy of doing them or the knowledge that they are helping others,
- in the church, the person recognized that their practical service releases others to operate in their gifts, especially leadership gifts.

Feedback On Love Cluster

1. Match each love gift with its central thrust by placing the capital letter in the blank next to the descriptive statement.

A Gifts of Governments   B. Giving   C. Mercy   D. Gifts of Helps
    ___(1)   a sensitivity to God to channel His resources to others
    ___(2)   supportive organizational abilities
    ___(3)   the attitude and ability to aid others in practical ways
    ___(4)   the empathetic care for those who are hurting

2. This manual is primarily dealing with leadership gifts so there is not as much focus on the love cluster which has more widespread manifestation among followers in a church situation. What do you think is a major problem for people who are dominantly gifted with gifts from the love cluster? Check any answers which you think may apply.

    ___a. Strong word gifted leaders project gifts which people with love cluster gifts don't have. This is not only guilt inducing but frustrating.

    ___b. These gifts, like the underrated lineman, don't get affirmed in a public way such as word gifts or the more spectacular power gifts do. All people need affirmation.

    ___c. People with love cluster gifts are usually so task oriented that they can not relate to people.

    ___d. People with love cluster gifts are usually not sensitive to the needs of others.

3. See if you can identify two people in your present church or parachurch group for each of the love cluster gifts. List them by specific name in the blanks.

A Gifts of Governments—supportive organizational abilities:
    (1) _____   (2) _____

B. Giving—a sensitivity to God to channel His resources to others:
    (1) _____   (2) _____

C. Mercy—the empathetic care for those who are hurting:
    (1) _____   (2) _____

D. Gifts of Helps—the attitude and ability to aid others in practical ways:
    (1) _____   (2) _____

ANSWERS———————
1.   _B_(1) _A_(2) _D_(3) _C_(4)
2.   _√ a. _√ b.
3. Your choice of course. Be prepared to share with someone, maybe even a word of thanks or affirmation to them. Here are some that I have seen along the way.
    A (1) Mo Whitworth (2) Christine Cervantes
    B. (1) Margaret Clinton   (2) Cathy Schaller
    C. (1) Jude Tiersma (2) Janet Boldt
    D. (1) Doris Wagner (2) Bill George

COMMENTARY ON LOVE CLUSTER

introduction	The love cluster is a very necessary group of gifts. Work will not be carried out and needs in the body will not be met if these gifts are not operating.
affirmation	Strong leaders need to couteract their natural tendency to project their own dominant word gifts on others. They especially must see to it that people with love gift clusters get the affirmation they deserve and sense fulfillment out of these gifts.
discipleship	Most discipleship programs, while supposedly designed for Christian growth for believers, are for the most part heavily weighted toward word gifted people. Non-word gifted people (power cluster and love cluster) usually struggle with these programs which are in effect projecting word gifts upon non-word gifted people. Discipleship should always be along the lines of gifts. That is, design various discipleship programs which help mature all kinds of gifted people and not just word gifted people.
overlap	I promised earlier to point out some of the overlapping symptoms so that when you see these symptoms happening in activities and ministry situations you may be aware of the various gifts that may be there.
Teaching and Exhortation	Teaching and exhortation both strongly related to Biblical truth. Frequently, manifestations of exhortation also clarify in order to apply.
Exhortation and prophecy	Exhortation has a three fold thrust: admonition (correction), encouragement, and comfort. It shares the admonition aspect with the prophetical gift.
Exhortation and mercy	Exhortation has a three fold thrust: admonition (correction), encouragement, and comfort. It shares the comfort aspect with the mercy gift.
Exhortation and pastoring	Exhortation has a three fold thrust: admonition (correction), encouragement, and comfort. It shares the encouragement aspect with pastoring—which encourages growth.
Prophecy and Word of Knowledge and Wisdom	Prophecy is often revelatory. Word of Knowledge and Word of Wisdom are also revelatory gifts. Frequently the word given via them may be futuristically oriented and seems like prophecy.
Apostleship ruling	Apostleship often involves vision casting, inspirational leadership which motivates people toward goals. It shares this aspect with ruling.
Pastoring and mercy	Pastoring involves care for growth of believers. This empathetic attitude is also part of the mercy gift.

evangelism and prophecy	Evangelism seeks to get breakthroughs with unbelievers to have them reconcile with God. It frequently carries a corrective force. This kind of strong challenge can overlap with the corrective aspect of prophecy.
revelatory gifts	All the revelatory gifts of the power cluster (word of wisdom, word of knowledge, faith, prophecy, discernings of spirits, all contain that common revelatory aspect. But the content of each and how it is used differentiates them.
faith and prophecy	Often the faith revelation concerns something well into the future so it may sound like a prophetic word.
gifts of healings	Two power gifts, gifts of healings and workings of powers frequently have overlapping symptoms. Both are always miraculous. In one sense gifts of healings are always workings of powers. But it is a special kind of workings of powers which is distinct in its own right.
use not identity	Remember in the last analysis it is the use of gifts that the Bible enjoins not identifying. If you have trouble identifying your own or other peoples gifting—first, ask yourself which cluster thrust, word, or love—to you most resonate with. That is the first major step. Then simply place yourself in activities and an environment were you can minister, whether or not you know exactly what gifting you are using. Identification will emerge over time as fruitfulness is seen both by you and others. Many times, others will be quicker to identify a gifting in you than you yourself.

SUMMARY LISTING OF GIFT DEFINITIONS

Introduction   From time-to-time you will find it useful to have all the definitions of spiritual gifts in one place, when you are showing them to someone. So they are listed in the order that they were given in this chapter.

GIFT	DEFINITION

THE 7 WORD CLUSTER GIFTS

teaching

A person who has the gift of teaching is one who has the ability to instruct, explain, or expose Biblical truth in such a way as to cause believers to understand the Biblical truth.
CENTRAL THRUST - TO CLARIFY TRUTH

exhortation

The gift of exhortation is the capacity to urge people to action in terms of applying Biblical truths, or to encourage people generally with Biblical truths, or to comfort people through the application of Biblical truth to their needs.
CENTRAL THRUST - TO APPLY BIBLICAL TRUTH

prophecy

A person operating with the gift of prophecy has the capacity to deliver truth (in a public way) either of a predictive nature or as a situational word from God in order to correct by exhorting, edifying or consoling believers and to convince non-believers of God's truth.
CENTRAL THRUST -
TO PROVIDE CORRECTION OR PERSPECTIVE ON A SITUATION

apostleship

The gift of apostleship refers to a special leadership capacity to move with authority from God to create new ministry structures (churches and para-church) to meet needs and to develop and appoint leadership in these structures.
CENTRAL THRUST - CREATING NEW MINISTRY

pastor

The pastoral gift is the capacity to exercise concern and care for members of a group so as to encourage them in their growth in Christ which involves modeling maturity, protecting them from error and disseminating truth.
CENTRAL THRUST - CARING FOR THE GROWTH OF FOLLOWERS.

evangelism

The gift of evangelism in general refers to the capacity to challenge people through various communicative methods (persuasion) to receive the Gospel of salvation in Christ so as to see them respond by taking initial steps in Christian discipleship.
CENTRAL THRUST - INTRODUCING OTHERS TO THE GOSPEL.

GIFT	DEFINITION

The 7 Word Cluster Gifts continued

ruling

A person operating with a ruling gift demonstrates the capacity to exercise influence over a group so as to lead it toward a goal or purpose with a particular emphasis on the capacity to make decisions and keep the group operating together.

CENTRAL THRUST - INFLUENCING OTHERS TOWARD VISION.

The 8 Power Cluster Gifts

word of wisdom

The word of wisdom gift refers to the capacity to know the mind of the Spirit in a given situation and to communicate clearly the situation, facts, truth or application of the facts and truth to meet the need of the situation.
CENTRAL THRUST - APPLYING REVELATORY INFORMATION

word of knowledge

The word of knowledge gift refers to the capacity or sensitivity of a person to supernaturally perceive revealed knowledge from God which otherwise could not or would not be known and apply it to a situation.
CENTRAL THRUST - GETTING REVELATORY INFORMATION

faith

The gift of faith refers to the unusual capacity of a person to recognize in a given situation that God intends to do something and to trust God for it until He brings it to pass.
CENTRAL THRUST - A TRUSTING RESPONSE TO A CHALLENGE FROM GOD.

gifts of healings

The gifts of healings refers to the supernatural releasing of healing power for curing all types of illnesses.
CENTRAL THRUST - RELEASING GOD'S POWER TO HEAL.

workings of powers

The workings of powers, gift of miracles, refers to the releasing of God's supernatural power so that the miraculous intervention of God is perceived and God receives recognition for the supernatural intervention.
CENTRAL THRUST -
THE RELEASING OF GOD'S POWER TO GIVE AUTHENTICITY.

discernings of spirits The discernings of spirits gift refers to the ability given by God to perceive issues in terms of spiritual truth and to know the fundamental source of the issues and to give judgment concerning those issues; this includes the recognition of the spiritual forces operating in the issue.
CENTRAL THRUST - A SENSITIVITY TO TRUTH AND ITS SOURCE.

THE 8 POWER CLUSTER GIFTS CONTINUED

Gift   **Definition**

tongues   The gift of tongues refers to a spontaneous utterance of a word from God in unknown words (to the individual giving the word) to a group of people.
CENTRAL THRUST - SPEAKING A MESSAGE IN AN UNKNOWN TONGUE.

**interpretation of
tongues**   The gift of interpretation of tongues refers to the ability to spontaneously respond to a giving of an authoritative message in tongues by interpreting this word and clearly communicating the message given.
CENTRAL THRUST - INTERPRETING A MESSAGE GIVEN IN TONGUES.

THE 4 LOVE CLUSTER GIFTS CONTINUED

gifts of governments The gifts of governments involves a capacity to manage details of service functions so as to support and free other leaders to prioritize their efforts.
CENTRAL THRUST - SUPPORTIVE ORGANIZATIONAL ABILITIES.

giving   The gift of giving refers to the capacity to give liberally to meet the needs of others and yet to do so with a purity of motive which senses that the giving is a simple sharing of what God has given to you.
CENTRAL THRUST -
A SENSITIVITY TO GOD TO CHANNEL HIS RESOURCES TO OTHERS.

mercy   The gift of mercy refers to the capacity to both feel sympathy for those in need (especially the suffering) and to manifest this sympathy in some practical helpful way with a cheerful spirit so as to encourage and help those in need.
CENTRAL THRUST -
THE EMPATHETIC CARE FOR THOSE WHO ARE HURTING.

gifts of helps The gifts of helps refers to the capacity to unselfishly meet the needs of others through very practical means.
CENTRAL THRUST -
THE ATTITUDE AND ABILITY TO AID OTHERS IN PRACTICAL WAYS.

CHAPTER SUMMARY

We have concluded the second of two chapters defining and describing spiritual gifts. If you have met the goals of this chapter you should be able
- to give the central thrust of each of the 19 definitions,
- to be familiar enough with our definitions to recognize them, and
- to recognize a given gift if we give you the symptoms for it.

Now I realize that you have been introduced to a large number of concepts and won't have mastered them all yet. That will come with time and use of them. But you are off to a good start. You are ready for the next chapter, which deals exclusively with leadership giftedness concepts. After that, we will be ready to talk about development.

CHAPTER 7:
LEADERSHIP GIFTS

INTRODUCTION

The original title of this book was **"Developing Leadership Giftedness"**. Thus far, we have talked in a preliminary way about *leadership* in chapter 2. We have talked about *giftedness* in chapters 3-6. Remember that in chapter 2, we laid the foundations for leadership thinking, prior to our getting into the giftedness concepts in chapters 3-6. Those leadership definitions paved the way for our understanding giftedness as it relates to leadership. *Turn about is fair play.* Now having studied the many details of giftedness we want to come back to leadership issues and tell how some of those giftedness ideas affect *leadership.* We have a special interest in understanding the issue of giftedness as it relates to leadership development. This present chapter comments on 8 observations relating giftedness issues to leadership issues. Each of these observations have implications for leadership. Pastors, missionaries, and denominational leaders will want to read these observations carefully with a view toward assessing the implications for their own ministries.

This chapter is written in a narrative format. It uses the old fireside chat approach. Its just two leaders chatting to other leaders about some things they have learned. We have dispensed with the information mapping format for the moment because we are not primarily defining but just chatting about implications of giftedness teaching for leadership. So I will simply give the observation in a conversational way and then suggest some implications. A simple format for each observation—chat and apply. But don't let that keep you from carefully studying this chapter. Take it just as seriously as if we had information mapped it.

KEY OBSERVATIONS ABOUT SPIRITUAL GIFTS AND LEADERSHIP

Observation 1. Leadership Gifts Versus *Offices*

Apostleship, prophecy, evangelism, pastoring and teaching are often called the leadership gifts. Because of their nature and function, the exercising of these gifts are directly connected to exercising leadership influence. Some would not call these gifts but would call them offices. Because of the way that these gifts are listed in Ephesians 4, it is easy to see how this viewpoint is formed. As we discussed when we covered the Ephesians 4 passage, we believe that Paul is using metonymy as he wrote the text on spiritual gifts. We believe that he is referring to individuals who are gifted in apostleship, prophecy, evangelism, pastoring and teaching not just to apostles, prophets, evangelists, pastors and teachers who hold that office in the church.[1]

Is it possible to operate with these gifts without the *office* or official position? We believe that it is possible. In fact, we have observed many leaders operating in these gifts without the *official* title or position. Often, those positions were not available to these individuals because of things like denomina

---

[1] We have some difficulties with the whole idea of these being just offices. What is the office of pastor? What kind of gifts would a person in that office have? What is the office of teacher? What kind of gifts would a person in that office have? What is the office of evangelist? What kind of gifts would a person in that office have? What is the office of prophet? What kind of gifts would a person in that office have? What is the office of Apostleship? What kind of gifts would a person in that office have? Why would these offices be in the church? If to equip and lead the body to maturity is that not needed today? Has the church reached the full maturity described in Ephesians 4 so that we can do away with these offices and the gifts entailed in them? Why would some of them disappear and not all of them? Are just some of them needed to take the body to maturity?

tional tradition, gender issues, or certain types of circumstances in their past. The fact that they were not in the position didn't stop them from exercising the leadership influence associated with the gift.

It is primarily these leadership gifts that have responsibility for maturing the body. Evidently they were needed to mature the church as described in Ephesians 4. Even if you don't believe them to be gifts you can ask yourself the question, what did each of these offices contribute to the maturing of the body? Even if the offices don't exist officially today, what functions did they represent? These functions will be needed today to mature the body. So what are these functions? You know what we will say. From chapter 6 we have given the central thrust of each of these gifts. Those central thrusts are essentially the functions that are needed to mature the body. Look at them again!

1. The Apostolic Function— **CREATING NEW MINISTRY**

2. The Prophetic Function— **TO PROVIDE CORRECTION OR PERSPECTIVE ON A SITUATION**

3. The Evangelistic Function— **INTRODUCING OTHERS TO THE GOSPEL.**

4. The Pastoring Function— **CARING FOR THE GROWTH OF FOLLOWERS.**

5. The Teaching Function— **TO CLARIFY TRUTH**

And to these we have added two other influence gifts—exhortation and ruling.

6. The Exhortive Function— **TO APPLY BIBLICAL TRUTH**

7. The Ruling Function—   **INFLUENCING OTHERS TOWARD VISION.**

It is our contention that God is still following the Ephesians 4 mandate of equipping the body and developing it toward maturity. And these kinds of functions are still needed.

Implications

1. All seven of the functions listed above are needed to bring a balanced maturity to the body.

2. In general over an extended time, no one of the functions should be overemphasized to the exclusion of others.

3. For a given contextual situation and for a given time, one or more of the functions may need to be overemphasized to meet crucial needs.

Application Question(s)

1. In my situation, which leadership functions are being accomplished? Which not?

2. Which of the leadership functions that are missing are most needed now?

3. Historically, what leadership functions have been overemphasized over an extended time? What functions have been omitted?

4. Over the long haul what can I do to move toward a more balanced approach to the leadership functions?

Observation 2. Leadership Gifts and Supplementary Gifts

We can display a person's gift-mix and show the relationship between the various spiritual gifts that he/she operates in.[2] All leaders we have studied are multi-gifted. In our research we have commonly seen that certain gifts frequently supplement other gifts. We want to demonstrate this by showing you several of the more common ways that certain gifts supplement the leadership gifts. We will give you several diagrams that illustrate the various relationships between gifts.

Diagram #1: Apostleship with supplementary gifts

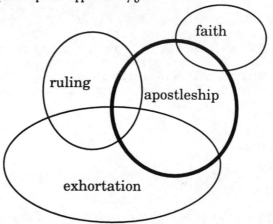

Comments: For a leader who operates in the gift of apostleship, it is common to find the gift of faith. This gift is needed because of the pioneering aspect of the apostleship function. The leader either operates in the gift of ruling or had strong natural abilities and acquired skills in leadership. Exhortation is an important gift because of the vision casting aspect of this type of leader. This is often the dominant gift in the leader's gift-mix.

Implication/Questions

1. Who are the multi-gifted leaders in my situation? Potentially multi-gifted leaders?
2. Who are the leadership people suggesting creative alternatives to meet ministry needs?
3. Who are the leadership people that can believe God to see something happen?
4. Who are the leadership people who can motivate others to do things?

---

[2] In fact we will do that in chapter 9. We will talk about Venn diagrams and tell you how to do your own.

Diagram #2: Prophecy with supplementary gifts

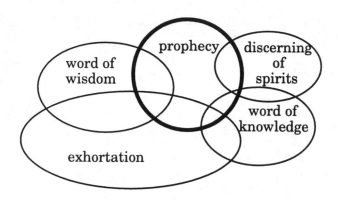

Comments: For a leader who operates in the gift of prophecy, it is common to see other *revelatory* gifts supplement the prophetic gift. For example, the word of knowledge and the word of wisdom gifts are frequently seen in the gift-mix. Also, there can be the discernings of spirits gift which allows the leader to discern the source of revelation. Exhortation is again a common gift because it is the gift that releases the revelation that God is giving this leader.

Implications/Questions

1.   Who are the leadership people pinpointing issues in our surrounding situation that needs to feel the impact of Christian influence?

2.   Who among the leadership people are prone to give God's word to us about the future and our place in it?

3.   Who in our situation frequently comes up with insights that break open what we are looking at?

4.   Who among our leadership frequently comes up with wise solutions to situations we face?

5.   Do our present structures and modes of operation hinder giftedness represented by the above profile? What can we do to foster giftedness represented by the above profile?

Diagram #3: Evangelism with supplementary gifts

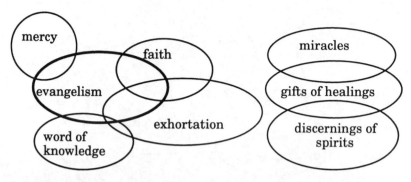

Comments: A leader operating with the evangelism gift can operate with a wide variety of supplementary gifts depending on his/her style, approach or even theology as it relates to the salvation of souls. Almost all of the leaders report a great burden for lost souls which can come out through a mercy gift. The gift of faith is important because of the nature of the work. Exhortation is common because it is often the gift the leader uses to share the message of the gospel. Healing, discerning of spirits, and miracles can also be an important part of a leader's gift-mix depending on theological perspective and if he/she operates in this capacity.

Implications/Questions

1.   Are we reaching lost people? If not, why not? Is there an absence of evangelistic giftedness and the related gifts that authenticate the Gospel?
2.   Who among us most typically links lost people to our situation? Can we come alongside and encourage them? Can we make changes that will enhance what they are doing?
3.   If there is an absence of evangelistic and supplemental gifts what would happen if God supernaturally laid such a person in our midst? Could that person operate in our midst or would our biases, our structures, our convictions mitigate against such a person?
4.   Are we willing to pay the price for evangelistic influence in our context and enable the breakthrough kinds of gifts that are needed?
5.   Are we willing to risk failure that goes along with these authenticity gifts that enhance evangelism?

Diagram #4: Pastoral gifts with supplementary gifts

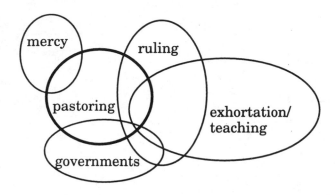

Comments: A person operating with a pastoral leadership gift will often have either the gift of ruling or strong natural abilities and acquired skills in leadership. He/she will also commonly have the gift of governments or have strong natural abilities and acquired skills in organizing, planning and administration. Because of the primary concern for people, compassion is often present in the gift of mercy. Either exhortation or teaching accompanies this gift. Because of the high concern and care of people, exhortation is a little more frequent in the gift-mix because exhortation focuses on the application of truth. However, most people operating in a pastoral gift have a *teaching* or *preaching* role and commonly see themselves as teachers.

Implications/Questions

1. Who among our leadership evince 3 or more of the above giftings?
2. Who among our potential leadership evidences a care for growth of followers?
3. Is pastoring only seen as a full time position in our situation? What can we do to promote pastoral gifted people in our midst?
4. In our situation how can we come identify and come alongside potential leadership with a mercy gifting?
5. In our situation how can we identify and come alongside potential leadership with ruling gifts (whether natural, acquired skills, or spiritual gift)? What can we do to incorporate them into our situation so that we don't have so many issues dropping through the cracks?

Diagram #5: Teaching with supplementary gifts

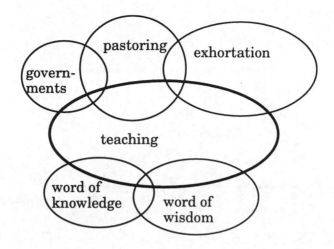

Comments: There are a number of supplementary gifts that operate alongside a person operating in teaching. It is common to see a leader operating in teaching who has pastoral gifting. Along with the pastoral gift comes governments or perhaps ruling or strong natural abilities and acquired skills in leadership. Depending on the type of teaching ministry, the leaders personality, his/her learning styles, the leader may operate in a number of different gifts such as word of knowledge or word of wisdom. Again, exhortation commonly operates in this gift-mix as the leader wants to see the truth that he/she is clarifying applied and acted on in the life of the person that he/she is teaching.

Implications/Questions

1. Do we have the means for identifying teaching giftedness? Do we know how to develop teaching giftedness even if we could identify those potentially gifted in teaching?
2. Do we have structures that enhance teacher/exhorters? What would we have to do to take advantage of this mix?
3. Do we have structures that enhance teacher/word of knowledge types? What would we have to do to take advantage of this mix?
4. Do we have structures that enhance teacher/word of wisdom types? What would we have to do to take advantage of this mix?
5. Is teaching only thought of in a public setting? Do we make it look like an office? What can we do to encourage teaching in small groups or a one-on-one individual way?
6. What teaching needs do we have in terms of subject matter? Who knows it? What can we do to enhance their communication of the needed subject matter?

Diagram #6: Natural Leadership and Spiritual gifts

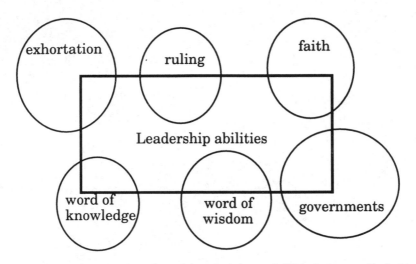

Comments: Sometimes, we have observed that a leader's natural abilities in the area of leadership dominate who they are. Spiritual gifts act as supplements to the leader's natural leadership gifts. This would include some of the so called leadership gifts such as pastoring, apostleship or teaching.

Implications/Questions

1.   Who are the natural leaders among us?
2.   Who are leaders out there in the business world?
3.   Who are the natural leaders among our young people?
4.   How can we help natural leaders to identify their supplemental spiritual gifts in order to develop and bring balance to their leadership influence among us?
5.   What in our situation turns natural leaders off from wanting to work with us?

Observation 3. Frequency of Gifts as They Appear in a Leader's Gift-Mix

Over the years we have been collecting data from leaders who study their own giftedness set and report their findings to us. One of the areas that we are studying is the frequency that certain gifts appear in the gift-mix of the various leaders who report to us. It is on the basis of our findings that we can make predictions about common relationships between certain gifts and those gifts that operate in a supplementary way.

Here is a preliminary report from data gathered over the past few years. There are 281 respondents covered in this survey. Each of the leaders report their own understanding of their gift-mix. The 281 respondents were all students, mid-career leaders, studying here at Fuller in the leadership courses in the School of World Mission. A large percentage of the students have been or are missionaries. Because of this, the percentages relating to the apostleship and evangelism gift are probably a bit higher than would be the average. Here are the statistics:

Percentage of leaders reporting this gift	Gift
53%	exhortation
51%	teaching
23%	apostleship
20%	pastoring
16%	evangelism
15%	faith
11%	word of wisdom
9%	prophecy
5%	ruling
4%	word of knowledge

It is too early in the research process to make any clear statement about the findings. We realize that only a certain type of leader comes to Fuller Seminary to study. As we continue to do research in this area, more insights will come. Two things stand out about this initial survey. First, there is an overwhelming abundance of word gifts in the leader's that we have surveyed thus far. *We can clearly see that every leader that we have studied thus far has at least one word gift.* Secondly, there seems to almost be a total lack of love gifts and power gifts. Now this may reflect the seminary's theological orientation and the contextual factors of western culture more than anything else. Or it may say something about leadership styles, roles or personality types. It is too early to say.

We thought that we would offer a slightly different perspective by giving you the research data from another brief survey. Recently, we taught a class on leadership development at a Pentecostal Bible college in the midwest. In the course, each student was required to identify and display their giftedness set. There were 30 students in the course. All but about 5-6 were pastors of Pentecostal churches. Here are the statistics on this group of leaders:

Percentage of leaders reporting this gift	Gift
80% (24 of 30)	exhortation
76% (23 of 30)	teaching
56% (17 of 30)	pastoring
36% (11 of 30)	faith
30% (10 of 30)	governments, word of knowledge
23% (7 of 30)	word of wisdom
20% (6 of 30)	apostleship, prophecy, evangelism
13% (4 of 30)	discernings of spirits
10% (3 of 30)	ruling
6% (2 of 30)	tongues, interpretation of tongues, giving, helps
3% (1 of 30)	mercy, healing

When you compare this group with the students at Fuller, it is amazing to see the similarities. Again, the word gifts are dominant, especially exhortation, although there are a few power gifts and love gifts that appear on the list.

The major finding thus far is that all of the leaders that we have studied thus far have at least one dominant word gift in their giftedness set.

Implication/Questions

1.   If we could do a survey of our leadership, like the above two surveys, what would the listing and per centages of gifts look like?
2.   Exhortation is one of the more dominant gifts among leaders. How do we identify such gifted people in our situation? What structures promote the use of the exhortation gift?

Observation 4. Word Gifts and the Bible—The Equipping Function

Remember, the word gifts have a primary function in the body of Christ

TO CLARIFY WHO GOD IS AND WHAT HE EXPECTS FROM US.

Because of the *fact that every leader we have studied so far has at least one word gift in their giftedness set,* we have looked at the word gifts and asked the question: how grounded in the Scriptures should a leader be if they operate in the word gifts? The answer to this question has strong implications for developmental thinking. It has repercussions for discipleship. It has repercussions for how we train others. It will affect gift projection, a tendency of all strong leaders.

We believe that there are various levels of word gifts in relationship to the importance of knowing the Bible. Every leader who operates in a word gift needs to be grounded in the Bible. It is our primary source and ultimate authority of revelation about who God is and what He expects. However, in our opinion, leaders operating in certain word gifts need to be grounded more thoroughly than other leaders operating in other word gifts. We have broken the word gifts up into three levels. Here is how we diagram this:

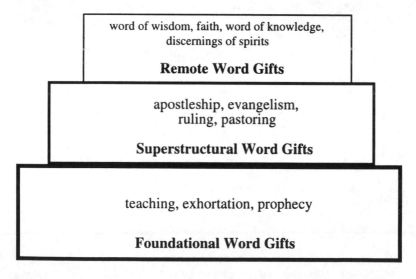

Foundational word gifts are said to be foundational because the major thrust of these gifts is the explanation of God and God's will. The operation of these gifts depend very much on one's knowledge of God's revelation of Himself and His ways in the Scriptures. Leaders with foundational word gifts must continually be deepening themselves in their knowledge of God by studying and understanding the written word of God. It must be their primary source for the operation of their gifts. They must have detailed disciplines for the study of the word of God on a regular and on-going basis. Foundational gifted people have a tendency to project their detailed disciplines on others; it seems so natural to them and they have profited and grown so much by doing them. But they should recognize these projection tendencies. They should see that rather than have all the other word gifted (and even non-word gifted) people emulating their programs they should see their place in the body and provide the rest with their gains and the fruit of their labor.

Superstructural word gifts are said to be superstructural because their major function is not the clarification of God's word but using God's word to accomplish other major tasks in the body of Christ. These leaders need to know the written word of God well enough to know that what they are building or accomplishing in ministry is firmly founded on the principles and revelation of God's word. For leaders with these gifts, carrying out the tasks related to their gifts is the focus rather than amassing an understanding of God's written word. These types of leaders need to rely on foundational word gifted leaders to provide correction, principles, values and guidance based on their more in-depth study of the word.

Remote word gifts are said to be remote because in the operation of these gifts the primary dependency is on the Holy Spirit and not an accumulated body of knowledge. This does not mean that these gifts should be inconsistent with the written word but the focus is on the immediate ministry situation. These gifts deliver a situational word from God in a specific ministry situation. Dependence on knowing the written word of God is secondary. Leaders operating with remote word gifts need to know the written word of God at a level so that the Bible operates as a tether or a yardstick for their situational words. God speaking to a situation through a leader would not contradict His written word or principles based on the written word of God.

Implications/Questions

1. Not all leaders need to be grounded in the word at the same level. There should be levels of depth of teaching and equipping in the word in a given situation.
2. Nor do all followers, non word gifted types, need the same level of teaching.
3. In terms of Bible study disciplines and goals, the various groupings of leaders will need different approaches and goals. Foundational will need the most exhaustive disciplines and approaches. Superstructural the next most and remote the least.
4. Almost all leaders are multi-gifted and will sometimes overlap among these three categories. The higher category should dominate their equipping philosophy.
5. All leaders are word gifted and need the equipping that can only come from the word.
6. Recognition of levels of word gifting will help ease the projection tendency of strong word gifted people.

Observation 5. Leadership Responsibility to the Body

Leaders have a responsibility to the followers that they are influencing on several different levels as it relates to giftedness.

- leaders are responsible to correct problems that come from wrong teaching or abuses in practice in the area of spiritual gifts. This requires a thorough knowledge and understanding of giftedness issues.

- leaders are responsible for the selection and training of emerging leaders. The recognition of giftedness early in the development greatly enhances the development and training process. Developing emerging leaders with an understanding of their unique giftedness allows you to focus their learning and maximizes the training efforts.

- leaders are responsible to recognize gift vacuums in the body and influence followers to use their gifts to meet those missing needs. This assumes that the Holy Spirit wants to meet the needs in the group.

- leaders are responsible to demonstrate the process of maturing in the use of giftedness. God uses leaders as models to influence followers.

Implications/Questions

1. Does our leadership know enough about giftedness to say that we are grounded? Do we know enough so that we can identify the strengths and weaknesses of different positions on giftedness, the abuses of giftedness, and perspectives on balance?
2. If we can not answer question 1 firmly, what can we do about it? In other words, does our leadership have a thorough knowledge and understanding of giftedness issues?
3. Do we even know what leadership selection and training is all about? Is this a priority with our leadership? What can we do to become proactive in leadership selection and development?
4. Are there gift vacuums in our situation? If so, are they serious? What can we do about it? Can our leadership trust God to bring in the needed giftings?
5. Who in our leadership is a model of a leader who is deliberately developing in giftedness? What can we do to model development?

Observation 6. Leadership Selection and Development

We have previously identified a major leadership lesson.

**EFFECTIVE LEADERS RECOGNIZE LEADERSHIP
SELECTION AND DEVELOPMENT AS A PRIORITY FUNCTION.**

By **leadership selection** we mean the processes by which God shapes emerging leaders and moves them into leadership. We are suggesting that effective leaders are aware of these ideas and hence sense what God is doing with a young emerging leader. They then move with God in deliberately affirming and developing that leadership.

By **leadership development** we mean the combination of opportunities, experience and training that a young leader needs if they are to mature to the potential gifting uniquely destined for them by God. And effective leaders will recognize the uniqueness of the emerging leaders and suggest the appropriate opportunities, experience and training that fits their giftedness.

Because these effective leaders know the processes and ways that God works they can stimulate these younger leaders by mentoring, suggesting informal training, and even designing training for them. They will know what non-formal training is available and needed. They will know whether or not formal training is needed and if so, when. As you can see this kind of thinking assumes these effective leaders are conversant with informal, non-formal, and formal means of training. They can assess each of the types and even design training, it if needed, to meet their unique situation.

Lets connect this thinking on leadership selection and development to giftedness. We have also repeatedly referred to the fact that our studies of mid-career leaders shows that all have at least one word gift in their gift-mix. In fact, our studies have shown that symptoms of these word gifts arise early in the process of the emergence of these leaders. Let me give some of the principles that have emerged from our observations. These include principles involving early recognition of word gifted leaders, potential relationships between young leaders and older leaders,[3] as well as implications flowing from these.

Symptoms of Those Who Emerge as Word Gifted Leaders

1. **WORD SYMPTOM**
   An appetite to learn the Word of God (shown by a person's response to the minsitry of Bible teachers and self-initiated study projects) is a good indicator of an emerging leader.

2. **APPLICATION SYMPTOM**
   A person who readily applies Scripture to his or her life in response to word checks, obedience checks, and integrity checks[4] is likely to emerge as a leader.

3. **RIGHTEOUSNESS SYMPTOM**
   A hunger for righteousness, a desire for personal integrity, and good response to these frequent process items dealing with these issues are good indications of an emerging leader.

4. **SPECIFIC PRAYER SYMPTOM**
   A potential leader prays specific prayers for his or her ministry and sees specific answers to prayer in such a way as to increase faith and expand the kinds of specific requests.

5. **GUIDANCE SYMPTOM**
   A potential leader will learn personal guidance lessons that serve as springboards for later getting group guidance.

6. **SELF-STARTER SYMPTOM**
   Leadership emerges at lower levels in self-initiated projects, ministry tasks, and experiences with God.

---

[3] We have determined in the past several years how important mentoring is in the development of leaders. Mentoring is a relational process in which one person empowers another by transferring or implanting resources that brings growth. We have developed materials that aid leaders in establishing relationships that will empower. Nine types of mentor functions have been identified and discussed in detail so that leaders can begin to use this information in training. See Stanley and Clinton, **Connecting** and Clinton and Clinton, **The Mentor Handbook**.

[4] These are technical names arising in leadership emergence theory which describe processes whereby God tests and shapes sensitivity to the Word, inner character, and desire to obey. See **The Making of a Leader** and **Leadership Emergence Theory**, both by Dr. J. Robert Clinton.

Nine Implications from the Leadership Symptoms

1. Leaders need to be aware of indicators of those who have an appetite for the word (such as marked Bibles, ordering and using tapes, buying Bible study books, attendance at Bible studies, producing of written studies, taking of notes at services, etc.).

2. Leaders should make available Bible study materials and other resources, which can be used to build skills and good Bible study habits.

3. Leaders should personally challenge potential leaders and lend or otherwise provide Bible study materials and resources to them.

4. Leaders need to be good listeners and know followers well, if they are to find out how Scripture is being applied in the lives of potential leaders.

5. Leaders need to provide potential leaders with adequate opportunity to testify concerning God's work in integrity checks, word checks, and obedience checks, and other processing focused on righteous living.

6. Leaders need to model a prayer life that demonstrates specific prayer requests and answers.

7. Leaders need to specify how they get guidance for the groups they lead and to encourage emerging leaders to seek guidance in the same way for their initial ministries.

8. Leaders must raise awareness of needs, challenge potential leaders concerning those needs, and release those potential leaders to solve them.

9. Leaders need to be aware that those who often engage in self-initiated projects do so to correct the status quo and often do so in an abrasive way.

Principles Involving Relationships With Leaders

1. **LIKE-ATTRACTS-LIKE GIFT PRINCIPLE**
    Frequently a gifted potential leader is attracted to a like-gifted leader who mentors him or her toward developing gifts.

2. **MODELING ATTRACTION PRINCIPLE**
    Frequently a potential leader is attracted to a leader who uses modeling as a means of influence.

3. **EXPECTANCY PRINCIPLE**
    A potential leader responds to genuine expectancy challenges from an older leader whom he or she admires.

4. **DIVINE CONTACT PRINCIPLE**
    God often brings one or more significant persons, divine contacts, across the path of an emerging leader at very opportune moments to perform some necessary mentoring which spurs him or her to develop leadership capacity.

Nine Implications from the Relational Principles

1. Leaders should recognize that those emergent leaders with gifts like their own frequently will be drawn to them. Informally a leader should be testing close followers for similarities to his or her gift-mix.

2. Leaders should model their use of a gift with an explanation of early indicators of the gift and of how the gift can be developed.

3. Leaders who use modeling as an important means of influence are demonstrating spiritual authority, which is a main reason potential leaders are drawn to certain leaders.

4. Leaders who use modeling should recognize they can play a vital part in moving potential leaders along the spiritual authority development pattern.

5. Leaders should be familiar with the spiritual authority development pattern and be prepared to have stimulating exercise and tasks that move potential leaders along it.

6. Leaders need to assess potential emerging leaders accurately for giftedness (natural abilities, acquired skills, and spiritual gifts).

7. Leaders must challenge potential emerging leaders with appropriate challenges—too great can discourage them, too little will not stretch them.

8. Leaders should seek to cultivate an awareness of sense of destiny in emerging leaders.

9. Leaders must be aware that God will often use them as divine contacts in the lives of emerging leaders. Hence leaders need to be thoroughly aware of the divine contact process item and mentoring process item.

Awareness of these symptoms, principles, and implications can make you sensitive to those developing around you. A thorough knowledge of giftedness will allow you early on to go from symptoms to specific word gifts. And knowledge of training and development methods[5] will allow you to speed up the process of development in young leaders.

Observation 7. Discipling Along Gifted Lines

This is a warning. This observation is really talking about giftedness projection—a very specific instance of it. And it is a form of projection that has been programmed and spread. A careful study of discipleship programs with a view to analyzing what they teach and require shows a heavy emphasis on word gifted skills and disciplines. When non-word gifted people are thrown into those situations or heavily recruited to do them they usually struggle in them. Many will drop out. This causes tension both with those running the programs and those leaving. Those leaving frequently have guilt feelings about not completing the program. On the other hand, word gifted people usually respond to these training programs and are greatly helped by them. In light of this analysis, let me give three suggestions which recognize this projection.

Suggestion 1.   Carefully pre-select those being trained in discipleship programs and screen out the non-word gifted people.

---

[5] In chapter 10 we will talk about specific ways that leaders develop in general and for specific gifts.

Suggestion 2.   Design other discipleship programs which disciple along the giftedness lines of those being trained.

Suggestion 3.   All discipleship programs should recognize the interdependence of the body. Word-gifted people clarify and help people know and relate to God. Love-gifted people meet needs and enable others to use their giftedness. Power-gifted people bring the spontaneity of God's interventions into groups. Cross-discipling may have adverse effects.

Now I recognize that there are some common things that are good for all being trained. But present discipling programs for the most part will train word gifted people and will screen out non-word gifted people.

Implications/Questions

1.   Discipleship involves a person's being completely available to God to use. It involves a commitment that works out in a process.
2.   A love-gifted disciple will need attitudes, skills, exercises for training, and encouragement that differs significantly from a word gifted disciple.
3.   A power-gifted disciple will need attitudes, skills, exercises for training, and encouragement that differs significantly from a love-gifted disciple.
4.   How do we disciple? Which cluster do we concentrate on? Can we adapt our discipling to meet all kinds of gifted people?

Observation 8. Giftedness and the Major Leadership functions

In chapter 2 we introduced some basic leadership ideas. General leadership research has identified several high level generic leadership functions. We listed 3 of these in chapter 2. Glance again at them to refresh your memory.

description   *Leadership functions* describe general activities that leaders must do and/or be responsible for in their influence responsibilities with followers.

description   *Consideration functions*, (relational behaviors) are those things leaders do to provide an atmosphere congenial to accomplishment of work, affirmation of persons, and development of persons.

description   *Initiation of structure functions*, (task behaviors) are those things leaders do to focus on accomplishing the organization's mission such as clarifying goals, forming organizational units, and holding people accountable for achieving.

description   *Inspirational functions* are those leadership activities that leaders do to motivate people to work together and to accomplish the ends of the organization.

The questions we want to ask are,

1.   Are any of the leadership gifts more likely to result in effective performance of relationship behaviors?

2.   Are any of the leadership gifts more likely to result in more effective performance of effective task behaviors?

3.   Are any of the leadership gifts more likely to result in more effective performance of effective inspirational behaviors?

The following table gives our best estimates as to giftedness which more effectively relates to one or more of these high level leadership functions. I am going to go beyond just leadership gifts because other gifts also play a part in accomplishing these leadership functions. Remember too, that certain natural abilities and acquired skills will contribute as well to the accomplishment of these functions.

Function	Gifts That Apply
Relational Behaviors	Pastoring helps
Task Behaviors	Apostleship Prophecy Evangelism Gifts of Governments
Inspirational Behaviors	Apostleship Evangelism Prophecy Exhortation faith

Teaching, ruling and exhortation are swing gifts. They can work to support all three kinds of functions. Most leaders are multi-gifted so will accomplish some portions of one or more of the functions because of their gift-mix. The main thing to recognize is that all of the functions need to be happening and certain gifted people may be needed to make them happen.

Implications

1.   Which of the generic leadership functions are we weakest in carrying out?

2.   Can we assess our leadership in terms of these functions?

3.   Can we in fact begin to deliberately assign responsibility for these functions to gifted leadership that are most likely able to carry them out effectively.

SUMMARY

We recognize that our research is limited. We continue to do research looking for new insights concerning spiritual gifts and leadership. There are a number of key observations that have been made thus far in our research. We believe that there are gifts that have inherent leadership influence in them: apostleship, prophecy, evangelism, pastoring, and teaching. We see these as gifts rather than offices or positions in the church. We also recognize that there are gifts that act as supplementary gifts to these leadership gifts. Certain gifts are commonly given in connection to other gifts and operate together in a leader's gift-mix.

Preliminary research is beginning to show that certain gifts occur more frequently in a leader's gift-mix than others. For example, exhortation is the most common gift followed by teaching, pastoring, and faith. Further research needs to be done in this area to see if these initial finding will hold up. The major finding thus far is the fact that every leader has at least one word gift in their gift-mix.

The last important observation that God is going to hold leaders accountable for how they operate in their giftedness and how the group of followers that they are influencing develop and operate in theirs.

As a final closure to the chapter why don't you read through the eight observations given below in summary form.

Observation 1.   All the leadership gifts are needed over time in order to bring the body to maturity.

Observation 2.   All leaders have gift-mixes which should be known and used to good advantage. Certain patterns of gifts and supplemental gifts are likely.

Observation 3.   A survey of the leadership and indeed the whole body can be helpful. Certain gifts will more likely appear in a body. Exhortation will be a gift that many leaders will have. Certain gifts are more rare for leaders, for example, mercy.

Observation 4.   Different word gifted people will need different challenges to develop their giftedness depending upon whether they are fundamental, superstructural or remote word gifts.

Observation 5.   Leaders are responsible to the body for applying giftedness concepts to the body.

Observation 6.   Leaders should be involved in the selection and development of emerging leaders. Giftedness concepts can be a help both in recognizing symptoms and helping pinpoint developmental assignments.

Observation 7.   One form of gift projection that should be corrected is discipling everybody along word gifted lines.

Observation 8.   Apply giftedness ideas as you assess and carry out the major leadership functions.

Chapter 8:
Identifying Your Spiritual Gifts

Introduction

We have now covered the material on spiritual gifts and it is time for you to begin identifying your spiritual gift(s). There are a number of different means by which you can work at identifying your spiritual gifts. We will suggest several of them. By the end of this chapter, you should have tentatively identified your gift-mix.

A Word About Gift Tests

Probably the most common means of identifying your spiritual gift(s) is using some type of gifts test or inventory.[1] There are many different kinds of spiritual gifts tests available. These can be very helpful and you will find some tests are better than others. However, we want to give you several words of caution about gifts tests that we hope will give you some better understanding of how the tests work.

1. Tests are usually based on *experience in ministry.* If a person has no experience, they will usually not do well on gifts tests. There are a few tests which are based on symptoms rather than experience. These kinds of tests are better for those who have little or no ministry experience. We know of only one that does this and it is not available to the public.

2. *Ego strength* affects how a person answers the questions. Low ego people tend not to have any gifts. (Their response is, "I knew it, I don't have any gifts!) High ego people tend to have most of the gifts. (Their response is, "I knew it, I have lots of gifts!) Keep this in mind when taking the test and giving tests to a group. There is the potential that the low ego people could be hurt. And the high ego people tend to feel prideful.

3. Testing tends to give people an *inoculation effect..* Because most people usually do not follow up the testing with ministry experience to confirm and develop their gifts, the testing process is wasted. The people feel like they have tried the *gifts* thing and it didn't make any difference. Ministry structures which provide places for people to operate in their giftedness need to be available after testing. People should be incorporated into structures and activities that let them confirm, text, experience, and develop their gifts.

4. Tests are only as good as *the definitions of spiritual gifts* which they use. Often the definitions are weak and the tests are not very beneficial. Poor definitions even though nicely worded can lead to confusion. We have already spoken of certitude of definitions. But when it comes time to test, one has to write down firm definitions whether they are correct or not. And so a test gives the feeling that these definitions are right, proper, and the real thing. And this may not be so.

5. Most gifts tests are not very sophisticated. Usually they are not well designed. There will be a set number of questions supposedly on one gift. Then the same set number on another gift. One well known test has every tenth question dealing with a given gift. There are ten questions for each gift. Now on this test and on many tests equal weight is given to each question. When in fact, some

---

[1] It is not necessarily the best, however. The best is confirmation by others, the body, as you repeatedly use your spiritual gifts to serve the body. This confirmation comes from those who have experienced your service to the body. It comes from those who are the leaders, responsible for the maturing of that body. They see your service and its contribution. Affirmation from these needs no written testing to confirm.

questions are much more important indicators than others. That is, few tests give weighting to more important indicators of gifts. Further, there is overlap between gift symptoms. So that, a given question may give information on more than one gift. Tests should be graded in terms of weighted answers and in recognition that several gifts have overlapping symptoms with other gifts. I know of only one test which weights and recognizes overlapping symptoms. And it is not available for public use.

6.   In our culture, *tests tend to carry to much weight.* If some test is printed and published with graphs, a results table, we tend to view this test as very official and it must be right! We need to beware of this tendency to give the test more importance than it deserves. God is a little bigger than a score on some spiritual gifts test!

Having said this, spiritual gifts tests are important tools for identifying your spiritual gifts.

3 STEPS IN IDENTIFYING YOUR SPIRITUAL GIFTS

Table 1 contains the summary procedure for identifying gifts that we will use in this chapter. Glance through it in order to get an overview. Then proceed through the detailed steps.

TABLE 1. 3 STEPS FOR IDENTIFYING YOUR SPIRITUAL GIFTS		
Step	**Basic Idea**	**Result**
1	**Do Your Own Reflection First**	Self-initiated list of spiritual gifts
2	**Work through the Identification tools.**	Comparative List of Gifts from Tools. Some are self-reflections using these tools. Others are confirmations from others.
3	**Summarize Your Findings**	Tentative gift-mix formed from analysis of self-initiated list with comparative list from tools.

Lets get to the details.

STEP 1: DO YOUR OWN REFLECTION

Take the list of short definitions that are given at the end of chapter 6, pages 177-179. Read through each definition and be sure that you are familiar with each gift. Pay particular attention to the thrust of each gift as it is used in ministry. If you need more information about the gift, review the gift as it is defined and commented on in chapter 6.

After familiarizing yourself with the definition and central thrust of each gift, think about how you operate around other people in your church or a group of believers. In ministry situations, what kind of things do you naturally lean toward doing?

Take some time and reflect. Begin to jot down the gifts that you believe that you operate in. You may want to begin by eliminating the gifts that you definitely know that you don't operate in. Then look at the remaining gifts on your list and focus in on those. Try to come up with some kind of a list and preferable two or three gifts that are primary gifts.

A helpful part of any spiritual gift testing is doing what we call a *discrepancy test*. Begin by getting someone who knows you fairly well or someone who has a chance to observe you in various ministry settings. Get them to do the same reflection exercise about you that you just completed (without your help of course). See what kind of list they come up with. If you are a high ego person, they will probably not have a list as large as yours. If you are a low ego person, they may have a larger list than yours. Either way, it is helpful to get input from others who know you.

It is important to start with this step rather than moving directly to a gifts test. Use the list that you come up with and check it against the results of the various gifts tests that you take.

STEP 2: WORK THROUGH THREE TOOLS.

Tool #1: Inward Conviction Questionnaire

Description:	This is a subjective exercise listing a number of items that can give indications of gifting essentially based on how God has made you and His inner leading of you.

Tool #2: The Outside Confirmation Form

Description:	This simply lists the gifts and gives a condensed list of definitions. You get confirmation from those who see you serving others in the body.

Tool #3: The Experience Questionnaire

Description:	This lists a number of typical expressions seen in western church life that reflect each of the gifts. Simply because you do these things does not necessarily mean you have the gifts, but its a good start. The more you have of them the better the indicator, provided the more important ones are seen.

We will introduce you each of these tools. You can use all of them or just the ones that will help you the most. Each of the tools is printed separately for ease in photo copying and using with others.

TOOL #1: INWARD CONVICTION QUESTIONNAIRE

Introduction

The inward conviction questionnaire seeks to gather information which relates to five basic principles often seen in the way that God leads people to identify and exercise their gifts.

- God honors personal desires. He has made you a certain way. If you are sensitive to Him he will give you both the desires you have and their fulfillment.
- A restless growing conviction to be involved in something may indicate that God will release a gift needed for your involvement in it.
- A God-directed specific call to a particular ministry indicates that you will have one or more gifts needed in that ministry.
- A forced situation may demand a certain gift or gifts to meet the needs of the situation. These gifts may already be there (latent) and will surface with the need or they may come spontaneously in answer to seeking them from God.
- Especially where leadership gifts are concerned, gifted leaders attract people who are potentially like-gifted.

The following questions should be answered with these basic principles in mind. Perhaps God is speaking to you right now in terms of one or more of these principles.

Fill out as many of the questions below as you can (i.e. those which really apply to you). Then follow the directions given after the questionnaire for instruction on how to use this tool. Use your own paper.

1. If I could do anything in the world that I wanted to (secular or spiritual), I would like to:

_____

_____

_____

_____

(describe in your own words what you would really like to do. In order to give absolute freedom to answer this question assume that whatever it is, it is in the perfect will of God for you to do).

2. Regardless of whether it is true that you possess them, check at least three gifts below that you would *like to have* in order of preference (1,2,3):

___Teaching	___Word of Wisdom	___gifts of governments
___Exhortation	___Word of Knowledge	___giving
___Prophecy	___faith	___mercy
___Apostleship	___gifts of healings	___gifts of helps
___Pastor	___workings of power	
___Evangelism	___discernings of spirits	
___Ruling	___tongues	
	___interpretation of tongues	

TOOL #1: INWARD CONVICTION QUESTIONNAIRE CONTINUED

3.   If you could have your choice of doing anything you wanted using one or more of the gifts that you checked in question 2, what would you like to do? (Describe it in your own words a ministry or role or Christian situation that would allow you to use the gifts you checked.)

4.   In my past experience with God, I have made the following promises or intents (either publicly or privately).

Where or when   Essence of the promise or intent

a.

b.

c.

5. I have had a growing restless conviction from within that,

a.   I should get involved in _____ or

b.   There is a special need that which I could help meet. Describe it:

c.   To what gift would this conviction best relate?

d.   In what way?

6. I am certain that God has definitely called me to a specific ministry.

a.   How do you know you are certain about this call? Describe your call (when, where, or how or any circumstances relating to it).

b.   Describe the gift or gifts that you feel are needed for this ministry.

c.   Which of these do you feel your are best fitted for?

TOOL #1: INWARD CONVICTION QUESTIONNAIRE CONTINUED

7.   I am in a situation at present (local church or other ministry) in which a certain gift or gifts are really needed. The situation demands this.

   a.   Briefly describe the situation as you see it.

   b. Name the gifts needed and why they are needed.

   c.   Can you see the gift(s) arising in any who are presently related to the situation? If so, why?

   d.   Do you feel God could develop this gift in you?

   ___ yes ___ no ___ unlikely ___ not sure

   e.   Are you willing to be a person God could use for this needed gift?

   ___ yes, definitely so ___ yes, if none of the others can

   ___ would rather someone else have this gift

8.   Have you ever made (or even thought) the following statement (or equivalent statement) concerning the ministry of some Christian.

   a.   I wish I could be like (name someone): _____ Even if I haven't, there are one or more persons that I could make that statement about. _____ _____

   b.   If so, describe what about the Christian (or Christians) or his ministry that prompted or could prompt you to make a statement.

   c.   What ministry, strengths, or spiritual gift(s) were demonstrated by the Christian(s) referred to?

9.   Of the Christians I feel drawn to or respect for their contribution to God's work, the two I most respect have the following gift(s). Use the number 1 for one of the Christians and use the number 2 for the other. Fill in the numbers alongside any of the gifts that apply.

___Teaching	___Word of Wisdom	___gifts of governments
___Exhortation	___Word of Knowledge	___giving
___Prophecy	___faith	___mercy
___Apostleship	___gifts of healings	___gifts of helps
___Pastor	___workings of power	
___Evangelism	___discernings of spirits	
___Ruling	___tongues	
	___interpretation of tongues	

TOOL #1: INWARD CONVICTION QUESTIONNAIRE CONTINUED

10.   If I could be associated with a gifted Christian for special on-the-job training in terms of the gift that he/she uses,

    a.   I would choose,

        I. Name the Individual: _____

        II. Somebody having this type of ministry: _____

        III. _____ I don't know anyone or any ministry that fits me.

    b.   If you choose a particular person,

        I. Why would you choose that person?

        II. What particular strengths, abilities, or spiritual gifts does that person operate in?

How To Assess Your Findings From the Inward Conviction Questionnaire

Assuming that you have filled out all the answers you can on the questionnaire, you are now ready to draw some possible conclusions from you answers.

Step 1: Fill out the chart below by examining your answers. You will sometimes have to do some reflection to see the connection between some of your answers and a gift related to the answer.

Step 2: After filling in the entire chart, put any gifts which occurred two or more times on the chart beside the summary of findings line.

POSSIBLE GIFTS BASED ON INWARD CONVICTIONS

Principle	Your answers to...	List any gifts reflected in your answers
God honors personal desires.	Questions 1,2,3,4	
A restless growing conviction may indicate a gift.	Question 5	
A God-directed call to a specific task entails a gift(s) needed for it.	Question 6	
My situation demands a gift(s) in order for it to prosper as God wants it to.	Question 7	
Gifted leaders attract people who will later exercise the same gifts that they do.	Question 8,9,10	

Summary of findings:

_____

INSTRUCTIONS FOR USING TOOL #2: THE OUTSIDE CONFIRMATION FORM

Introduction   What do other Christians think your spiritual gift(s) are? The leaders and people who know you well and have observed you operating in ministry situations can really help you identify your spiritual gift(s). The key to using this tool is involvement in ministry situations. A *sit and soak* Sunday Christian will probably never know his/her spiritual gifts. If you have been involved in a church where there is freedom to exercise gifts (and it is encouraged), then others in the group that you are involved with can help you identify your gift(s).

Comments about using this tool

1.   If you have not had much church or ministry related experience, or no one really knows that much about you...don't give out this form. It won't really help you. We would encourage you to get involved in a ministry.

2.   If the group that you are a part of does not encourage the use of spiritual gifts or believe in them...don't give out the form. You might cause controversy or questions to be raised. Trust that God can give you some outside confirmation through some other means.

3.   We would encourage you to give the form to someone who knows you and is considered one of the leaders of the ministry. Then give out at least two other forms to friends that know you and have observed you in ministry situations.

4.   If it is possible, after the forms have been filled out, talk with those who filled them out and discuss their answers. Seek their advise about using your gifts and how you might go about developing them.

TOOL #2: THE OUTSIDE CONFIRMATION FORM

Outside Confirmation Form for: _____

Filled out by: _____   Circle one: leader in ministry

friend

other (explain)

The following list of spiritual gifts will be referred to in the questions below. Please see the definitions on the following pages for the sense in which these words are used.

___ prophecy	___ tongues	___ evangelism
___ teaching	___ interpretation of	___ miracles
___ knowledge	tongues	___ healing
___ pastoring	___ discernment	___ mercy
___ exhortation	___ faith	___ governments
___ giving	___ apostleship	___ helps
___ wisdom		

Use your background knowledge and experience with the person named above to answer the following. Use the back of the page for additional space.

1. Mark with a C any gift listed above which you are definitely <u>Certain</u> the person operates in.

2. Mark with a P any gift listed above which you think might be a <u>Potential</u> gift for that person.

3. Mark with an F any gift above which you have actually observed the person using <u>fruitfully</u>.

4. For each gift you marked with a C, tell why you feel it to be a gift.

5. For each gift you marked as P, tell why you feel it is a potential gift.

6. For each gift you marked F, illustrate what you meant.

7. Which gift that you have marked above do you feel should be the priority gift used by this person? Why?

8. Would you advise how this person could train or better us this gift in the ministry?

9. Would you mark with an O your own gifts?

SUMMARY LISTING OF GIFT DEFINITIONS

Instructions	Give out this form with your Outside Confirmation Form so that people will know what is meant by the list of gifts on the questionnaire.

Gift	Definition
teaching	A person who has the gift of teaching is one who has the ability to instruct, explain, or expose Biblical truth in such a way as to cause believers to understand the Biblical truth. CENTRAL THRUST - TO CLARIFY TRUTH
exhortation	The gift of exhortation is the capacity to urge people to action in terms of applying Biblical truths, or to encourage people generally with Biblical truths, or to comfort people through the application of Biblical truth to their needs. CENTRAL THRUST - TO APPLY BIBLICAL TRUTH
prophecy	A person operating with the gift of prophecy has the capacity to deliver truth (in a public way) either of a predictive nature or as a situational word from God in order to correct by exhorting, edifying or consoling believers and to convince non-believers of God's truth. CENTRAL THRUST - TO PROVIDE CORRECTION OR PERSPECTIVE ON A SITUATION
apostleship	The gift of apostleship refers to a special leadership capacity to move with authority from God to create new ministry structures (churches and para-church) to meet needs and to develop and appoint leadership in these structures. CENTRAL THRUST - CREATING NEW MINISTRY
pastor	The pastoral gift is the capacity to exercise concern and care for members of a group so as to encourage them in their growth in Christ which involves modeling maturity, protecting them from error and disseminating truth. CENTRAL THRUST - CARING FOR THE GROWTH OF FOLLOWERS.
evangelism	The gift of evangelism in general refers to the capacity to challenge people through various communicative methods (persuasion) to receive the Gospel of salvation in Christ so as to see them respond by taking initial steps in Christian discipleship. CENTRAL THRUST - INTRODUCING OTHERS TO THE GOSPEL.
ruling	A person operating with a ruling gift demonstrates the capacity to exercise influence over a group so as to lead it toward a goal or purpose with a particular emphasis on the capacity to make decisions and keep the group operating together. CENTRAL THRUST - INFLUENCING OTHERS TOWARD VISION.
word of wisdom	The word of wisdom gift refers to the capacity to know the mind of the Spirit in a given situation and to communicate clearly the situation, facts, truth or application of the facts and truth to meet the need of the situation. CENTRAL THRUST - APPLYING REVELATORY INFORMATION
word of knowledge	The word of knowledge gift refers to the capacity or sensitivity of a person to supernaturally perceive revealed knowledge from God which otherwise could not or would not be known and apply it to a situation. CENTRAL THRUST - GETTING REVELATORY INFORMATION
faith	The gift of faith refers to the unusual capacity of a person to recognize in a given situation that God intends to do something and to trust God for it until He brings it to pass. CENTRAL THRUST - A TRUSTING RESPONSE TO A CHALLENGE FROM GOD.
gifts of healings	The gifts of healings refers to the supernatural releasing of healing power for curing all types of illnesses. CENTRAL THRUST - RELEASING GOD'S POWER TO HEAL.
workings of powers	The workings of powers, gift of miracles, refers to the releasing of God's supernatural power so that the miraculous intervention of God is perceived and God receives recognition for the supernatural intervention. CENTRAL THRUST - THE RELEASING OF GOD'S POWER TO GIVE AUTHENTICITY.

SUMMARY LISTING OF GIFT DEFINITIONS CONTINUED

Gift	Definition

discernings of spirits
The discernings of spirits gift refers to the ability given by God to perceive issues in terms of spiritual truth and to know the fundamental source of the issues and to give judgment concerning those issues; this includes the recognition of the spiritual forces operating in the issue. CENTRAL THRUST - A SENSITIVITY TO TRUTH AND ITS SOURCE.

tongues
The gift of tongues refers to a spontaneous utterance of a word from God in unknown words (to the individual giving the word) to a group of people. CENTRAL THRUST - SPEAKING A MESSAGE IN AN UNKNOWN TONGUE.

interpretation of tongues
The gift of interpretation of tongues refers to the ability to spontaneously respond to a giving of an authoritative message in tongues by interpreting this word and clearly communicating the message given. CENTRAL THRUST - INTERPRETING A MESSAGE GIVEN IN TONGUES.

gifts of governments
The gifts of governments involves a capacity to manage details of service functions so as to support and free other leaders to prioritize their efforts. CENTRAL THRUST - SUPPORTIVE ORGANIZATIONAL ABILITIES.

giving
The gift of giving refers to the capacity to give liberally to meet the needs of others and yet to do so with a purity of motive which senses that the giving is a simple sharing of what God has given to you. CENTRAL THRUST - A SENSITIVITY TO GOD TO CHANNEL HIS RESOURCES TO OTHERS.

mercy
The gift of mercy refers to the capacity to both feel sympathy for those in need (especially the suffering) and to manifest this sympathy in some practical helpful way with a cheerful spirit so as to encourage and help those in need. CENTRAL THRUST - THE EMPATHETIC CARE FOR THOSE WHO ARE HURTING.

gifts of helps
The gifts of helps refers to the capacity to unselfishly meet the needs of others through very practical means. CENTRAL THRUST - THE ATTITUDE AND ABILITY TO AID OTHERS IN PRACTICAL WAYS.

Tool #3: The Experience Questionnaire

Introduction God has given us gifts so that we can serve the body of Christ and bring forth results that are pleasing to Him. It is primarily through the use of our gifts that there are results and recognition of those gifts. If you think that you have some gift, ministry experience and the results of that ministry will either confirm it or deny it. The experience questionnaire is designed to force you to think back over your Christian experience and activity to help you confirm the gifts that you have been operating in.

Instructions

Recognize that the statements which are given are not all the possible statements that could be given. Hopefully they are representative. Perhaps a statement as given does not exactly fit you but by changing it slightly it would be true for you. Feel free to credit yourself with a modified statement or even a substitute statement which implies the same kind of outward expression of the gift.

The questions are grouped according to the gift. Go through each section for each gift and check off any statement that is true for you. At the end of the test, tally up the statements for each gift and record it in this chart.

Questions	Gifts	Results
1-14	teaching	___ of 15
15-27	exhortation	___ of 13
28-41	prophecy	___ of 14
42-55	apostleship	___ of 14
56-69	pastoring	___ of 14
70-95	evangelism	___ of 26
96-105	ruling	___ of 10
106-118	word of wisdom	___ of 13
119-128	word of knowledge	___ of 10
129-141	faith	___ of 13
142-155	gifts of healings	___ of 13
156-171	workings of powers	___ of 14
172-186	discernings of spirits	___ of 14
187-198	tongues	___ of 12
199-203	interpretation of tongues	___ of 5
204-216	gifts of governments	___ of 13
217-225	giving	___ of 9
226-240	mercy	___ of 15
241-250	helps	___ of 10

Summary of Findings

List any gifts on which you checked 1/2 or more of the statements. If you didn't check at least 1/2 on any of the gifts, pick the 2 gifts with the highest percentage of true statements.

Gifts: 1. _____ 2. _____ 3. _____

    4. _____ 5. _____ 6. _____

The Experience Questionnaire

Place a check mark beside each statement which is true for you.

_____ 1. I have taught regularly in a Sunday School class and know my teaching has helped clarify the thinking of those I taught.

_____ 2. I have taught regularly in a small group situation and can definitely point out several people who have mentioned they saw truth clarified for them.

_____ 3. I have read the Bible through a number of times.

_____ 4. I have made a special study of Jesus' parables to gain principles to use when I taught.

_____ 5. I have used the lecture method with such success that I can maintain attention spans of groups for 50 or more minutes.

_____ 6. I have led discussion groups so that people discover truth for themselves and apply it to their lives.

_____ 7. I have studied a number of books of the Bible on my own.

_____ 8. I have planned my teaching period to accomplish measured objectives and have evaluated these periods for effectiveness.

_____ 9. It has been my experience that I can usually hear a question, interpret it correctly, and give an answer which gives information which explains the point of the question.

_____ 10. I have been called upon by various groups outside my own church to teach various subjects to them.

_____ 11. I have repeatedly received comments after some class in which I participated to the effect that my contribution sure helped clarify and explain points in the discussion.

_____ 12. I have made it a point to study educational books or magazines and communication books or magazines in order to sharpen my own skills in communication.

_____ 13. I have tried some unusual things or methods in order to communicate effectively. Some have really failed while others have really succeeded.

_____ 14. It has become habitual for me to seek feedback whenever I am communicating to a group in order to know what has been learned and what I must do to correct my communication in the future.

_____ 15. I have often corrected another believer by showing him his error and giving him a Scriptural principle to help him with the result that the correction was applied to life.

_____ 16. I have written letters from time-to-time to friends in which there were comments which proved to be very encouraging to these friends.

_____ 17. I have found it my experience that I am easy to talk to and often have people share with me heart-to-heart talk.

_____ 18. Sometimes in waiting rooms (like waiting for dentist or doctor) a stranger will talk with me and soon even share some deep things being faced.

_____ 19. In small groups with which I have been associated it is not uncommon for someone to tell me that something I said has been a real comfort to them.

_____ 20. I often am the one to urge the group to action especially when they are bogged down and indecisive on some issue.

_____ 21. People often look to me to console someone who is facing a hard time.

_____ 22. I find it my experience that I am very sensitive to people and can recognize that they are hurting though others in contact with these people never know they are hurting.

_____ 23. I try to go out of my way to give a cheerful word to people around me and find that I usually encourage people in a general way.

_____ 24. Many times things I say, whether to groups or individuals, cause people to become convicted.

_____ 25. I know for certain that a number of things have happened in individuals' lives and in my church situation in general because I have given a Scriptural admonition which was heeded.

_____ 26. I often counsel with people.

_____ 27. I have read a number of books dealing with psychology on a popular level in order that I might better understand people and be able to talk with them in a way to help them.

_____ 28. I have been asked by my church to speak publicly to the church on a given issue of importance to the church.

_____ 29. I have shared my testimony before a large church or other group and know that God used it to move people.

_____ 30. I have spoken before groups containing believers and unbelievers and have given messages (not evangelistically oriented) which have caused unbelievers to assert the truth of what I said and to recognize God for who He is.

_____ 31. I have more than once become convinced that God was giving me a message to meet a given situation and I have given that message authoritatively to the group concerned with the result that they were moved by God.

_____ 32. I have experienced that when I speak most people listen and there is a definite dichotomy of response: some definitely for and some definitely against what I have said.

_____ 33. I have been compelled when in a group in which discussion was taking place to interrupt and give an impassioned speech taking a definite stand on some issue. Often I have felt that God pressed me to speak.

_____ 34. I find that when speaking publicly I often speak with deep emotional tones which God uses to break hearts so that there is a hearing to my message.

_____ 35. I have felt that God has given me a word concerning some future event or some word telling my church or group what to do in the future.

_____ 36. It has happened several times to me that when I spoke to a group (even though I didn't know their needs) that many have commented to me afterwards that what I said must have been from God because it dealt perfectly with a situation in the group.

_____ 37. It has been my repeated experience to admonish a group when I know there is something wrong because I want to face the situation rather than let it ride.

_____ 38. I have received what I felt was a vision from God, which was an analogy of something that was to happen in my church situation. I knew I should share it with my group.

_____ 39. I have from time-to-time had dreams which were vivid and deeply impressed upon my mind—so much that I knew them clearly when I awoke and knew they had significance for others—about things that were to happen.

_____ 40. I have from time-to-time intuitive-like impressions of something that is about to happen (like a certain person coming to see me or the like).

_____ 41. Upon occasion my impressions are such that they become deep seated convictions which I feel I must share.

____ 42. I instigated the movement to begin a new church.

____ 43. I started a new church which exists today.

____ 44. I am a charter member of a church.

____ 45. I am certain that God has called me to do church planting.

____ 46. I have been involved in selecting leaders for church work.

____ 47. I have been commissioned or ordained or licensed or have otherwise been authoritatively recognized for a full-time gospel ministry.

____ 48. In church situations I am looked upon to give an authoritative word which will clarify a problematic situation.

____ 49. I have selected and appointed leaders to ministry.

____ 50. I have seen the need for a new ministry and found a way to bring it into existence.

____ 51. I am challenged by the unreached, the yet undone, the needs around me and I have enough self-initiative to do something about it.

____ 52. I have had God confirm what I said or did with a demonstration of His power.

____ 53. I have brought discipline to a church situation which needed an authoritative resolution if it was to survive.

____ 54. When I speak to a Christian or a group of Christians I receive their respect and am treated as an authoritative Christian.

____ 55. My ministry takes me broader than just a local church; I frequently have ministry to leaders of groups and different churches.

____ 56. I am presently serving as a pastor of a church..

____ 57. I am presently serving as a member of the leadership group of my church.

____ 58. I am presently responsible for the spiritual welfare of a group of people.

____ 59. In my past experience in the controlling group of our church I have been able to avert crises situations because I thought through possible consequences of decisions and was able to choose the best decision.

____ 60. My example in Christian living has had a decided impact on the group for whom I feel spiritually responsible.

____ 61. In my church group I am often called upon to listen to people's problems because my counsel is generally well-balanced and good for the group as a whole.

____ 62. I have personally discipled several people of the group I am responsible for so that their progress toward maturity is evident.

____ 63. I am considered by a number of people in my church as a spiritual leader.

____ 64. I have repeatedly motivated groups of people toward goals or to carry out plans which I originated.

____ 65. I am one of the people most concerned with the spiritual progress of my church and by virtue of my influence will be able to do something about it.

____ 66. I am concerned when people in my church are being led astray by teaching I don't think is truth.

____ 67. I am concerned that my ministry helps people grow.

____ 68. I feel the responsibility for groups of people; though I have no official position I have a deep concern and care for people in groups of which I am a part.

____ 69. I am in the process of recognition by a denomination for leadership.

_____ 70. I have been influential in a number of people becoming Christians and later church members.

_____ 71. I get excited at the thought of someone hearing about the Gospel.

_____ 72. I have done door-to-door *cold-turkey* witnessing and have seen some make decisions.

_____ 73. I have witnessed on my job with the result that several people are now Christians who would not be so if I hadn't helped them along.

_____ 74. I have helped set up an evangelistic thrust requiring serious planning.

_____ 75. I have gone through an evangelism training program and loved it.

_____ 76. I have taken part in an evangelistic thrust in which I individually challenged people with the salvation message and saw positive results.

_____ 77. I have had freedom to turn natural conversations with individuals into witnessing situations and have seen individuals come to Christ.

_____ 78. I am in contact with numerous non-believers.

_____ 79. I have invited people to various evangelistic activities several times and have seen several come to Christ.

_____ 80. I have shared my testimony at a public evangelistic thrust with the result that my participation helped bring about positive results.

_____ 81. I have prayed specifically for several lost people by name and have seen them come to Christ.

_____ 82. I have been the main speaker at public evangelistic meetings and have seen people come to Christ.

_____ 83. I have participated in a small group which met regularly and was used by God to influence many to come to Christ.

_____ 84. I have used tracts or booklets with many people and have seen several come to Christ.

_____ 85. I frequently recognize that I have a deep burden for those who do not know God; I have even wept for them.

_____ 86. I have written letters to people in which I witnessed to them and have seen positive results through this letter writing.

_____ 87. I have used some plan for presenting Christ to individuals such as the Roman Road, the Bridge, the 4 Spiritual Laws or like technique and have seen a number of people make actual committals to discipleship.

_____ 88. I have shared my conversion testimony or other present testimony about God's working in my life with many individuals.

_____ 89. I can frequently sense when God has been previously working in a person's life and I make myself available to God to talk to that person.

_____ 90. I often carry tracts with me and hand them out when I have a good occasion.

_____ 91. One of the most exciting things for me is seeing someone make a decision for Christ. That brings joy.

_____ 92. I love to watch television evangelism specials like the Billy Graham crusade.

_____ 93. I have trained as a follow-up counselor and participated as such in a Billy Graham crusade.

_____ 94. I have been involved in telephone evangelism.

_____ 95. I have been involved in door-to-door surveys canvassing for opinions regarding Christianity.

___ 96. Though not a full time pastor I am part of the leadership group for my church.

___ 97. In a group situation I can see what ought to happen and am called upon to help clarify what we should do.

___ 98. I can motivate people to follow through on ideas that I introduce to the group.

___ 99. I often present things to the church as a whole though I am not a full time Christian worker.

___ 100. I choose to be in leadership positions in the church because I feel a call to do so and a sense of responsibility for people.

___ 101. When people in my group select someone in my group to head up some task force, committee, or problem solving group I am usually one of those selected.

___ 102. When I make decisions for a group I find myself thinking of the betterment of the group as a whole.

___ 103. Though I am often now called upon to fill leadership roles in the church I did not have leadership responsibilities as I grew up.

___ 104. I find that I have studied 1, 2 Timothy and Titus because I feel they help me understand more clearly what I can do in a church situation.

___ 105. Given a choice of leading or following I would rather lead.

___ 106. I have studied Job, Psalms, and Proverbs to the extent that it is almost second nature for me to transfer principles seen in them to life situations.

___ 107. It has often been my experience in group situations that I could clearly, though admittedly intuitively, see what must be done and was able to communicate this to the group by applying correct Scriptural principles to the situation.

___ 108. I have often had individuals ask me for my opinion concerning some situation they faced and amazing as it may seem some Scriptural phrase or passage or other "advice" came to mind which I was able to convey to them convincingly so that they saw it as a word from God for their problem.

___ 109. I have often been convinced in my own mind that the Holy Spirit has given me an answer and led me in my choice of words in order that what I said would be received well.

___ 110. People have often remarked to me that they have taken some comment that I made as a word from God to them concerning some issue or decision that they must make.

___ 111. Many times I have thought the following (or equivalent), "It is clear how God sees this thing; why don't these people see things God's way?"

___ 112. I have received deep satisfaction when people have applied my advice to their situations and later received clear confirmation that the advice was God-given.

___ 113. It is easy for me to match some current situation with a Biblical character or historical event in Bible times and draw out some application for the current situation.

___ 114. Sometimes in a one-on-one situation I get a clear impression of some answer that I feel should be given the person. I do so and get almost immediate feedback that the word I had was from the Lord for that person.

___ 115. Sometimes I will get an impression about some Scriptural passage. I will turn to it and read it and see that God has something in it for the group of which I am a part.

___ 116. In a committee when we are grappling for a solution to some complex situation, in a flash something will come to me and intuitively I sense it from God so I will share it with the group and have it accepted as the solution to the situation.

___ 117. James 3:17,18 have been a blessing to me and I have taken it as the standards for what I want my answers to situations to be like.

The Experience Questionnaire continued

___ 118. I am at home in the wisdom literature and know that my spending time in this portion of Scripture is partially the reason why I can give good advice.

___ 119. I have several times had strong impressions when in a group meeting of some idea that related to the group. The idea related to something that I would not have known had not God given it to me.

___ 120. Sometimes I see pictures in my mind of something that I feel God wants me to communicate to a group.

___ 121. In healing situations I often seem to know, spontaneously, that someone has a certain kind of health problem that God wants to heal.

___ 122. I have suddenly known things that are needed by the group—though I didn't know how I came to know them.

___ 123. In talking with a person in a Christian setting I have sensed information about the person's personal life regarding problems or a sinful condition or the like.

___ 124. I have been used by God to affirm someone by revealing something from their past known only to them and giving a message from God that He knew of that and would give victory in spite of it.

___ 125. I resonate with the passage about woman at the well. When Jesus told her, "You have well spoken. For you have had five husbans; and the one you are now living with is not your husband," the woman immediately recognized Jesus as one getting revelation from God. This has happened to me on a number of occasions—I suddenly have information about a person that gives me a hearing.

___ 126. Paul's knowledge of the Philippian jailer's suicidal intent has always struck a chord with me. He knew, even without lights or anything of what was going on. I know this kind of thing has happened to me too.

___ 127. Though it has happened very rarely, it has happened that I stood and spoke in a group setting and I didn't know what I would say as I stood. I just knew I was to stand and speak. It just came out. And it was received as from God.

___ 128. I have a close inner relationship with God and am sensitive to His inner voice prompting me.

___ 129. I have often prayed the *prayer of faith*. God has answered many of these prayers. He will answer the rest.

___ 130. A number of times in my personal Bible reading times I have been convinced that God would have me claim certain promises for certain given situations. I have done this and have seen many of these promises fulfilled.

___ 131. Most of my prayers are specific because I want to know when the answer comes.

___ 132. People often come to me and ask me to pray for some situation because they feel my prayers get answered.

___ 133. I have read many times the Old Testament accounts which picture God doing miraculous things for his people. These passages have encouraged me to trust God in tough situations that my church has faced. God did it for them and He can meet us too.

THE EXPERIENCE QUESTIONNAIRE CONTINUED

___ 134. When problems arise my natural inclination is to trust God to somehow meet it while most in my church first try to analyze the problem or seek some way to solve it.

___ 135. There have been times when I have a conviction that I am sure is from God. I recognized that what God wanted done would require a *risk* in faith. In those times I learned to trust God to do those things. Our whole group has been encouraged to trust God more because of my example of stepping out in faith.

___ 136. It is not my nature to brag about my various exercises of faith and many of them are unknown to people, but even so, I am certain that God has used some of my experiences of trusting in unusual ways to encourage others to believe and pray with expectancy.

___ 137. The reason I feel I pray so effectively is that I first seek what God has to say about the situation or what He wants to do. Then I pray along those lines and believe it will happen.

___ 138. I resonate with that great faith-act by Joseph in Genesis 50. I find it exciting to think that my trusting God for something can have a motivational impact on others.

___ 139. 1 John 5:14,15 are favorites with me and give the reason for my confidence in praying.

___ 140. I have been involved in projects for raising a large amount of finances for a Christian cause that I felt God was backing.

___ 141. The angel's word to Mary, Luke 1:37, is one of my mainstays: For no word from God is void of His power.

___ 142. I am frequently asked along with other leaders in the church to lay hands on someone and pray for them to be healed.

___ 143. I have known God's power as I prayed for someone and saw the person healed of a physical ailment.

___ 144. I have sensed the power of God present for healing in a service and as a result have felt an increased faith within to believe God for healing.

___ 145. I have felt a tingling in my hands, or have felt a strange warming flowing through my hands when I am praying for someone.

___ 146. I have been part of a prayer team trained to help in ministry time in a large church service where healing is expected to happen.

___ 147. I have observed many healings such as inner organs being made healthy, backs straightened, or soreness in muscles taken away.

___ 148. I have commanded a word of healing to a person and seen that person healed.

___ 149. I frequently pray for inner healing—that is, dealing with persons who have dysfunctional backgrounds or history's of problems.

___ 150. For me to see someone receive healing and to know it was God's power is to bring tremendous joy.

___ 151. When a television healer prays for people I often enter in and pray for them too.

___ 152. I believe that God can heal through supernatural means as well as through medical means, but my first inclination when someone says I'm sick is to ask, "Has someone prayed for you?"

___ 153. I resonate with passages like Acts 27:8,9 where Paul healed people on Melita. I think, that's wonderful. And God is still doing that today, and I'm part of it.

___ 154. I have prayed for people who were not healed as well as many who were and yet I still believe God heals and that I should seek His healing power in situations.

___ 155. Often when I see the sick or hurting, a feeling of compassion wells up within me and I want to do something to help them.

____ 156. I resonate with a passage like Acts 13:9-12 Paul's encounter with Elymas the sorcerer, or Elijah's confrontation on Mount Carmel. For these power encounters allow God to be shown for who He is.

____ 157. I believe God uses signs and wonders today to display His power and reality and I have faith to believe He uses me in this way.

____ 158. God has used me to bring power to bear in an unusual way. This gave me great joy that the living God would use me in this way.

____ 159. God has used me to answer a prayer like Samuel's prayer for rain in the dry season. I saw God answer and He was vindicated.

____ 160. I have been involved in a power encounter with the demonic world and saw God bring power to bear to deliver someone from demonic control.

____ 161. I have been used to pray about and believe God for various weather conditions (clearing of fog, abating of rain, rain in a time of drought, etc.).

____ 162. I have been used in church planting situations to pray to break the spiritual control in the region, with the result that there was a breakthrough and the church was planted.

____ 163. I have seen God work in a primitive missionary situation with the result that animistic peoples were willing to burn their spirit world phenomena.

____ 164. I have spoken a word of discipline to a person, who was absent, and saw God bind that person and clear up a situation and see the person come back to God.

____ 165. I have seen drug addicts delivered instantly in my ministry.

____ 166. I have seen God miraculously protect in an inner-city situation where His character and power were on the line.

____ 167. I have believed God to over ride a government decision and seen it happen in such a way as to promote His work.

____ 168. I have seen God miraculously reveal a word of judgment in a physical way (similar to the situation in Daniel with Belshazzar).

____ 169. I have been involved in a supernatural phenomena where God protected via angelic beings— similar to Elisha's situation in 2 Kings 6:16ff.

____ 170. I have seen God provide food miraculously in a needy situation.

____ 171. I have seen God bring back to life a person who was dead or dying or was thought to be dead as a result of an outpouring of God's power.

____ 172. I have often been able to recall many passages throughout the Bible which in some way relate to some given topic.

____ 173. It is almost second nature for me to analyze what a person says to see if it matches what I think Scripture teaches.

____ 174. People have often remarked to me that I have a way of cutting through all the cobwebs and getting to the real issue.

____ 175. I have a number of times corrected comments where they disagree with the tenor of Scripture with the result that the modified truth was accepted by all.

____ 176. It has been my repeated experience for people to ask me a question similar to the following, "Is it really true what he said?"

___ 177. Though I don't always comment on it, I am bothered by much public ministry because I notice very quickly when preachers or teachers misinterpret or misapply Scriptural truth. It doesn't seem to bother others.

___ 178. I often catch myself not paying attention to some conversation because I have become interested in analyzing in detail something spoken in the conversation.

___ 179. I am often the one who has to bring it to the attention of others that a particular practice is inconsistent with some Scriptural imperative.

___ 180. I often catch subtle errors in religious books which if not caught could cause real trouble with believers.

___ 181. Upon occasion I recognize that in a situation I am being confronted by a spirit power and I am able to sense what kind of spirit is involved.

___ 182. Though I do seem to have a critical bent and am misunderstood by some people I know for certain that a number of issues on which I have given modified or different views have turned out to be correct and have helped our church avoid pitfalls.

___ 183. I have upon occasion entered a room and known immediately that there was an evil presence.

___ 184. I have been prompted from within that a certain person in a Christian gathering was false and could bring harm to the group—like a voice or strong impression telling me to watch out.

___ 185. Sometimes I see physical manifestations about people (like a gray aura, or green/black coloring on a face) that indicate to me something is not true or right about the person or that the person is empowered from the demonic world.

___ 186. People often come to me and share their dreams or visions or thoughts in prayer and want my assessment of it or interpretation of it.

___ 187. In a situation not influenced by anyone, God gave me tongues. I suddenly began to speak in syllables which I did not control or understand.

___ 188. When faced with a crisis or need for discernment I often pray immediately in tonuges as a first response. This usually brings a sense of calmness or focus after which God meets me in the situation.

___ 189. When I don't know how to pray for a situation I pray in the Spirit trusting that God is hearing and that the Spirit is leading in the intercession.

___ 190. In worship situations where it is appropriate I often sing in tongues and find that what I sing harmonizes with others to produce a worshipful experience and sound.

___ 191. When I am asked to pray for healing for someone when I lay hands on them I first begin, sometimes inwardly, to pray in tongues. I may later pray outwardly in words understood by all.

___ 192. I have upon occasion in a ministry time, stood and given a word in tongues. It was interpreted and was seen to be a prophetic word of encouragement about what God was going to do in the body.

___ 193. Rarely, for me, I have stood in a ministry time, and simply opened my mouth and out came a word. I didn't even know I was going to do it.

___ 194. I frequently use a prayer language, a special gift of tongues given to me, in my private prayer when no one is around. It is a special time of closeness with God.

___ 195. I have often wanted to give a word of tongues in a situation but the people in the group inhibited that possibility because of their convictions about such a gift.

The Experience Questionnaire continued

___ 196. I can speak in tongues whenever I want.

___ 197. I can not give a public word in tongues whenever I want. I always make myself available to do so. And I do from time to time give a word. My words have always been interpreted.

___ 198. A leader imparted the gift of tongues to me by the laying on of hands and special prayer for me.

___ 199. In a public meeting, during a ministry time, a person stood and gave about a 2-3 minute word of tongues. As they were giving it, I heard in my mind, like simultaneous translation what they were saying. I immediately stood and gave the interpretation.

___ 200. I have given interpretations of tongues in small groups repeatedly.

___ 201. I am sensitive to God's revelatory voice and often hear God speaking so that I have no problem believing God can get our attention through a word of tongues.

___ 202. I enjoy giving authenticity to God's unusual messages given in tongues by giving the translation.

___ 203. When I give an interpretation it is not like I am receiving a simultaneous translation. I simply get the whole thing and once and give it.

___ 204. I presently serve as a deacon(ess) of my church.

___ 205. I have served as a church clerk or treasurer or other such position.

___ 206. I have served as a Sunday School superintendent or other such position requiring my organizational ability.

___ 207. I have overseen the church property in some supervisory responsibility.

___ 208. I have been in charge of distributing benevolence funds in several church projects to needy people.

___ 209. I have been chosen on several committees which were formed to solve some administrative problems in conjunction with our church programs.

___ 210. I often am asked to arrange for the details of meetings, making sure everything is ready.

___ 211. I have been placed in charge of several programs (like Vacation Bible School, Awana or other youth ministries, etc.) which require organizational ability.

___ 212. I like to see things done orderly and want to pitch in to make it go well.

___ 213. I easily see where there are missing pieces in a plan to do something. I can suggest what ought to be done.

___ 214. I have successfully organized a number of different ministries.

___ 215. I have stepped in when something was failing due to lack of follow through and turned it around.

___ 216. I love innovative people who come up with great ideas. For I find I can step in behind them and make it work. Many times they can not.

___ 217. I have at times given to help others with money that I needed. Some would probably think that foolish if they knew.

___ 218. I would have been able to do without things (for me they are luxuries anyway) that others consider necessary in order to give more to God's work.

___ 219. God somehow seems to bring to my attention financial needs of people in my church (many times unintentional ways). I have given to people like this. Few know about some of these gifts.

___ 220. I have consistently given more than 1/3 of my income to God's work.

___ 221. There have been times when I sensed some special financial need but did not have the finances to meet it. And then money came in some non-normal way. I knew that God wanted me to meet the need. So I gave.

___ 222. I have an inward joy in giving to meet a need. And it doesn't make any difference to me whether anyone ever knows about it or not.

___ 223. I am certain that God has given me special abilities to make money. I know that this is because he expects to use me as a channel to give large amounts to his cause.

___ 224. I find that I have a liberal spirit not only with money but with time or any of my possessions or resources. I love to help others out.

___ 225. When I see people in need, I want to find a way to give them help.

___ 226. I have been involved in a social outreach program in a large city which sought to help needy people.

___ 227. I have helped down-and-outers through some church related program.

___ 228. I have helped physically handicapped people; I cheer them up.

___ 229. I have been involved in a literacy program or other educational program to help underprivileged children or adults.

___ 230. I have taken food baskets to poor people.

___ 231. I have helped distribute clothing to needy people.

___ 232. I have ministered to people through some medical activity and know that my ministry done cheerfully has helped others.

___ 233. I have contributed financially to programs helping orphans or other underprivileged.

___ 234. I have served as a house parent (or other equivalent worker) in some orphanage program.

___ 235. I have worked on a regular basis with alcoholics and become empathetically involved with them, and helped several to recover.

___ 236. I have been involved in a prison rehabilitation program and know my cheerful influence has helped some.

___ 237. I have been involved so as to practically help drug addicts.

___ 238. I have helped unwed mothers face their problems and seen some of them straighten up their lives as a result of my help

___ 239. I resonate with Jesus' feelings in the passage, Matthew 9:36-38, when he looked on the multitudes and saw their needs and had compassion (was filled with tenderness for them) on them. I want to be one of those He sends out to meet their needs.

___ 240. I know that I am a sensitive person and feel peoples needs, more than most others.

The Experience Questionnaire continued

___ 241. I am very skillful with my hands and enjoy doing maintenance jobs on church property.

___ 242. I can fix almost anything and have gladly used my skill to help church members who needed my help.

___ 243. I have helped a number of people in my church with practical things even though it meant I put off something I needed to do for myself.

___ 244. I don't mind doing some task, menial or not, if I know it will free some other church member to exercise his gift.

___ 245. I have often been one of the first to volunteer for something the pastor felt was needed concerning the church.

___ 246. I don't mind unexpected guests in the home if I know we are helping them.

___ 247. Several times the pastor or someone else in the church has asked me to help accommodate guests. I gladly accepted the call.

___ 248. I find real satisfaction in doing practical things that will help others and try to seek opportunities to do so joyfully.

___ 249. Often people remark to me what a helpful spirit I have; I do love to help others.

___ 250. I frequently see things that need to be done; I find ways to help get them done.

STEP #3: FINALIZE YOUR FINDINGS

Based on your own reflections and any tools that you might have used, list your 3 top spiritual gifts.

Spiritual gifts: 1. _____

                     2. _____

                     3. _____

Others:

At this point you have assessed your entire giftedness set including, natural abilities, acquired skills, and spiritual gifts. You are ready to consolidate your findings and display them. The next chapter will introduce you to the process of displaying your giftedness set with a Venn diagram.

CHAPTER 9:
DISPLAYING YOUR GIFTEDNESS SET

INTRODUCTION

By now you should have identified the basic elements of your giftedness set. You should have the two or three top natural abilities, acquired skills, and spiritual gifts. In this short chapter, we are going to teach you to display your giftedness set using a Venn diagram. A Venn diagram is a pictorial diagram which uses symbols, spacing and sizes to communicate information. By the end of this chapter, you should be able to draw your Venn diagram and display your giftedness set.

Explaining the Venn Diagram

This diagram uses three elements to communicate information.

Symbols: We use three different symbols to display giftedness.

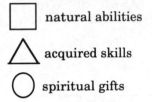

Size: The size of the symbols is important. Bigger size denotes more importance. Smaller size denotes lesser importance. For example:

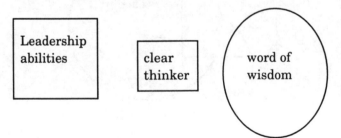

In this example, there are two natural abilities listed and one spiritual gift. The leadership abilities are being displayed as more important than the natural ability of clear thinking. The word of wisdom gift is larger than the leadership abilities and the clear thinking natural ability. It is the most important. The natural abilities next most important.

Spacing: Spacing is the most complex feature of a Venn diagram. When you space the symbols on the diagram you are showing the relationship between the symbols. If two elements of the giftedness set are seen as working together, they would be placed in such a way as to demonstrate the relationship. Overlap means that some of both occur simultaneously. Where there is no overlap it means that the item also occurs alone. The most important elements are the largest ones and are placed in the center of the diagram. For example:

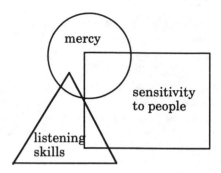

In this example, this person is demonstrating a relationship between three different elements of the giftedness set. The dominant feature is the natural ability called, sensitivity to people. It is placed in the center of the diagram and is the largest symbol. The spiritual gift of mercy enhances the operation of this natural ability in ministry situations. God takes the person's natural sensitivity and empowers this with His Holy Spirit and releases the love of God in the situation. This person has acquired some skills in the area of listening. One would summarize this diagram by saying that this person uses his/her natural ability to release a spiritual gift usually through listening to others.

Here's another example:

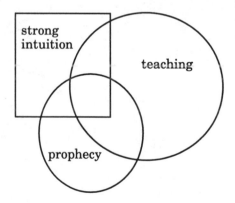

In this example the person is demonstrating that there are three elements that relate closely. The spiritual gifts work hand in hand together. There is a large amount of teaching that is not prophetical. But there is a strong overlap between teaching and prophecy meaning the teaching has strong admonition or correction and/or could be actual teaching on prophecy. The teaching gift is dominant but has a prophetic touch to it. The natural ability of intuition influences both the teaching and the prophetic gifts. But there is a large part of intuition which takes place out of the teaching and prophetic context.

DRAWING YOUR VENN DIAGRAM

STEP 1: GATHERING YOUR DATA

At this point you should have identified the most important elements of your giftedness set. List them here. See page 88 for your summary of natural abilities and acquired skills. See page 227 for your summary of spiritual gifts.

Your Natural Abilities:

Your Acquired Skills:

Your Spiritual Gifts:
(List only your primary gifts)

STEP 2: THE FOCAL ELEMENT

Before you can actually start drawing your giftedness diagram, you need to decide which element is the focal element or the element that dominates your giftedness. Whichever element it is, you will make it the biggest. Occasionally there will be two elements which are equally important but this is not common.

STEP 3: DETERMINING THE RELATIONSHIPS AND IMPORTANCE OF EACH PART.

Begin with the focal element. Determine how dominant each component is. For example, if spiritual gifts are the focal element, then look at your list of gifts and determine which one of those is dominant and make it the biggest. Then decide how the other gifts relate to that gift. When you overlap symbols the overlap area indicates that all the items that are overlapping operate together. Then move to the other two elements of the giftedness set and repeat the process.

STEP 4: BEGIN DRAWING YOUR DIAGRAM

By now you should have assigned some degrees of importance and some degree of relationship between the various components of your giftedness set. Begin drawing and start with your focal element. Make the dominant component the largest and place it in the center. Then begin to add the other components according to the importance and relationships as you see them. It will probably take you two or three tries so do the first few in pencil.

STEP 5: GET FEEDBACK

Once you have drawn a rough draft. Contact some people who know you and have observed you in ministry. Share your diagram with them. Talk through the relationships of the various components and describe how you see the importance of each component. Get feedback. As you share the diagram and talk about it, you will see more or learn more. You may want to modify your diagram based on what you have learned.

STEP 6: PREPARE YOUR FINAL DRAFT

Once you have gotten some feedback, you can draw your final draft. Recognize that giftedness development is not static. Your giftedness set will change over the years as you grow and mature. From time to time, review your giftedness set and modify it as you see fit.

EXAMPLE 1 OF GIFTEDNESS DIAGRAM--LEADER A

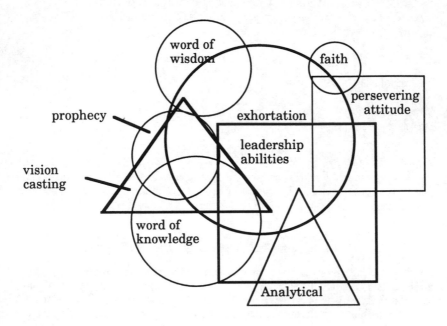

Natural Abilities: leadership abilities, persevering attitude

Acquired skills: Analytical thinking, vision casting

Spiritual Gifts: Exhortation, Word of Knowledge, Word of Wisdom, Prophecy, Faith

Focal Element: Spiritual Gifts
Dominant gift: Exhortation

COMMENTARY ON EXAMPLE 1—LEADER A

background   Leader A is a 34 year old male with about 12 years ministry experience. He has church planting experience and pastoral experience. He did research and writing of public presentation materials for an international leader. He has training design experience. He has done non-formal training in workshops, seminars, and conferences around the U.S.

focal element   Lets be clear on terminology as we discuss these sample diagrams. When we refer to *element* we are speaking of the elements of the whole giftedness set. That is, natural abilities, acquired skills, and spiritual gifts. When we talk about an *item* we are talking about some member of one of those elements. In this diagram, two items stand out as larger than the rest: the leadership abilities item of the Natural Abilities element; the exhortation item of the spiritual gifts element. In determining the focal element the first thing you look for is the largest single item on the diagram. In this case two are equal. But a closer look at the diagram as a whole shows that a number of spiritual gifts are listed and cluster around the large exhortation item. It is this overall effect that would allow us to declare **spiritual gifts as the focal element**, closely followed by natural abilities.

tightness   This is a relatively *tight* diagram. By tightness we mean a close-knit, focused diagram in which there is much overlap between elements and items. A *loose* diagram is one in which some of the items do not overlap much or are even away from the central focus of the diagram. Frequently, this means that the ministry tasks, ministry assignments or Christian roles probably have not enhanced the giftedness so that the loose element or item occurs generally outside the ministry context. One value of Venn diagrams is to discover this looseness and determine ways to tighten up the diagram.

spiritual gifts   In terms of spiritual gifts, exhortation is the **dominant gift** of the gift-mix. The total gift-mix is exhortation, word of knowledge, prophecy, word of wisdom, and probably faith used occasionally, notice how small and not tightly placed. The word of knowledge is obviously frequently used as the basis for exhortation—having a clear word from God on something adds authority to the exhortive ministry. Because we are keeping the clutter down, we don't show secondary or tertiary gifts. In this case, Leader A in the past has exercised gifts of healings, most likely a role enabled gift, while in a church planting ministry. During a period of 7 years in church planting and pastoral work he prayed for more than 5000 people for healing. But now that gift is rarely used. Discernings of spirits has been evident also.

natural abilities   Leadership is a strong natural ability. Seeing it as a *dominant natural ability* and not a spiritual gift (ruling) probably indicates that Leader A exercised leadership during childhood and teens before recognition of spiritual gifts. Notice the importance of persevering attitude to leadership—what an asset!

acquired skills   Vision casting, the skill of organizing strategic thinking and motivating others with it, is an important skill. Note it overlaps almost entirely the prophecy spiritual gift. This means that a lot of the vision is probably based in revelation from God. But the acquired skill of vision casting means that he has learned how to frame the thinking and present it so as to promote it well and motivate followers toward it. The analytical skill has to do, for the most part with discerning leadership situations.

EXAMPLE 2 OF GIFTEDNESS DIAGRAM--LEADER B

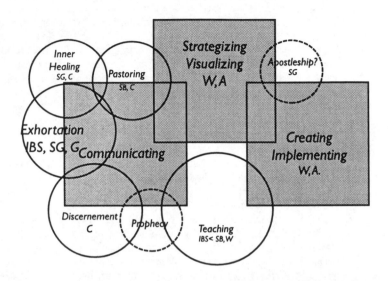

Self-Directed Learning
Foundation for development
of other gifts and abilities

☐ = *Natural Abilities*

◯ = *Spiritual Gifts*
(Dotted Circles = secondary & tertiary gifts)

Aquired Skills:
IBS = Inductive Bible Study
SG = Small group Leadership
W = Worship Leadership
C = Counseling Skills
A = Art Skills

COMMENTARY ON EXAMPLE 2—Leader B

background	Leader B is a 32 year old female with about 9 years of ministry experience with a two year break in the middle for formal mid-career training—including completion of the leadership concentration at the School of World Mission of Fuller Seminary. Her experience is almost totally focused on campus ministry. She has operated as a single person on a team as well as a married person on a team. Presently her husband and her operate in the co-ministry social base pattern—meaning both are full time Christian workers who share responsibilities in the home and in ministry.
exception in standards	Because of the larger number of acquired skills this person has, she chose to represent them with large capital letters, rather than triangles. This reduces clutter. She locates each of the acquired skills with the item it most closely relates. Not using triangles means we can't tell how influential the acquired skill is. But choosing not to use the triangle probably means any of the acquired skills are supplementary to the items they relate to and not dominant. Since this person is a creative person with heavy communication skills we can certainly allow her this leeway. I don't know what is meant by the IBS<SB, W symbol.
focal element	The largest items are three natural abilities. This forms the **focal element**. Spiritual gifts, particularly clustering around the natural communication ability, are a close second. Notice how she places the communication ability at the focus of the spiritual gifts. The communication ability is the dominant item of the natural ability element. Notice her distinctive labels for natural abilities—two of them are combinations.
possible gifts	Notice that the diagram has two dotted spiritual gifts—apostleship, prophecy. She has dotted them to indicate she is as yet uncertain about them. She labels them as secondary and tertiary. But most likely they are either embryonic or they are actually part of the natural abilities to which the relate. That is, apostleship may really be part of her creative instinct. Prophecy may be part of her communications skill of telling things plainly as they are.
overall impression	Most of the Spiritual gifts cluster around the communication ability. There is some creativity in teaching flowing from that natural ability. The exhortation gift takes place in counseling or in relation to small groups. There is much looseness in the diagram.
questions	Some things we might want to ask this person if we were in a face-to-face situation are:

What kinds of healings have you experience described as *inner healing*?
Why does not the discernings of spirits overlap with that inner *healing*?
Does the non-overlap between Strategizing/Visualizing and teaching mean that you have not attempted to train others concerning this important natural ability element?
Is the looseness in the diagram due to lack of roles which will allow enhancement of these and integration of them?

FEEDBACK ON EXAMPLE 2—LEADER B

1.   If you were to reduce the number of spiritual gifts in this diagram to the three most important, which ones would you include—in order of importance?

2.   If you were to reduce the number of acquired skills to three important ones which ones would you include?

3.   In the commentary about this display it was mentioned in the overall impressions that, "There is much looseness in this diagram." Give comments about this diagram which describe looseness.

4.   What suggestions would you give for tightening up the diagram? What implications would that have for ministry?

5.   What might be an ideal role for a person with this diagram if it were tightened up? List some tasks that would fit this giftedness.

ANSWERS————————-
1.   Teaching, discernment, exhortation
2.   SG = small group leadership (occurs three times on entire diagram); c = counseling skills (also occurs three times); W = worship leadership (also occurs three times)
3.   The natural abilities of Strategizing/Visualizing and Creating/Implementing have little overlap with each others. Two of them have no overlap. Apostleship is way off from the cluster of other spiritual gifts. Teaching should be a dominant part of communicating—it is the largest spiritual gift and communicating is the dominant item of the focal element. Yet there is little overlap. Usually prophecy and exhortation have an overlap (they do share an admonition focus—but these don't but probably could).
4.   First, the natural abilities of Strategizing/Visualizing and Creating/Implementing should be moved toward the left so that they have more impact on the communicating. Teaching should move up and to the left to centralize it more with communicating exhortation and discernment overlaps.
5.   An ideal role would be one which had the following kinds of tasks:
    •   strategic planning for long term ministry goals which involve innovative structures and ministry means,
    •   a teaching/training ministry which is dominantly that of writing materials for small groups and thoroughly testing these materials in small groups, said training should be in harmony with implementing the overall strategic planning of task 1.
    •   career planning for emerging leaders, including laying out a developmental analysis based on their giftedness sets.
    •   counseling with these emerging leaders concerning their lives and developmental plans.

I would call this role a trainer/ consultant specialists.

EXAMPLE 3 OF GIFTEDNESS DIAGRAM--LEADER C

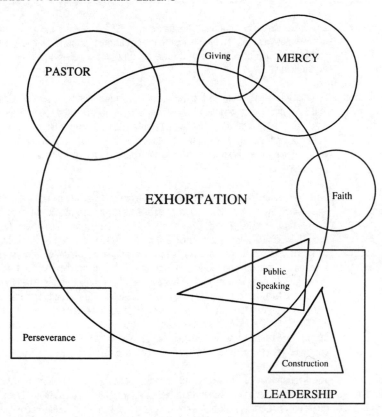

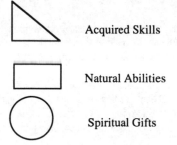

Acquired Skills

Natural Abilities

Spiritual Gifts

COMMENTARY ON EXAMPLE 3—Leader C

background
: Leader C is a male bi-vocational Christian worker. He has been in ministry for about 40 years, now being 65. He has planted churches, pastored them, and now supervises a district of other bi-vocational and some full time pastors. He is in a Pentecostal denomination.

focal element
: Spiritual gifts stand out as his **focal element** with exhortation being very **dominant** in the gift-mix. Other spiritual gifts include pastoring, mercy, faith and giving in that order. Leadership is the dominant natural ability with perseverance (an ability/value) a close second. Acquired skills involve public speaking which complements well his exhortation gift and construction which allows him to financially support himself in his leadership.

special remarks
: This man's ministry takes place in a wide geographical expanse in Texas where he has planted churches, pastored them, and pastored the pastors of many of them. He has supported himself with construction jobs. His faith gift has allowed him to repeatedly start new works and to trust God for finances as they were built. He has a pastor's heart which helps him relate to the leaders under him, many of whom are bi-vocational pastors. Giving has helped him financially support these works. It takes perseverance to stay with small churches and keep them going. It takes perseverance to continue to travel year after year the many miles it takes to visit and care for all the churches in his district. I would say this man's ministry has been tailored to his giftedness set. I might add he has a very supportive wife who has given herself to helping him in this pastoral oversight ministry. But he told me that he no longer has the energy to keep up the persevering visitation involved in overseeing the district.

overall impressions
: The diagram is loose. If I were to question him or counsel him about it my guess is that we would see more overlap than he has shown. I am amazed that this leader shows only one charismatic gift. Obviously, in his long ministry he has undoubtedly seen a number of Pentecostal secondary and tertiary gifts needed to plant churches and break open new fields.

clarity
: He has simplified well his diagram. He has reduced clutter by concentrating on the very most important elements and items. He could have given much more information with a corresponding loss of clarity on the diagram. When doing Venn diagrams the tendency is to overkill. That is, give too much information which clutters the diagram and makes it hard to interpret the overall. There is a delicate balance that must be maintained between giving too much information and losing clarity or underling clarity at a loss of information that might explain. If you have to err, do so on the clarity side. One can always follow-up and ask questions about more information.

FEEDBACK ON EXAMPLE 3—LEADER C

1. Identify the one power cluster gift that Leader C has.

2. How do you explain the lack of sign gifts in a denomination which in the past has certainly advocated at least some of them?

3. I mentioned in the commentary that the diagram is loose. Give evidence of what I mean by that.

4. How would you suggest correcting this looseness, that is, can anything be done to tighten up the diagram?

5. In light of Leader C's remark to me that he no longer has the energy (nor does his wife) to travel the many miles necessary to keep up the ministry, what would you suggest to him?

ANSWERS—————-

1. faith, normally in this denomination tongues would be there as well as some gifts of healing.

2. As I mentioned in the commentary, he has opted for clarity and the other power gifts that he may have exercised in a role/enablement pattern are not on-going gifts. His role now is dominantly that of pastoring pastors and helping them begin new works and maintain them.

3. The spiritual gifts have very little overlap. You would expect mercy to overlap with the pastoral gift since both have normally have a caring thrust. You would expect faith and giving to overlap with the natural ability of leadership since he has been involved in church planting in the past. You would expect the perseverance ability to overlap with the leadership.

4. Here's what I think ought to be the ideal. Keep the exhortation gift in place and shift the leadership and acquired skills upward to the left and move the pastoral gift around the circumference till it had strong overlap with mercy. Then move both mercy and pastoring on around the circumference downward to the right. Move the giving around to overlap mercy and leadership. The faith should move down toward the leadership.

5. I told him he should concentrate over the next few years in mentoring several of his top leaders to replace himself. Split the big geographical district up into about three major areas and find an emerging leader in each to work with him to learn how to supervise. Then simply mentor, lot of co-ministry but also releasing for ministry alone.

Example 4 of Giftedness Diagram—Leader D

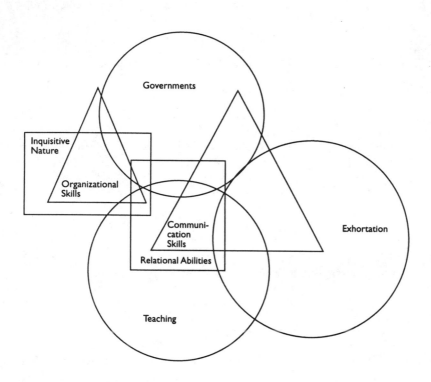

Acquired Skills

Natural Abilities

Spiritual Gifts

COMMENTARY ON EXAMPLE 4—LEADER D

background
Leader D is a male in his late 30s who is now a training specialist in a denomination. He has a number of years of pastoral experience but now is involved in Christian education for several districts of churches in his denomination.

focal element
Spiritual gifts are the focal element. Exhortation is the dominant gift of the gift-mix with teaching a close second. Governments is the third gift of the gift-mix.

fit
Note the way his giftedness goes together. Natural abilities include relational abilities which he encloses in his teaching gift meaning that his teaching is most likely very personal. He would relate individually to people he teaches. He probably also does informal teaching as well as formal. His acquired communication skills fit with his teaching (better teacher) and with exhortation (motivational skills most likely). He naturally has an inquisitive ability or bent. He shows it as primarily going hand-in-hand with his organizational skills which supplement the spiritual gift of governments.

tightness
This is a relatively *tight* diagram. It is a relatively close-knit, focused diagram with one exception which I will call to mind in the feedback exercises.

skill/attitude
This diagram illustrates the broad view we hold on natural abilities. A natural ability may involve an attitude or bent of mind that affects thinking or doing as well as some innate talent for accomplishing. Here there is the label, inquisitive nature. Probably as a kid growing up and as a student in school Leader D was always asking questions. This demonstration of a God-given learning posture can stand him in good stead. Learning to ask the right questions about organizations and how they operate is a step forward to a better organization. Asking questions about learners, the processes of learning, learning outcomes, and evaluation of communication is a major step forward for a teacher. Previously we saw another skill/attitude on two other leaders— perseverance or persevering attitude.

questions
If you were to question this leader concerning his giftedness Venn diagram what might be your questions? Let me suggest several,

Wherein lies your spiritual authority from a giftedness standpoint? There is no evidence at all of a power cluster gift?

How do your relational abilities fit with your teaching gift? You show almost total overlap.

How has your communication skills buttressed your teaching gift and your exhortation gift?

FEEDBACK ON EXAMPLE 4—Leader D

1. I mentioned in the commentary that with one exception this was a tight diagram, a very focused display. What is that one exception?

2. What would it mean in emphasis for Leader D to bring the diagram more into focus?

2. Note my statement in the commentary, *Wherein lies your spiritual authority from a giftedness stand-point? There is no evidence at all of a power cluster gift?*

definition   *Spiritual authority* is the right to influence conferred upon a leader by followers be-cause of their perceived spirituality seen in the leader.

That perceived spiritual comes in three basic ways:

     a.   a godly lifestyle which emulates the character of God, that is, the leader is per-ceived as a godly person,
     b.   the leader knows God experientially as well a theoretically. He/she has had deep experiences with God, in which God meets the leader,
√   c.   and gifted power.

The question as I stated it is focusing on spiritual authority from a giftedness standpoint.   From this definition what do you think I mean by the question? And how possibly could Leader D answer it?

ANSWERS———————
1. The exhortation gift is the dominant gift in the gift-mix according to the size given it. Yet most everything else focuses to the left. The exhortation gift is sort of out in right field. If it really is the dominant gift then it needs to be moved left so that the natural abilities and acquired skills can supplement it.
2. To move the exhortation gift to the left means that Leader D must recognize that in his teaching and in his organizational issues it is the exhortation aspect that should be strongest. In his teach-ing he should deliberately design his teaching for application and allow for example, ministry times in which concepts are used. In organizational issues his questions and organizational skills along with governments are to be used not just to analyze and pinpoint strengths and weaknesses but there must be a push through to action. Leader D is only part way there when he sees things. He must implement things if the exhortation gift is to become dominant.
3. Normally gifted power is seen first in a power cluster gift. If a person does not show a power cluster gift (and Leader D doesn't) then it must come through the word gift s(normally a govern-ments gift would not normally be perceived as gifted power). Leader D could answer the question by saying. My teaching gift combined with exhortation has repeatedly been anointed with gifted power as perceived in the learners who are being influenced by my teaching and application. Or he might say my basis for spiritual authority is not dominantly coming through my gifted power but through my character and my deep experiential knowledge of God.

EXAMPLE 5 OF GIFTEDNESS DIAGRAM—LEADER E

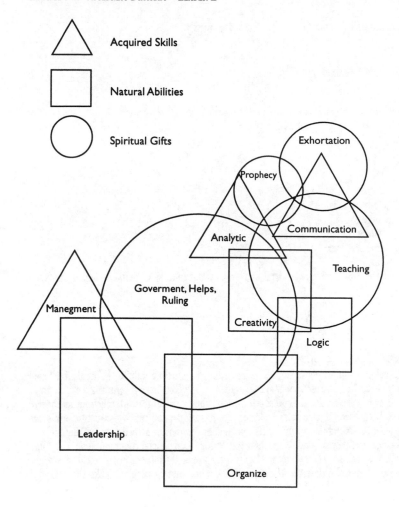

△ Acquired Skills

▢ Natural Abilities

◯ Spiritual Gifts

Natural Abilities: *Creativity, Leadership, Logic, Organization*

Acquired Skills: *Analytical, Communication, Computer, Design, Management, Planning, Woodworking*

Spiritual Gifts:

    Primary ~ *Exhortation, Government, Helps, Prophecy, Teaching, Ruling*

    Secondary ~ *Word of Wisdom, Word of Knowledge, Interpretation*

FEEDBACK ON EXAMPLE 5—Leader E

1. What is the focal element of Leader's E giftedness set?

2. What is the dominant spiritual gift?

3. Notice that there appears to be two major constellations (i.e. focus points) on the diagram? What are they? What might this mean?

4. What cluster of gifts is more prominent?
   ___ a. word cluster
   ___ b. power cluster
   ___ c. love cluster

5. What advice would you give Leader E, as a result of your study of his Venn Diagram on Giftedness?

ANSWERS—————-
1. Spiritual gifts with strong supportive under girding from natural abilities. Notice there are really
2. Leader E combines three together and gives them the biggest circle: government, helps, ruling.
3. There is one focus around the government, helps, ruling spiritual gifts. Management and analytical skills and natural abilities of leadership, organize, logic, and creativity seem to form a tight constellation around the spiritual gifts combination—government, helps, ruling. But there is a second constellation around the teaching gifts focus. Analytic and communication skills along with natural abilities of creativity and logic cluster around the spiritual gift of teaching. Prophecy and Exhortation also cluster on the edge of this gift and with the acquired skills. I see two possibilities of meaning. In either case we are talking about a very gifted person. Possibility 1 is that this person is a late bloomer and this second constellation which is strongly word gifted is beginning to emerge and will actually become dominant as role adaptation occurs. Possibility 2 is that the person has been involved in a forced role situation which utilizes the present larger constellation (mostly supportive gifts) but does not enhance the word gifted constellation. In that case, Leader E is probably a frustrated person just waiting his chance. Can the two constellations move together. Probably not without a major role change which focuses on the smaller constellation.
4. √ c. The major constellation revolves around love cluster gifts. The secondary constellation revolves around word gifts. Notice at the bottom of the page Leader E does show secondary gifts in the power cluster. This shows that from time-to-time where needed power gifts have authenticated his ministry.
5. Be ready for a major role change which will bring the minor constellation into prominence. In fact, be praying for it. Be looking for it. Watch for some faith challenges from God which will lead to this change.

EXAMPLE 6 OF GIFTEDNESS DIAGRAM—LEADER F

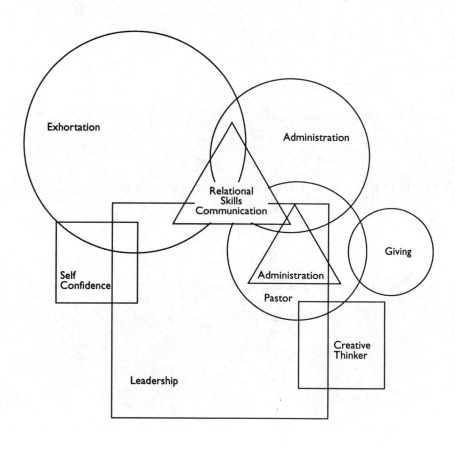

△ Acquired Skills

□ Natural Abilities

○ Spiritual Gifts

FEEDBACK ON EXAMPLE 6—Leader F

1.   What is the focal element of the giftedness set displayed by Leader F?

2.   What spiritual gifts are given? List them in order of importance.

3.   Would you expect this person to have a strong ego or weak ego? Why?

4.   What one item is almost an exclusive item and probably exercised out of the context of the other items? What might this mean?

5.   What observations might you have on the diagram as a whole?

ANSWERS————————-

1.   natural abilities; the natural ability of leadership is the dominant item on the display. Exhortation, a spiritual gift is a very close second.
2.   Exhortation, administrations (which I call governments), pastor, giving
3.   strong ego. note the natural abilities of self confidence, dominant leadership, creative thinker.
4.   the spiritual gift of giving. It has little overlap with anything else (slight with pastor). I am not sure. This is a question I will ask this leader when next I see him. It may mean he has a personal giving fund (outside the church benevolent fund)
5.   I think it is incongruent that exhortation is the dominant spiritual gift and is almost as large as the focal element yet it does not form a constellation . It is off to the upper left with little overlap. If it is really that dominant it should have more of the other items clustering around it.

EXAMPLE 7 OF GIFTEDNESS DIAGRAM—LEADER G

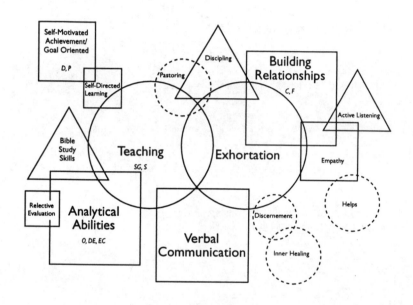

LEGEND

⭘	= Spiritual Gifts
☐	= Natural Abilities
△	= Primary Acquired Skills
⭘ (dashed)	= Tertiary Gifts or Gifts to be explored

C = Correspondence
DE = Delegation
DI = Discipline
EC = Experimentasl Research & Computer Skills
O = Organization
P = Prayer
S = Sermon Preperation
SG = Small Group Leadership

FEEDBACK ON EXAMPLE 7—LEADER G

Background   Leader G is a Japanese-American female leader around thirty years of age. She has
                 had excellent training via a number of mentoring relationships during her collegiate
                 days. She in turn has mentored others.

1.   What stands out as you first view Leader G's Venn Diagram?

2.   In your opinion is the diagram loose or tight?

3.   List the natural abilities in order of importance.

4.   How many kinds of acquired skill items are listed or indicated on the diagram?

5.   Knowing nothing more than the information I have given and her Venn diagram what role(s)
     could you suggest for this obviously gifted person?

ANSWERS————————-
1. The twin dominant spiritual gifts of teaching exhortation. Both are the same size. They fill up the
    middle of the diagram and are the center of gravity for a constellation.
2. Your opinion. Your are just as right as me. But here's mine. With the exception of tertiary gifts
    being explored and one set of natural abilities in the upper left-hand corner, it is a tight diagram.
    There is a major constellation with twin-centers. Each of the acquired sills or natural abilities
    connects naturally to something that it supplements.
3. Verbal Communication, analytical abilities, and building relationships are all about equal and the
    most important of the natural abilities. Empathy and self motivation are equally important and
    next behind the top three. Reflective evaluation and self-directed learning are about equal and
    next in importance.
4. Eight are given in abbreviated form (C, DE, DI, EC, O, P, S, SG. Three are indicated as fairly impor-
    tant in pictorial form: Active Listening, Bible Study Skills, and Discipling.
5. Since females are not usually allowed any strong leadership in the Japanese-American context of
    church life she will have to most likely find a role in a parachurch set-up. If she were a male she
    could easily pastor a church in the Japanese-American culture. She could probably teach in a Bible
    School which had a mixed Asian faculty. Or she could become involved in a campus ministry.

SUMMARY

At this point you have identified your giftedness set and displayed it. You have identified your dominant gift in the spiritual gift-mix. You have identified the focal element for the whole giftedness set.

From the feedback exercises you have learned the importance of understanding a person. You have considered overlaps and non-overlapping implications. You have looked at what might bring the whole diagram toward a focused one. You have seen the importance of looking at a role that takes advantage of the gifting being displayed. As a leader you are probably seeing the importance of giftedness Venn diagrams for selection and development of your people as well as assigning of roles to match who they are.

Let me summarize it for you. You have learned the importance of a Venn diagram. Venn diagrams do at least the following 6 things:

1. They force you to think through which elements and items are most important.
2. They force you to think in what way these elements and items overlap—how do they support each other; how do they operate in an exclusive fashion.
3. From an overall standpoint, they force you to see how you can tighten up the diagram, that is, get more out of the overlap.
4. From an overall standpoint, they force you to see how the exclusive action of the elements and items can contribute.
5. From an overall standpoint, they help you think toward a role which best enhances the totality of giftedness represented by the diagram.
6. If you are a leader, and you have these available for your followers and especially the emerging leaders they help you think through ministry tasks, roles, and training that best develops them in terms of their whole giftedness.

In short, they help you to **MINISTER OUT OF BEING** as you understand more of how God made you to be. And they can help you to move others to minister out of their being also.

Now you are ready to take seriously the Stewardship Model. God has indeed blessed you with resources. What will you do with them? The following chapters help us think about development of the resources we have.

CHAPTER 10:
HOW LEADERS DEVELOP IN GIFTEDNESS

INTRODUCTION

In this chapter, we discuss the issue of developing in your giftedness. By this point, you have identified and displayed your giftedness set. How can I develop to use my gifts more effectively? That's what this chapter is all about. We'll give some suggestions for development for each of the spiritual gifts.

WHAT IS DEVELOPMENT?

When we talk about development in the context of giftedness, we mean moving toward maturity. By maturity, we mean that a person is operating in maximum potential as it relates to his/her giftedness set. Maximum potential is measured in several ways. First, a person operating in maturity in his/her giftedness does it in a Godly way. The character of God is revealed in all that is said and done. Secondly, the various elements of the giftedness set are operating in balance, harmony and synergistically. Each person's giftedness set is unique to him/her so maturity in this regard looks different for each person. Thirdly, a person operating in maturity in his/her giftedness bears appropriate fruit and is accomplishing the things that God has set out for him/her. The process of development involves anything that helps move us along in any of these three areas.

Many spiritual gifts writers focus on defining the gifts; a few in helping the readers identify their own gifts. We go a step further: know, yes; identify, yes; but also develop. The stewardship model and its values spur us on to be developing toward maturity in our giftedness. And we are to be proactive and deliberate in this pursuit.

When a person looks at his/her giftedness set, the question is: what can be developed? Can you develop a natural ability? In our opinion, no. Natural abilities are not developable. God had sovereignly given us our natural abilities. You can't sit down tomorrow and say, "I think I'll develop a natural ability!" You either have it or you don't. However, it is possible to discover some latent natural abilities and when you discover them it feels like you are developing it.

By definition, all acquired skills are developed and learned. Some acquired skills enhance our natural abilities. Some acquired skills enhance our spiritual gifts. This arena is an important one in terms of developing in our giftedness set.

Can you develop a spiritual gift? Many would say no. We say...a qualified yes. We believe that you can develop (remember, moving toward maturity) in the area of spiritual gifts. Experience is a great teacher. If a person is oriented to learning from experience, then he/she can learn a great deal about the use of spiritual gifts in ministry. And it is definitely possible to acquire skills which enhance the use of spiritual gifts.

Here is our plan for the chapter. We'll review the patterns for development of giftedness. This will help us think in terms of development. Then we will introduce to you the three major modes of development which we interweave in all our suggestions for development which we will give each spiritual gift.

You should examine your Venn diagram. Choose one of the gifts from your gift-mix that you want to work on for the next several months. Then read the suggestions for development of that gift. Choose several of them. Or perhaps these suggestions will stimulate you to design your own. In any case, lay out a plan for developing a gift.

THE GIFTEDNESS DEVELOPMENT PATTERN

introduction   A spiritual gift is a unique capacity for channeling a Holy Spirit led ministry in and
                 through the life of the believer. Wagner (1979) coined the term gift-mix to talk about
                 multi-gifted people. How a gift-mix is discovered and matures as a gift cluster is the
                 focus of this pattern.

description   The *Giftedness Development pattern* refers to the process a leader goes through in
                 moving from initial discovery of a gift to convergence.

stages   The pattern includes: (read —> as "may lead to")
                 1. ministry experience —>
                 2. the discovery of gift/natural abilities —>
                 3. increased use of that gift/abilities —>
                 4. effectiveness in using that gift/abilities —>
                 5. more ministry experience or new ministry roles
                 6. which stimulates further discovery of gifts in order to meet the new situation —>
                 7. which over time eventuates in the identification of the gift-mix —>
                 8. the development of a gift-cluster —>
                 9. convergence (maturity in giftedness).

explanation   Gift-mix is a phrase which is used to describe the set of spiritual gifts a leader repeat-
                 edly uses in ministry. Gift-cluster refers to a gift-mix which has a dominant gift, sup-
                 ported harmoniously by other gifts and abilities. The giftedness discovery process
                 item describes any significant advance along the giftedness discovery pattern and the
                 stimulus (trigger incident) that brought the discovery. This might be an event, per-
                 son, or reflection process. The repetition with increased clarity of this giftedness dis-
                 covery process item is an important feature of the ministry phase.

inclusive   The pattern actually refers to all elements of the giftedness set. The latter stages
pattern   refer only to spiritual gifts since most natural abilities and acquired skills are discov-
                 ered or obtained in the early stages of ministry. As one matures in giftedness, the
                 emphasis primarily involves the development of spiritual gifts or supplementary skills
                 related to them.

natural   If natural abilities are the focal element, then steps 5,6,7 most likely collapse into
ability   one step. In this step, acquired skills and spiritual gifts are recognized as
as focal   supplements which support the natural abilities.

THE GIFTEDNESS DEVELOPMENT PATTERN

Viewed pictorially the giftedness development pattern looks like the following.

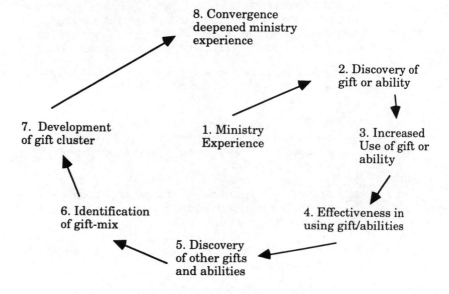

THE GIFT-CLUSTER RIPENING PATTERN

introduction	A leader moving toward convergence in the middle to later part of ministry frequently operates in a mature gift cluster. Operating in gifted power is habitual. The supportive gifts of the cluster synergistically support the dominant gift to produce the clustering effect. The cooperative interaction between the gifts of the gift-mix is such that the total effect is greater than the sum of the effects of each gift taken independently.
description	The *Gift-cluster Ripening pattern* expands in detail the advanced stages (7,8) in the giftedness development pattern and includes the following:

Step 7:
a. the selection of a ministry based on the dominant gift —>
b. experiencing supportive gifts operating in concert with the dominant gift —>
c. gaining of insights into how the supportive gifts relate to the dominant gift —>

Step 8:
a. selection of ministry opportunities based on the total gift-cluster —>
b. modifying the ministry role to allow for the supportive gifts to operate in concert with the dominant gift.

explanation	Gift-cluster denotes a dominant gift supported by other gifts so as to harmonize the gift-mix and to maximize effectiveness.
5 examples	• exhortation (dominant), teaching, word of wisdom • apostleship (dominant), word of knowledge, teaching • governments (dominant), exhortation, mercy • giving (dominant), governments, teaching • discerning of spirits, (dominant), miracles, mercy
gifted power shift	A major shift occurs in terms of a leader operating in gifted power at the culmination of this gift-cluster ripening pattern. The leader shifts from power pattern 1, the Temporary Acquisition Pattern to power pattern 2, Confident Usage Pattern.
explanation power pattern 1	The **temporary acquisition pattern** is as follows: 1. the leader is not aware of or has no need for the special use of power 2. the leader recognizes the need for gifted power 3. a ministry situation forces the leader to obtain power 4. there is an insightful moment when God meets the leader and releases power 5. the leader returns to normal ministry in terms of gifted power
explanation power pattern 2	The **confident usage pattern** is as follows: 1. the leader is constantly aware of the need for power 2. the leader has an insightful moment when God prompts the leader to operate in power which is followed by, 3. the confident acceptance of gifted power by faith 4. God's release of power through the leader.

VARIOUS MEANS FOR DEVELOPING GIFTEDNESS

When you think about using various means to develop your giftedness, there are a number of different contexts and relationships that could be utilized. As you plan for your own development, recognize that there is a wide variety of choices to be made in terms of creating a development plan. Here are some of the means that we have seen utilized in giftedness development plans.

DEVELOPMENT MEANS

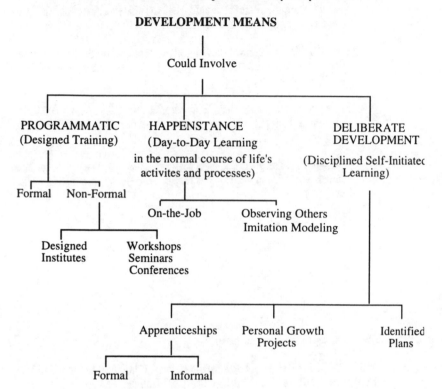

DEVELOPMENT IDEAS FOR SPIRITUAL GIFTS

All development ideas fall somewhere in the three major means above: programmatic designed training, happenstance in the course of life, or deliberately planned for. In this section, we are simply going to brainstorm ideas for development. There will not be any order or importance to the ideas. We will just list them. We will look at each gift. In the suggestions we give for each gift you will see the three means above interwoven many times. We are suggesting that you should be deliberately developing your gifts whatever the means.

How To Develop The Gift Of Teaching

introduction   Remember that the teaching gift is one of the Word Cluster gifts. Each of these gifts all contribute to the major aims of that cluster which is

Word gifts clarify the nature of this unseen God and what He expects from His followers. People using these gifts both communicate about God and for God.

The gift of teaching is central to this Word Cluster thrust. As you think through developing yourself for a more effective use of this gift always remember the central thrust to which it is contributing.

Before you work through the ideas for development, refresh yourself with the definition of the teaching gift. Keep it in mind as you ponder the developmental suggestions.

teaching   A person who has the *gift of teaching* is one who has the ability to instruct, explain, or expose Biblical truth in such a way as to cause believers to understand the Biblical truth.

CENTRAL THRUST - TO CLARIFY TRUTH

Here are some GUIDELINES to help you to develop in this gift.

6 Major Guidelines

1. Hermeneutics (science of interpreting the Bible)

MAKE CERTAIN YOU HAVE A FOUNDATIONAL UNDERSTANDING OF INTERPRETIVE PRINCIPLES TO GUIDE YOU IN YOUR STUDY OF THE BIBLE.

Explanation
You need to master a system of hermeneutical principles based on the grammatical-historical approach to the Bible. Teachers need to be consistent in their approach to the study and interpretation of the Scriptures.[1]

---

[1] You may want to get into a class in hermeneutics in a formal training set-up such as a Seminary or Bible College. See Dr. J. Robert Clinton. **The Bible and Leadership Values** available through Barnabas Publishers, P.O. Box 6006, Altadena, CA, 91001. See the introductory pages 7-10 which lists a hermeneutical system of principles. The rest of the handbook studies each book of the Bible using this approach.

How To Develop The Gift Of Teaching continued

2. Bible Study

SYSTEMATICALLY BEGIN A PROGRAM TO MASTER THE BIBLE, KEEPING IN MIND THAT YOU SHOULD BE A CONTINUAL SEARCHER FOR TRUTH.

Detailed Suggestions:

1. Determine to master as much of the Bible as you can in your lifetime. If you lack discipline to study, ask God to give you a hunger to learn and ability to study. By master is meant you can give the overall theme and purpose of a book and see your way completely through the book in order to relate structure to the theme.

2. Have a Bible reading program which you repeatedly use to familiarize yourself with the entire Bible.

3. Set up a plan to study in depth individual books of the Bible applying your hermeneutical system.

4. Make it a practice to try to do your own original study of a book before going to commentaries or other aids.

5. Use commentaries which follow the basic hermeneutical principles that you use.

Explanation
There are many kinds of projects that could be worked on as it relates to gaining Bible knowledge. For people who have a teaching gift, there should always be an emphasis on this area. Teaching is one of the foundational word gifts and demands that the teacher be immersed in the Word of God at a deep level throughout life. Teachers should have a plan to systematically master the Bible over their lifetime.

Every year new *personal growth projects* should be set and tackled. For example,

- learning tools and principles to use when interpreting the Scriptures,
- gaining an overall understanding of each book in the Bible. There are numerous books that present overviews of each book of the Bible that are helpful in this regard,[2]
- learning to study each book for theme and structure,
- looking at each book and seeing what it contributes to a particular theme (the person of God, leadership, justice, healing, etc.),
- studying a book of the Bible comprehensively,
- learning to interpret various types of literature in the Bible (parables, figures and idioms, Hebrew poetry, etc.).

---

[2] See G. Campbell Morgan's books: **The Analyzed Bible—The Books of the Bible Outlined by the Prince of Expositors**, Westwood, N.J.: Fleming H. Revell. See his **Handbook for Bible Teachers and Preachers—Applications to Life From Every Book of the Bible**. Grand Rapids: Baker Book House. See Henrietta C. Mears, **What the Bible Is All About**, Ventura, CA: Regal Books.

How To Develop The Gift Of Teaching CONTINUED

3. Teaching Philosophy

LEARN AS MUCH AS YOU CAN ABOUT THE DUAL PROCESSES OF TEACHING
AND LEARNING.

Explanation
There are a number of books on teaching that are excellent. In our opinion, there are some helpful books on teaching that are worth studying. The classic book is Gregory's **The Seven Laws of Teaching**. Carl Scafer has written a modern abridgment of Gregory's book called **Excellence in Teaching** which may be easier to get. Howard Hendrik's book, **Teaching to Change Lives** is excellent as well. These books and others like them will help a teacher understand the dynamics involved in teaching and communicate principles which will help the emerging teacher become more effective. Through the Bible Ministries of Atlanta, Georgia puts out Video series on the Laws of the Teacher and Laws of the Learner.[3]

4. Communicational Skills

DELIBERATELY STUDY COMMUNICATION THEORY.

Detailed Suggestions:
1. Use a receptor oriented communication model.[4]
2. Master feedback techniques and use them in all your teaching. Never be satisfied to only think that learning is going on.
3. Be conscious always of the learners in the teaching process. When you sense they aren't learning, find out why. Remember as a teacher you are responsible for the learner learning.
4. Discipline yourself to prepare thoroughly for a teaching session.
5. Be flexible enough to change any teaching plan or methodology.

Explanation
Teaching involves study and hard work to get valuable life changing information for people. But that is only one half the battle. The other half is communicating it to people with impact. It will usually take twice as much time to design your communication approach in a given situation than it did to study the material. Anything that can be learned about communication and the dynamics involved is helpful.

---

[3] An excellent help for teachers who want to learn also about preparing instructional materials is Susan Markle's book, **Frames—Good or Bad**. It is teaching about how to write programmed instruction, an auto-didactic methodology. But more than that it teaches the psychology of learning, the principles of learning. I personally found this greatly increased my teaching skills.
[4] Charles H. Kraft of the School of World Mission, Fuller Seminary in Pasadena has several books out on receptor oriented communication. His **Christianity in Culture** defines in detail receptor oriented models of communication.

5. Observing Various Teaching Models—Getting Formal or Informal Mentoring

IF AT ALL POSSIBLE SPEND AN EXTENDED PERIOD OF TIME INVOLVED WITH A SUCCESSFUL TEACHER AND LEARN WHAT YOU CAN FROM HIM/HER.

Detailed Suggestions:
1. Analyze every teacher for his/ her good and bad features. Avoid the bad ones in your own ministry. Use the good ones if they can become a natural part of you.
2. Talk a lot with other teaches and discuss successes and failures and teaching techniques, etc.
3. Be particularly on the lookout for anyone who communicates on the affective (emotional/ value) and conative (volitional) level. Learn techniques for doing this.

Explanation
One of the best ways to learn good principles about teaching is observing good teachers in action. Make a survey of *teachers* in your area. Find ways to listen and watch. Observe and study their methodologies. If you can form some kind of mentoring relationship with them, go for it.

6. Gaining Experience

USE YOUR GIFT OFTEN BOTH IN SMALL GROUPS OUTSIDE THE CHURCH SETTING AND IN THE CHURCH SETTING ITSELF.

Explanation
There is nothing that beats gaining experience in teaching. In order to get the most out of every situation, you need to get some honest feedback and do some honest evaluating of your teaching efforts. Maintain a learning posture. Learn to be sensitive to the Holy Spirit's empowering of your teaching. Watch for what the Holy Spirit is doing to the listeners. There will be cultural cues. But there will also be a spiritual understanding that comes to a person operating in gifted power. A teacher operating in gifted power can expect to sense the moving of the Holy Spirit during a time of teaching. This special sense of anointing will allow you to move freely in your teaching, to modify it to follow the Spirit's prompting. Such a sensitivity will allow you to see empowered teaching.

How To Develop The Gift Of Exhortation

introduction   Remember that the exhortation gift is one of the Word Cluster gifts. It is a primary word gift since it deals so directly with using the Word of God with others. Each of these gifts all contribute to the major aims of that cluster which is

Word gifts clarify the nature of this unseen God and what He expects from His followers. People using these gifts both communicate about God and for God.

Whereas teaching focuses on *clarifying*, Exhortation focuses on *what He expects from His followers*. The gift of exhortation like the teaching gift is central to this Word Cluster thrust, for it motivates people to use God's truth. As you think through developing yourself for a more effective use of this gift always remember the central thrust to which it is contributing.

Before you work through the ideas for development, refresh yourself with the definition of the exhortation gift. Keep it in mind as you ponder the developmental suggestions.

exhortation   The *gift of exhortation* is the capacity to use Biblical truth to urge people to action, or to encourage people generally, or to comfort people with truth that meets their needs. **CENTRAL THRUST - TO APPLY BIBLICAL TRUTH**

Here are some areas to work in to develop in this gift.

8 Major Guidelines

1.   General Bible Study of Applicational Passages

STUDY REGULARLY THE PASSAGES OF SCRIPTURE WHICH ARE HEAVY IN APPLICATION.

Detailed Suggestions:
1.   Your regular Bible reading program should focus on application passages. Your devotional life should focus on Scriptures which are applicational in nature. See the Table of Passages Focusing on Application of Truth to Life, p. 264.
2.   Seek to apply these Scriptures to your own life. Write down your personal applications and note your personal obedience to God.[5]
3.   Be particularly sensitive to the Holy Spirit. He will quite often emphasize Scriptures which will apply to current situations around you.

Explanation
Exhortation is one of the foundational word gifts and demands that the person be immersed in the Word of God at a deep level throughout life. Every year new projects should be tackled. In particular,

---

[5] A simple procedure for becoming sensitive to application of truth is given in the booklet by Dr. J. Robert Clinton, **How To Apply the Word of God**. Available through Barnabas Publishers. You can use this five step procedure with othrs as well as yourself.

How To Develop The Gift Of Exhortation CONTINUED

a focus on applying Biblical truth should be the theme of study. In order to get Biblical truth, much needs to be studied and learned from the Scriptures about how truth is applied.

2. Specific Bible Books and Passages Focusing on Application Skills

STUDY BIBLE BOOKS WHICH WILL HELP YOU BECOME SENSITIVE TO PEOPLE'S NEEDS.

Detailed Suggestions:
1. Read regularly in the Psalms and note:
   - The moods and changing experiences faced by people as they walk with God,
   - God's method of meeting men in these situations,
   - How you can use the various Psalms to bring comfort to those facing the same kind of situations.
2. Study Job to note:
   - How to and how not to empathize with those in suffering,
   - The stress on the sovereignty of God—this will be a foundational principle in comforting and encouraging people.
3. Study Ecclesiastes to see areas in which people seek satisfaction.
4. Study especially the Parables and Jesus discourses. In almost each of them Jesus is applying truth to real life situations.
5. Other passages that put special emphasis on the application of truth include: Proverbs, Romans 12-16, the book of 1 Corinthians, many of Paul's other epistles such as Galatians, Ephesians 4-6, Philippians and Colossians, the books of Hebrews and James.

Explanation
The more you are familiar with application of truth to life such as described in Biblical situations the more you will find yourself modeling what you have learned in life.

3. Apply Scripture From Memory

MEMORIZE VERSES WHICH WILL PROVE HELPFUL TO YOU AS
YOU USE YOUR EXHORTIVE GIFT.

Examples:
Proverbs 9:8 10:17 11:14 15:28,31 17:10 20:5 25:11,12 26:4,5 27:5,6,9,17 John 14:26 16:13 2 Corinthians 1:3,4 12:9 Hebrews 10:24,25 James 1:22 and many others.

Explanation
Exhortation can have a powerful impact when truth which fits a situation is sensitively applied. When a person knows Scripture and get bring it to mind orally it carries great authority. Often the Holy Spirit will bring to mind Scripture that has been tucked away at a timely moment when it is needed.

4. Study Motivational Skills

DELIBERATELY ACQUIRE MOTIVATIONAL SKILLS.

Explanation
Exhortation because of its applicational nature deals a great deal with motivation. You should study communication skills which deal with motivation.

5. Linking Up With a Mentor

SEEK OUT A MENTOR WHO HAS AN EXHORTATION GIFT

Explanation
A mentor is a person who empowers you with God-given resources. In this case, the resources would be anything that relates to the gift of exhortation. People who operate in this gift in a mature way are extremely important as models. Watch how they exhort, how they communicate, how they are sensitive to the people they are exhorting, etc. Form a relationship with the person if you can and watch them in action.

6. Learn To Be Sensitive to the Holy Spirit

BE READY TO BE PROMPTED TO EXHORT BOTH IN SMALL GROUPS
AND INDIVIDUAL SITUATIONS.

Detailed Suggestions:
1. Be alert to the Holy Spirit in small groups and one-on-one situations for promptings. He will call your attention to situations or problems to which He has previously given you help.
2. The experiences you face will be particularly used of God to teach you lessons to be used with others.
3. You will find that you are unusually sensitive to lessons learned from others' experiences also. You will also notice quick recall of verses, past experiences and principles from tome-to-time in your discussions with others.
4. Share these with others always in love and with the principles of Philippians 3:15, 16 in mind.

Explanation
Modeling is a dominant way that exhortation happens. God will teach you lessons which He will also use with and for others. You must learn to share your experiences when opportunities arise.

How To Develop The Gift Of Exhortation continued

7. Exploit Opportunities

TAKE ADVANTAGE OF OPPORTUNITIES IN SMALL GROUPS AND THE GATHERED
CHURCH TO SHARE YOUR CURRENT EXPERIENCES WITH GOD.

Detailed Suggestions:
1. Because of the nature of your gift you can expect an unusual sensitivity to God in everyday circumstances.
2. Your sharing of your everyday experiences will be used by God to meet others facing similar situations though you many not even be aware of their situation. Your sharing may involve critical timing for them.
3. Share in a God-centered way rather than an experience-centered way or a self-exalting way.

Explanation.
There is nothing that beats gaining experience in ministry situations. In order to get the most out of every situation, you need to get some honest feedback and do some honest evaluating of your exhortation efforts. Maintain a learning posture.

8. Self-analysis of Your Exhortation Gift (working on the weak side)

RECOGNIZE THAT THERE WILL BE GROWTH IN YOUR EXHORTATION GIFT OVER TIME.

Explanation.
As you begin to gain experience in ministry, you will probably notice that you tend to exhort others in primarily one of the three types of exhortation (either admonishment, encouragement or comfort). Most people with exhortation gifts either begin with a strong admonition bent or a comfort bent. The admonition types are usually confrontive. The comfort types are those who seek peace. Over time God will move you toward picking up some of the other thrusts. For example, those people that start out dominant in admonishing and correction will usually mellow somewhat in their abrasive nature (via shaping processes of God) and move toward the encouragement thrust of exhortation. Those with the comfort thrust will become more active in moving the people to action. They move toward the encourage thrust also. So a good general rule is to set up some growth projects which will focus you on developing exhortation skills in your weaker areas.

TABLE OF PASSAGES: FOCUS ON APPLICATION OF TRUTH TO LIFE

introduction   For each passage be alert for truth for your current situation.

Books or Passages	As You Read or Study You Should Focus on:
Proverbs	• practical advice for all kinds of daily living, • verses telling how to give advice.
parables and Jesus' other discourses	• various central truths taught by each parable, most of these are fundamental principles of Christianity, • Jesus' method in applying truth to situations, • the thrust of Jesus' exhortation: whether admonition, encouragement, or comfort.
Romans 12-16	• principles of interrelationships between Christians, • principles concerning disputed practices,[6] • principles concerning government.
1 Corinthians	• The entire book illustrates Paul's approach to various problems. Note principles for applying truth to problems.
Galatians 1:6-10; 2:1-21 3:1-5; 5:13-6:10	• intensity needed when correcting serious problems • importance of taking a stand if essential truth is involved, • fervor in admonishing and example of admonishing.
Ephesians 4:1-6:23	• examples of exhortive teaching.
Philippians	• how to share from your present experience to meet the needs of others, • exhortations to unity,
Colossians 3,4	• examples of admonitions.
Hebrews 2:1-4; 3:7-4:13; 5:11-6:20; 10:26-39; 12; 13	• examples of admonition, the book contains cycles of truth followed by warnings—note especially the corrective aspect in the warnings, • the importance of prefacing admonition by teaching.
James	• practical use of Scripture to life situations, • use and misuse of tongue, • description of practical wisdom and principles for applying it, • truth for current situation.

---

[6] See the booklet by Dr. J. Robert Clinton, **Disputed Practices—Guidelines for Christian Liberty**, which deals with Romans 14 and 1 Corinthians 8-10 and gives applications for this important subject. This booklet also treats the whole concept of assessing principles of truth. Available through Barnabas Publishers.

How To Develop The Gift Of Prophecy

introduction   Remember that the prophecy gift is one of the Word Cluster gifts as well as a power cluster gift which authenticates the reality of God today. Notice the two aims it seeks to fulfill.

Word gifts clarify the nature of this unseen God and what He expects from His followers. People using these gifts both communicate about God and for God and *Power gifts* demonstrate the authenticity, credibility, power and reality of the unseen God.

Prophecy will bring God's present revelation to bear in a corrective way as well as give indications of future work of God. And when God reveals something in an authoritative way it will lend authenticity to His reality and existence.

Before you work through the ideas for development, refresh yourself with the definition of the prophecy gift. Keep it in mind as you ponder the developmental suggestions.

prophecy A person operating with *the gift of prophecy* has the capacity to deliver truth (in a public way) either of a predictive nature or as a situational word from God in order to correct by exhorting, edifying or consoling believers and to convince non-believers of God's truth.

CENTRAL THRUST - TO PROVIDE CORRECTION OR PERSPECTIVE ON A SITUATION

Here are some areas to work in to develop in this gift.

6 Major Guidelines

1. Bible Study
There are many kinds of projects that could be worked on as it relates to gaining Bible knowledge. For people who have a prophetic gift, there should always be an emphasis on this area. The gift of prophecy is one of the foundational word gifts and demands that the person be immersed in the Word of God at a deep level throughout life. Every year new projects should be tackled. Here are some places to start (note these first several suggestions apply generally to all foundational word gifts):
- learning tools and principles to use when interpreting the Scriptures,
- gaining an overall understanding of each book in the Bible. There are numerous books that present overviews of each book of the Bible that are helpful in this regard.
- learning to study each book for theme and structure,
- looking at each book and seeing what it contributes to a particular theme (the person of God, leadership, justice, healing, etc.),
- studying a book of the Bible comprehensively,
- learning to interpret types of literature in the Bible (parables, figures and idioms, Hebrew poetry, etc.),
- focus your study specifically on the predictive passages or the books that deal with the operation of this gift. For example, 1 and 2 Kings provide historical background on the Biblical prophets as they emerged, the 17 prophetical books are important, the Gospels (specifically Jesus as a prophetic voice), Romans 9-11, 1 and 2 Thessalonians, 1 Timothy 4:1-10, 2 Timothy 3:10-17, 2 Peter, Jude and Revelation.

How To Develop The Gift Of Prophecy continued

2. Study Other Books on the Gift of Prophecy

There are numerous books that are written about the operation of this gift during Biblical times and the gift of prophecy today. See the annotated bibliography at the end of the manual for a few references. Gather every available piece of information from magazines, etc. There are several *prophetic* ministries that publish newsletters. Also, there are numerous teaching tape series on prophecy. Study everything that you can get your hands on.

3. Observing Others and Getting Mentoring

I would highly encourage you to get around people who operate in the gift of prophecy and observe them. If you can, build relationship with them and get them to mentor you. There are numerous ways of expressing this gift and there are many *prophetic* models out there. Expose yourself to as many as possible.

4. Keeping A Journal

Because the gift of prophecy involves getting and releasing revelation from God concerning situations, it is extremely important to keep accurate records of both the receiving and giving of revelation. This record keeping allows you to be accurate in your evaluating and provides a place for reflection. We would suggest keeping a running journal which tracks *prophetic* activity.

5. Communicational Skills

This is a crucial area of development in this gift. There are many mistakes and/or possible abuses of this gift. Learning to communicate sensitively, carefully and accurately with integrity are all skills to be learned.

6. Gaining Experience

Just as with any other gift, this gift is developable. You can get better at releasing this gift to the Body. Experience is a great teacher. Because of the potentially *dangerous* use of this gift, it is important to structure accountability into your ministry situation.

How To Develop The Gift Of Apostleship

introduction   Remember that the apostleship gift is one of the Word Cluster gifts.

Word gifts clarify the nature of this unseen God and what He expects from His followers. People using these gifts both communicate about God and for God.

Apostleship operates with authority to clarify what God wants to do in situations needing ministry. It will usually work in conjunction with other word or power gifts. Power gifts particularly give authenticity and authority to the apostleship gift.

apostleship   The *gift of apostleship* refers to a special leadership capacity to move with authority from God to create new ministry structures (churches and para-church) to meet needs and to develop and appoint leadership in these structures.

CENTRAL THRUST - CREATING NEW MINISTRY

Here are some areas to work in to develop in this gift.

6 Major Guidelines

1. **Bible Study**
   You need to be an all around Bible student. You need to especially focus on the passages that deal with the working of this gift. For example, the pastoral epistles, the church epistles, leadership passages throughout the Bible, the book of Acts. You basically need to know the bounds within which you will operate in introducing new works, appointing leaders, and evaluating works for genuiness. You need to study every apostolic function such as Barnabas' evaluation of Christianity at Antioch, the Jerusalem council's evaluation of possible heresy, Titus' apostolic role in appointing leaders, training them, Timothy's role in correcting the problems in Ephesus, etc. Particularly focus on Paul's burden for churches and sensitivity to starting new works, establishing leadership, and problem solving. Study also Peter's *door opening mandate*.

2. **Study The Church And The Para-Church**
   You should have a clear understanding of the nature of the church along with its purposes, functions and growth processes. You should also have a clear understanding of the nature of the para-church along with its purposes, functions and growth processes. You should understand how the two relate. There are numerous books and materials on these subjects.

3. **Develop Leadership Skills[7]**
   - how to develop strategies,
   - how to plan and implement a plan,

---

[7] You probably would profit from some formal training in these leadership areas. The leadership concentration at the School of World Mission of Fuller Seminary deals with many of these leadership focuses. Some courses are taught in intensive one week or two week formats. Some materials available from Barnabas Publishers which deals with some of these areas include: **A Short History of Leadership History, Coming To Conclusions on Leadership Styles, Bridging Strategies—Leadership Perspectives for Introducing Change.** All authored by Dr. J. Robert Clinton.

- develop change agent skills,
- develop expertise in leadership styles,
- how to inspire and motivate followers,
- develop mentoring skills,
- develop organizational skills especially focusing on foundations,
- team building skills,
- learn to identify and develop emerging leaders.

4. Communicational Skills

Depending on the type of ministry situation that you are going into, you need to develop the appropriate communicational skills to your situation. Most important are motivational skills via communication.

5. Learn From Other Models

- Christian biographies are a great source of learning regarding apostolic personalities.
- Try to observe and study others who have founded new works.
- Try to establish mentoring relationships with other similarly gifted people.

6. Develop Intimacy With God

This gift needs a great deal of faith to operate effectively. Deep faith comes from deep relationship with God. This kind of relationship needs to be cultivated intentionally. There needs to be a special attention given to hearing the voice of God, obedience to that voice and the demonstration of power that comes with that. Spiritual authority ought to become the prime power base. Remember, spiritual authority is the right to influence conferred upon a leader by followers because of their perceived spirituality of that leader. It is delegated from God in its essence but is manifest in the leader via three elements: 1. experiential knowledge of God—His person, character, ways, purpose; 2. godliness in character—the effects of knowing God personally result in a character which is god-like; 3. gifted power—the leader operates in ministry with an aura and with manifest results of the supernatural upon the giftedness set (natural abilities, acquired skills, and spiritual gifts).

How To Develop The Gift Of Evangelism

introduction
Remember that the evangelism gift is one of the Word Cluster gifts, though not a foundational one.

Word gifts clarify the nature of this unseen God and what He expects from His followers. People using these gifts both communicate about God and for God.

Evangelism operates especially to clarify what God wants in terms of relationship with Him.

evangelism
The *gift of evangelism* in general refers to the capacity to challenge people through various communicative methods (persuasion) to receive the Gospel of salvation in Christ so as to see them respond by taking initial steps in Christian discipleship. CENTRAL THRUST - INTRODUCING OTHERS TO THE GOSPEL.

Here are some areas to work in to develop in this gift.

7 Major Guidelines

1. Bible Study
You need to be an overall student of the Bible. You should especially study the passages which relate to the doctrine and process of salvation. There are key verses which should be memorized and the story of Jesus and salvation should be second nature. A particularly important topic is the study of people coming to Christ in the book of Acts. What did they have to believe? What did they have to do? How were power gifts used in conjunction with evangelism? How were love gifts used in conjunction with evangelism? What other word gifts were seen operating with the evangelism gifts?

2. Develop Sensitivity To Peoples Needs
Any type of relationship training that helps you become sensitive to peoples needs is helpful. Most people today think of evangelism in terms of confrontive, that is, presentations that call for a decision or commitment. In contrast to that, there is a growing movement toward friendship evangelism. That is, relating to people over the long haul, demonstrating God's love, care, and concern for them as well as witnessing to the truth of their need for salvation. Training in friendship evangelism is especially important for people having this gift, who do not operate in the public realm with it.

3. Communicational Skills
Recognize that people *hear* and respond differently. Gain skills in various methods and means of communicating the Gospel. Be receptor oriented in your communication planning but Spirit sensitive as you communicate.

4. Relational Skills
Gain skills in relating to a wide diversity of people. Learning to identify and develop emerging leaders in the area of evangelism. Learn as much about personality types, various approaches to learning, and how different types of people respond differently as you can.

HOW TO DEVELOP THE GIFT OF EVANGELISM continued

5. Study Other Approaches

Survey various evangelistic approaches. Discern strengths and weaknesses. Learn as much as you can.

6. Get Mentoring.

Develop relationships with people who have this gift and are operating more effectively than you. Get them to take you with them. Learn all that you can. Get historical mentoring. Read about men and women who have been successful evangelists. Be challenged by them. Get insights from their ministry.

7. Gain Experience

Pray for God to open opportunities for you. Be sensitive to the leading and prompting of the Holy Spirit. Try, try, try. Do feedback and evaluation from time to time and learn from your mistakes and your successes.

How To Develop The Gift Of Pastor

introduction   Remember that the pastoral gift is one of the Word Cluster gifts, a superstructural one. It functions also in the love gift cluster.

Word gifts clarify the nature of this unseen God and what He expects from His followers. People using these gifts both communicate about God and for God.

Love gifts are manifestations through practical ways of God's love that can be recognized by a world around us which needs love. They demonstrate the reality of relating to this God.

Pastoring is a gift which demonstrate God's loving care for people. It functions also as a Word Cluster gift since so much of what it means to protect and care for a group of people is tied up in the Word.

pastor   The *pastoral gift* is the capacity to exercise concern and care for members of a group so as to encourage them in their growth in Christ which involves modeling maturity, protecting them from error and disseminating truth.

CENTRAL THRUST - CARING FOR THE GROWTH OF FOLLOWERS.

Here are some areas to work in to develop in this gift.

6 Major Guidelines

1. Bible Study
   You need to be an overall student of the Bible. If teaching the Bible is part of your role, you need to study the Bible in-depth. Studying the leadership passages in Scripture should be a priority; especially study the texts related to servant leadership and stewardship. These were mentioned in chapter 2. Also, the pastoral epistles, church epistles and the book of Acts should be focused on. Focus particularly on passages which help you understand the process of growth in the life of a believer. You want to have a strong overall understanding of how people move toward maturity in their faith and life.

2. Develop A Clear Philosophy Concerning Church
   If you have the role of pastor as well as the gift, you need to develop a clear understanding of the church, its nature, purpose, function and growth processes. You need to begin articulating ministry values as it relates to the church.

3. Expose Yourself To Many Different Models Of Church
   One of the most helpful things that you can do to understand your own values and philosophy concerning church is to observe a lot of other models of the local church. As you learn and evaluate the other models, key values and insights will come into view. Don't just examine models within your theological framework, examine models of other persuasions as well.

4. Get Mentoring

There are a lot of people who operate in the gift of pastoring in a variety of ways. Some have the official role of pastor in a church but others do not. It is helpful to get perspective from others about how to pastor people effectively. Accountability and honest feedback are two critical elements to get established in these mentoring relationships. They will help you evaluate your growth in the gift of pastoring and will provide encouragement along the way. Most small groups, no matter, what the function they are set up for, will need pastoring. These will be unofficial roles that people with the pastoral gift will immediately be drawn to.

5. Develop Leadership Skills

Take special courses or training which relates to any aspect of pastoring. Especially focus on training which deals with conflict resolution, problem-solving, relationship building, change agent skills, vision-casting, team building, learning to identify and develop emerging leaders, etc.

6. Gain Experience

Once again, experience is a great teacher. Start caring for people. Get involved in small groups. Help nurture the people that God gives you to influence. Be attentive to learning from your experience.

How To Develop The Gift Of Ruling

introduction   Remember that the ruling gift is one of the Word Cluster gifts, but only a tangential one.

Word gifts clarify the nature of this unseen God and what He expects from His followers. People using these gifts both communicate about God and for God.

Ruling is a gift which demonstrate God's concern for the welfare of the church as a whole. A ruling gift helps communicate how God wants to organize the local church to accomplish His purposes.

ruling   A person operating with *a ruling gift* demonstrates the capacity to exercise influence over a group so as to lead it toward a goal or purpose with a particular emphasis on the capacity to make decisions and keep the group operating together.

<u>**CENTRAL THRUST**</u> **- INFLUENCING OTHERS TOWARD VISION.**

Here are some areas to work in to develop in this gift.

5 Major Guidelines

1. Bible Study
You need to have a general knowledge of the Bible. There are a number of leadership passages that are important. Look at the organizational passages concerning the worship of Israel, the organization of Israel through Moses, etc. Look at key leaders in the Bible and learn leadership lessons from their lives (Moses, David, Nehemiah, Daniel, Joseph, Paul).

2. Leadership Skills
You will have to understand how to apply leadership principles at a local church level.
Here are some of the things you can do to gain expertise in leadership issues:

- how to develop strategies,
- develop change agent skills,
- how to inspire and motivate followers,
- develop mentoring skills,
- team building skills,
- learning to identify and develop emerging leaders.

How To Develop The Gift Of Ruling

3. Organizational Skills
You will especially need to hold things together in terms of structural needs. Here are some of the things you can do to tighten up the local church organizationally:

- running meetings efficiently,
- setting up a committee,
- designing job descriptions and responsibilities,
- planning and implementing plans,
- crisis handling.

4. Communicational Skills
People will not automatically buy your ideas about organizing the local church. You will need to learn how to communicate in such a way as to motivate people and implement your ideas. Here are some topic that can aid you in this:

• communicating objectives, goals, and plans clearly,
• writing skills.

5. Relational Abilities
You will need to relate to leaders over you, peer leaders, and supportive leadership under you. Relational skills are imperative. Here are some:

- conflict resolution,
- learning how to skillfully negotiate,
- learning sensitivity as it relates to motivation,
- learning how to encourage and build up personnel.

How To Develop The Gift Of Word Of Wisdom

introduction | Remember that the word of wisdom gift is a power cluster gift which authenticates the reality of God today. It is also a remote Word Cluster gift. Notice the two aims it seeks to fulfill.

Word gifts clarify the nature of this unseen God and what He expects from His followers. People using these gifts both communicate about God and for God and *Power gifts* demonstrate the authenticity, credibility, power and reality of the unseen God.

A solution from God to a situation, which receives authentication from those receiving it does much to cause people to believe in the concern of God for their situations and to believe in His reality.

Before you work through the ideas for development, refresh yourself with the definition of the Word of Wisdom gift. Keep it in mind as you ponder the developmental suggestions.

word of wisdom | The *word of wisdom* gift refers to the capacity to know the mind of the Spirit in a given situation and to communicate clearly the situation, facts, truth or application of the facts and truth to meet the need of the situation.

<u>CENTRAL THRUST</u> - APPLYING REVELATORY INFORMATION

Here are some areas to work in to develop in this gift.

5 Major Guidelines

1. **Bible Study**
   You need to develop an overall mastery of Biblical truth. Wisdom usually increases with experience and maturity. This is especially true of a person who has been spending time in the Word on a consistent basis. Your devotional life and interaction with the Word at this level is important. The book of Psalms, Proverbs and James are important books for someone operating in this gift. The truth of the James 1:5,6 passage should be an ongoing practice for one using this gift. The James 3:15-17 should describe the tenor of the word of wisdom.

2. **Work On Your Weak Side In Using This Gift.**
   Remember a person using the gift of word of wisdom usually operates along the continuum given below. Most likely you will do so toward one side or the other more often than the other. The other side is called the weak side.

   Word of Wisdom   Wisdom
   |————————————————————————————————————|
   situational word   accumulated wisdom
   a sovereign word   comes from experience

   Figure out where you operate most often. Intentionally work on the other end of the continuum.

To work on the wisdom side, do a special study of Proverbs, which applies truth to life and sets the pattern or applied spiritual common sense. Study James and not his emphasis of applying truth to everyday actions, dependence upon God for the wisdom to do this, and the description of wisdom and qualities of one how has it. To work on the Word of Wisdom side, be alert in small group discussions and individual conversations to the promptings by the Holy Spirit in which he will call your attention to situation or problems for which He will give you clear solutions. Sometimes the solutions may come from past ideas that are modified. But sometimes they will be entirely new. In either case, there will be a sense of an idea or series of ideas that come. You should take advantage of ejaculatory praying in the midst of talking to others *a la Nehemiah* (Nehemiah 2:4). Expect God to give on-the-spot answers. Sometimes in the midst of a problem you will see as if by intuition the way to untangle the situation. Expect this to happen. It is likely that the gift of wisdom, will be coupled with a leadership gift in order that decision-making in the church will be influenced by this gift.

3. Get Mentoring.
Find someone who operates in this gift effectively. Get them to mentor you and observe how they operate in ministry situations. Ask them how they got the word of wisdom, how they knew to give it, etc.

4. Develop Some Spiritual Disciplines.
Silence, solitude, prayer (especially intercession), and meditation are all important disciplines for someone who wants to operate in this gift. Learning to hear from God are all critical elements of these disciplines. Because this gift does require a developed inner life with God and a quiet mystical sense of God's moment-by-moment presence in direction of one's actions and thoughts, you will have to be particularly careful of guarding your devotional life. Learn to spend much time in prayer with God. Specifically focus on books like Psalms and Proverbs in your devotional life. The gift, word of wisdom, becomes increasingly effective with maturity in your Christian life as you build up the wisdom side of the continuum. Therefore, you should spend frequent times of evaluating your life with God to make sure no barriers are hindering your spiritual growth.

5. Gain Ministry Experience.
Be ready in every situation for God to use this gift. Be sensitive to the prompting of the Holy Spirit.

How To Develop The Gift Of Word Of Knowledge

introduction

Remember that the word of knowledge gift is a power cluster gift which authenticates the reality of God today. It is also a remote Word Cluster gift. Notice the two aims it seeks to fulfill.

Word gifts clarify the nature of this unseen God and what He expects from His followers. People using these gifts both communicate about God and for God and *Power gifts* demonstrate the authenticity, credibility, power and reality of the unseen God.

Word of knowledge is more spectacular say than the word of wisdom gift, especially when the revelation involves something that can only be known by God and some individual. As the revelation is authenticated by the person who knows it to be true there is a tremendous sense of the reality of God. He does care. He does exist. He has shown Himself to us again. In addition to authentication of God's reality, this gift has great potential for evangelism, if you use it with unbelievers. It also has a strong place in the love cluster when you use it in conjunction with healing.

Before you work through the ideas for development, refresh yourself with the definition of the Word of Knowledge gift. Keep it in mind as you ponder the developmental suggestions.

word of knowledge

The *word of knowledge* gift refers to the capacity or sensitivity of a person to supernaturally perceive revealed knowledge from God which otherwise could not or would not be known and apply it to a situation.

<u>CENTRAL THRUST</u> - GETTING REVELATORY INFORMATION

Here are some areas to work in to develop in this gift.

5 Major Guidelines

1. Bible Study

You need to be aware of the general content of Scripture. This can be done at a devotional level. The guidelines of the Scriptures are important in helping set boundaries for this gift. There is one area of study that would be worth focusing on. Study any passage where this gift is possibly operating (Acts 5:3ff; 16:28; 18:9; 20:25,29,30; 21:10; 27:22-26). Begin with these but also identify any other possible incidents as well.

2. Work On Your Weak Side In Using This Gift.

Remember a person using the gift of word of knowledge usually operates along the continuum given below. Most likely you will do so toward one side or the other more often than the other. The other side is called the weak side.

Word of Knowledge   Knowledge
|———————————————————————————————————|
situational word   accumulated knowledge
a sovereign word   comes from what you've learned

Figure out which side you tend to operate on most frequently and work to develop skill in the other side. For example, if you operate in the word of knowledge side, you might want to set up some study projects that will give you understanding and perspective on various ministry situations. If you operate on the knowledge side, you may want to learn to hear God speak in situations and open to learning how to hear His voice in that way.

3. Get Mentoring.

People get words of knowledge in all sorts of ways. People have reported getting words from God by seeing newspaper headlines in their mind's eye, hearing an audible-like inner voice, seeing pictures in the minds-eye, or on occasion in healing situations actually feel someone else's symptoms or pain. There are other ways that people get words of knowledge. Investigate, observe, ask questions and learn everything you can from people who operate in this gift. Watch them in ministry.

4. Gain Experience.

Experience is a good teacher. Open yourself to being used by God and allow Him to speak to you and through you in situations. Track your progress by writing up what you are learning in some sort of journal. Be willing to try as you sense promptings. You will become more sensitive to those which are truly words of knowledge.

5. Develop Some Spiritual Disciplines.

Silence, solitude, prayer (especially intercession), and meditation are all important disciplines for someone who wants to operate in this gift. Learning to hear from God are all critical elements of these disciplines.

How To Develop The Gift Of Faith

introduction
Remember that the gift of faith is a power cluster gift which authenticates the reality of God today. It is also a remote Word Cluster gift. Notice the two aims it seeks to fulfill.

Word gifts clarify the nature of this unseen God and what He expects from His followers. People using these gifts both communicate about God and for God and *Power gifts* demonstrate the authenticity, credibility, power and reality of the unseen God.

The faith gift acts in the word cluster when the revelation concerns information about a situation or prophecy about the future or some other challenge by God. But it is usually not so much the content of the word that is important, it is the challenge to trust God in it that is important. But when God reveals something, a person with the gift of faith believes it, and by faith sees it come to pass there is tremendous recognition of the reality of God. There is nothing like having God reveal something and believing it in to existence as He said.

Before you work through the ideas for development, refresh yourself with the definition of the faith gift. Keep it in mind as you ponder the developmental suggestions.

faith
The *gift of faith* refers to the unusual capacity of a person to recognize in a given situation that God intends to do something and to trust God for it until He brings it to pass.

CENTRAL THRUST - A TRUSTING RESPONSE TO A CHALLENGE FROM GOD.

Here are some areas to work in to develop in this gift.

6 Major Guidelines

1. Bible Study
You need to increase your general knowledge of the Great Miracle Working Faithful God. You need to focus on the concept of faith as it is mentioned throughout the Bible. Focus especially on the books that contain historical narrative. Learn all the great stories of the Bible. There are several books in particular which inspire faith: Joshua, Habakkuk, Daniel, and John. Beyond this there are several passages which are note-worthy: Numbers 13,14; Deuteronomy. 1; 2 Kings 6:8-7:20; 1 Chronicles 4:9,10; Luke 11:1-13, 18:1-8; Romans 4; Hebrews 11. Do a special study on the promises of God in the Bible. Do a special study on the person of God in the Bible (the object of our faith). And remember the main emphasis is on

TRUSTING **GOD**,

not **T**RUSTING GOD.

How To Develop The Gift Of Faith continued

2. **Christian Biographies.**
   One of the great sources of inspiration and lessons on God's faithfulness comes from reading stories about God's faithfulness over an entire lifetime. Reading biographies is a way of consciously
   stirring up faith. George Muller's biography should be read by all who have this gift. J. Hudson
   Taylor's biography is also a must. Henrietta Mears is worthy of study in this regard too.

3. **Developing Spiritual Disciplines.**
   An spiritual discipline which promotes intimacy with God is worth developing. Learning to hear
   clearly from God is one of the keys to developing faith. The disciplines that are related to prayer
   are central.

4. **Keeping A Record Of God's Faithfulness.**
   Keep a record of God's answers to prayer. Don't forget the *Stones of Remembrances* of Joshua. You
   need your own *Stones of Faith* to remember. This collection of answered prayers will go a long way
   to stir faith and help maintain faith in difficult times. From time-to-time go back and review the
   major faith happenings that were completed. Just seeing them afresh will increase your level of
   faith again.

5. **Develop Mentoring Relationships.**
   Develop relationships with like minded people who can pray with you, encourage you, hold you
   accountable.

6. **Ponder These Things In Your Heart.**
   Like Mary, you will find that a lot of your ministry will be inward and alone with God. Many of
   your acts of faith, which represent your exercise of this gift may never be known by others. This is
   an unsung gift by those down here. But not in heaven. God will someday honor you for your
   faithfulness in this gift.

How To Develop Gifts Of Healings

introduction

Remember that gifts of healings is a power cluster gift which authenticates the reality of God today. It also operates as a love cluster gift in that it openly demonstrates the mercy of God to those being healed.

Power gifts demonstrate the authenticity, credibility, power and reality of the unseen God. *Love gifts* are manifestations through practical ways of God's love that can be recognized by a world around us which needs love. They demonstrate the reality of relating to this God.

This gift is probably the most spectacular of the power gifts. And it is probably the most abused. Exercised properly it both demonstrates God's love and His power. When God heals there is such a sense of His reality and His care. Remember there are gifts (most likely varied forms—like inner and physical) of healings (different degrees of healings, most likely). Inner healing as well as physical healing are both needed in our world today. God uses this gift to reach out to that world.

Before you work through the ideas for development, refresh yourself with the definition of gifts of healings. Keep it in mind as you ponder the developmental suggestions.

gifts of
healings

The *gifts of healings* refers to the supernatural releasing of healing power for curing all types of illnesses.

<u>CENTRAL THRUST</u> - RELEASING GOD'S POWER TO HEAL.

Here are some areas to work in to develop in this gift.

6 Major Guidelines

1. Bible Study

You want to immerse yourself in every incident of healing recorded in the Bible. There is much to be learned from these stories. In particular, study the issue of faith. Study especially the passages in the Gospels that deal with the conception of the power of the Lord being present for healing. Evidently one can discern when this condition is present. Developing sensitivity to this will increase the level of faith.

2. Study What Others Have Written.

There is a wide variety of books written in this area. Pick up a wide selection of them. Look at various viewpoints regarding the theology and practice of this gift. Build a foundation of knowledge that will allow you to operate with confidence before God. Read broadly in the inner healing literature. Read also about inner healing via an acquired skills framework of counseling.

How To Develop Gifts Of Healings continued

3. Observe The Gift In Others.
There are many healing approaches and models. We would encourage you to observe as many different ones as possible. Get around people who are praying for the sick. Learn everything that you can. Explore and investigate.

4. Get Mentoring.
Find someone who operates in this gift and develop a mentoring relationship. Go to ministry situations and learn from their example.

5. Practice Spiritual Disciplines.
Any discipline that helps you focus in on what God is doing will help. Learning to see or discern what God is doing in a situation is key to operating in effectiveness. Also, faith is so crucial to the release of this gift. Any discipline that inspires, encourages or increases faith is very helpful.

6. Get Experience.
Pray for as many sick people as you can. Learn from each experience. Keep notes and reflect on what you are learning in each situation. Try to join a ministry team and travel to a campaign with a noted healer.

How To Develop Workings Of Powers

introduction   Remember that workings of healings is a power cluster gift and that, *power gifts* demonstrate the authenticity, credibility, power and reality of the unseen God.

This gift is probably most commonly seen in two different forms: 1. power encounters in which there is need for the living God to vindicate Himself against evil powers represented in many forms: governments, religion, and even societal structures; 2. in connection with exorcism or power encounters with demons. Like gifts of healings this is one of the more spectacular of the power gifts. It frequently accompanies apostolic work to break open a ministry. The God of Elijah still demonstrates His reality through those who exercise this gift.

Before you work through the ideas for development, refresh yourself with the definition of workings of powers. Keep it in mind as you ponder the developmental suggestions.

workings   The workings of powers, gift of miracles, refers to the releasing of God's supernatural
of powers   power so that the miraculous intervention of God is perceived and God receives recognition for the supernatural intervention.

<u>CENTRAL THRUST</u> - THE RELEASING OF GOD'S POWER
TO GIVE AUTHENTICITY.

4 Major Guidelines

1. Bible Study.
You want to immerse yourself in every incident of a miracle that is recorded in the Bible. There is much to be learned from these stories. In particular, study the issue of faith. Study the end result of these demonstrations of God. Study the person through whom it came. Study its connection to spiritual authority.

2. Study Any Materials That You Can Find On This Topic.
Especially read stories about miracles and how God has met needs in unusual ways. Christian biographies are a great source in this regard.

3. Interview And Talk To People Who Have Experienced A Miracle.
Go to places where people believe in the miraculous and find out who has experienced a miracle. Listen to the stories. Learn. Let your faith be raised.

4. Casualties.
Be aware that a number of people who use this gift, especially against the spirit world often become casualties. In the end those spirit beings they overcome them. One thing you should do if you are involved in an on-going ministry working of powers, especially in terms of exorcism, is to have a solid core of prayers behind you. You should also seek the gift, discernings of spirits, or team up with someone who has it.

Explanation:
All of the things mentioned above serve to do one thing. Build your faith which in turn raises your expectations. In this context, God does miracles. Can you develop the gift of miracles? We don't think you can make a miracle happen but we do know that you can definitely stop God from releasing a miracle through unbelief and doubt.

How To Develop The Gift Of Discernings Of Spirits

introduction   Remember that discernings of spirits is a power cluster gift and, *power gifts* demonstrate the authenticity, credibility, power and reality of the unseen God.

This gift is an important gift that works in an ancillary fashion with several other gifts. It is used in conjunction with prophecy to determine its accuracy or at least the source behind it. It is used in conjunction with tongues and interpretation of tongues to check validity. It is used with teaching to determine source behind it. It is used when dealing with the spirit world either in inner healing or via workings of powers.

Before you work through the ideas for development, refresh yourself with the definition of discernings of spirits. Keep it in mind as you ponder the developmental suggestions.

discernings   The *discernings of spirits gift* refers to the ability given by God to perceive issues in
of spirits   terms of spiritual truth and to know the fundamental source of the issues and to give judgment concerning those issues; this includes the recognition of the spiritual forces operating in the issue.

CENTRAL THRUST - A SENSITIVITY TO TRUTH AND ITS SOURCE.

Here are some areas to work in to develop in this gift.

7 Major Guidelines

1. Bible Study.
Develop an overall mastery of the Scriptures. You need to develop a knowledge of the Scriptures at an in-depth level. The Biblical knowledge serves as a backdrop for the operation of this gift. Also, focus on any passage where there is mention of evil spirits operating.

2. Developing The Weaker Side.
Remember a person using the discernings of spirits gift usually operates along the continuum given below. Most likely you will do so toward one side or the other more often than the other. The other side is called the weak side.

Discernings of spirits   Discernment
|———|
Holy Spirit revealed   Based on accumulated
knowledge and experience

Determine which side is you tend to operate on and work to develop the other side.

3. Develop Analytical Skills.
Work to learn skills which will allow you to break things down and look at the individual parts as well as the whole. Having the right kind of questioning spirit is very important. The following types of questions are important:

- what is God doing or saying here?
- what assumptions are being made?
- is this based on sound Biblical foundations?

4. Develop Spiritual Disciplines.
Any of the spiritual disciplines which help you quiet your own voice and center in on what the Holy Spirit is saying is important. In this context, it is important to learn to distinguish between God's voice, your own voice, and the enemies' voice.

5. Use Available Research.
Study materials written by practitioners in the area of dealing in spiritual warfare and/or healing of the demonized. There are an increasing number of books being written in this area. Some are more helpful than others. Recognize that it is not possible to be dogmatic about dealing with spirits and spiritual power. Everyone writes from their own experience. Remember this while you are studying.

6. Get Mentoring.
This is crucial to developing maturity in this gift. It is in the context of interaction with others, accountability and feedback that growth can occur in this gift. Many, many problems occur in the development and practice of this gift occur because there is not any objective feedback or accountability.

7. Gain Experience.
Recognize that this gift is needed to bring checks and balances to a number of other gifts (e.g. 1 Thessalonians 5:20,21; 1 John 4:1-3). Try to put yourself in situations where you can work in an ancillary fashion with: prophecy to determine its accuracy or at least the source behind it, tongues and interpretation of tongues to check validity; teaching to determine source behind it; ministries of inner healing or workings of powers. Not all that we see is of God. This gift is desperately needed to authenticate what is and what isn't of God.

How To Develop The Gift Of Tongues and
          The Gift Of Interpretation Of Tongues

introduction   Remember, tongues and interpretation of tongues are power gifts and, *power gifts* dem-
                onstrate the authenticity, credibility, power and reality of the unseen God.

                Tongues particularly has been a controversial gift because of the abuse which identi-
                fies the gift with a superior form of Christianity. When used in its public form, and
                properly interpreted, it can come in the form of prophecy, knowledge, or teaching and
                can encourage and edify the body. Tongues when used privately, praying or singing, it
                can be a source of peace and confidence and will often pave the way for God's speak-
                ing or acting.

tongues   The *gift of tongues* refers to a spontaneous utterance of a word from God in unknown
                words (to the individual giving the word) to a group of people.

                <u>CENTRAL THRUST</u> - SPEAKING A MESSAGE IN AN UNKNOWN TONGUE.

interpretation The *gift of interpretation of tongues* refers to the ability to spontaneously respond
  of tongues   to a giving of an authoritative message in tongues by interpreting this word and clearly
                communicating the message given.

                <u>CENTRAL THRUST</u> - INTERPRETING A MESSAGE GIVEN IN TONGUES.

                                    5 Major Guidelines

1. Bible Study.
Study the 1 Corinthians passages, chapters 12-14, concerning this area of gifting in detail. Come
up with a clear Biblical understanding of these gifts.

2. Expose Yourself To Other Literature Concerning These Gifts.
Learn about the different *kinds of tongues*. Learn about the different viewpoints regarding these
gifts. Cover this from as many different viewpoints as possible. Don't just read the material that is
written by *your group*. Why have these gifts been so controversial? What are the issues?

3. Explore The Practice Of These Gifts.
Go visit as many different places where these gifts are practiced and observe them in action. Ask
questions of the leaders overseeing the meeting. Ask individuals who are operating in these gifts.
Explore and investigate. There are many different approaches and models that are used. How do
they work? Why? How do you know when to release it or not? How do you recognize an interpretation?

4. Be Open To God Using You In This Way.
Learn to be obedient. Get feedback after each ministry situation where you release one of these
gifts.

5. Validity.
From time-to-time ask a person operating in discernings of spirits to check up on your use of
tongues for validity.

How To Develop Gifts Of Governments

introduction   Remember that gifts of governments is a love cluster gift.

Love gifts are manifestations through practical ways of God's love that can be recognized by a world around us which needs love. They demonstrate the reality of relating to this God.

One or more persons with Gifts of governments often provide the glue that holds the whole thing together. It is the unselfish loving spirit with which they serve that is remembered even more than the service which helps the local church as a whole operate more smoothly.

gifts of   The *gifts of governments* involves a capacity to manage details of service functions
governments   so as to support and free other leaders to prioritize their efforts.

CENTRAL THRUST - SUPPORTIVE ORGANIZATIONAL ABILITIES.

6 Major Guidelines

1. Bible Study.
Study the passages that deal with servanthood and serving. Work on developing a godly inner character. Work on purifying your motives and serving cheerfully.

2. Leadership Skills.
Frequently, you will be working alongside a pastor or a person with ruling gifts and you will need to supplement needed leadership expertise such as:
- how to develop strategies
- develop change agent skills
- how to inspire and motivate followers
- develop mentoring skills
- team building skills
- learning to identify and develop emerging leaders

3. Organizational Skills.
More usually these are things that you will have to be good at and repeatedly do:
- running meetings efficiently
- setting up a committee
- designing job descriptions and responsibilities
- planning and implementing plans
- crisis handling

4. Communicational Skills.
- communicating objectives, goals, and plans clearly
- writing skills

5. Relational Abilities
- conflict resolution
- learning how to skillfully negotiate
- learning sensitivity as it relates to motivation
- learning how to encourage and build up personnel

6. Get Experience.

How To Develop The Gift Of Giving

introduction   It is easy to remember that the gift of giving is a love cluster gift. Like Paul in writing to the Philippians, if you have ever been on the beneficial side of this gift, you know it is a love gift.

Love gifts are manifestations through practical ways of God's love that can be recognized by a world around us which needs love. They demonstrate the reality of relating to this God.

One or more persons with this gift can work wonders both in supplying resources and in modeling for others in the body. Recognizing that God is the source and owns all, makes all the difference in having a liberal giving spirit. Developing sensitivity to hear God direct the giving is the key to effective use of this gift.

giving   The *gift of giving* refers to the capacity to give liberally to meet the needs of others and yet to do so with a purity of motive which senses that the giving is a simple sharing of what God has given to you.

CENTRAL THRUST - A SENSITIVITY TO GOD TO CHANNEL HIS RESOURCES TO OTHERS.

6 Major Guidelines

1. Bible Study.
Study the texts related to giving. For example, the parables of the Unjust Steward and the rich man and Lazarus; the book of Acts and instances of giving; 2 Corinthians 8,9; Philippians 4:10-19; 1 Timothy 6:3-10; James 5:1-6; the book of Malachi; the Old Testament passages dealing with the offerings.

2. Dedicate Yourself To God.
Use your natural abilities and acquired skills to maximum potential so that you have resources to give to others. Dedicate your business and personal finances in a special way. Determine early that your resources will make a significant contribution to Christianity.

3. Get Mentoring.
Get someone who can hold you accountable for your giving. Enter into partnerships with others who are like minded.

4. Work Hard On Inner Character.
Develop strong integrity, honesty, and obedience as lifestyle characteristics. Develop cheerfulness in giving and work on giving with pure motives. Sometimes after resources and power have accumulated a person will stray from those first convictions and promises to God. Guard your heart about your promises to God.

5. Develop Sensitivity To Special Needs.
Learn to be directed in your giving by God. He will use circumstances to prompt you. He will use inner promptings, restless feelings, and resonant feelings with some mission thrust to move you to give. Learn to hear His voice about giving.

6. Get Involved In Ministry.
Start giving as God directs you and learn to grow in faith and giving.

How To Develop The Gift Of Mercy

introduction   Those with this gift know what Jesus meant when he said in, Matthew. 9:13 "But go
                and learn what this means: `I desire mercy, not sacrifice.'"

                Love gifts are manifestations through practical ways of God's love that can be recog-
                nized by a world around us which needs love. They demonstrate the reality of relating
                to this God.

                A hurting world needs to know that God loves them. This gift probably more than any
                other demonstrates that love.

mercy   The *gift of mercy* refers to the capacity to both feel sympathy for those in need (espe-
                cially the suffering) and to manifest this sympathy in some practical helpful way with
                a cheerful spirit so as to encourage and help those in need.

                <u>CENTRAL THRUST</u> - THE EMPATHETIC CARE FOR THOSE WHO ARE HURTING.

                Here are some areas to work in to develop in this gift.

5 Major Guidelines

1. Bible Study.
   Gaining general knowledge about God's dealings with people is helpful. There are many stories
   where God's mercy is evident. Focus on the texts where God releases mercy. There are at least 67
   contexts in the Old Testament where mercy is mentioned. There are at least 54 contexts in the New
   Testament where mercy is mentioned. The 21 such contexts in the synoptic gospels are especially
   important. Study them all.

2. Imbibe The Atmosphere.
   Get around people and places where mercy centered ministry is going on. There are individuals,
   groups, churches or organizations which operate in mercy centered ministry. Catching the spirit
   of what is being done can help develop your own sense of compassion for those who are hurting.

3. Enter Into Mentoring Relationships.
   If you can find an individual who operates in this gift, try to establish a mentoring relationship
   with him/her. Especially try to be with them in ministry situations and observe how mercy is
   released. People with these gifts often work in communities which minister in the inner city.

4. Relational Skills.
   Develop skills that will allow you to be sensitive to people and to relate to people who are hurting.
   This will probably already be *natural* to you. But it is the sense of the various needs that you will
   grow in.

5. Gain Experience.
   Get involved and learn to release mercy. A good place to start is a small group which has a caring
   concern as one of its main agenda items. Internships or at least on-the-job training in communities focusing on people's needs would be a next step.

HOW TO DEVELOP THE GIFT OF HELPS

introduction

Unselfishly coming to the aid of a person in need demonstrates the love of God. Some people in the body are gifted both with the inner attitude and the abilities to help others in need. Such people demonstrate God's love over and over in their lifetimes.

Love gifts are manifestations through practical ways of God's love that can be recognized by a world around us which needs love. They demonstrate the reality of relating to this God.

People with ruling gifts and government gifts can do much to help other leadership gifts out. But still, much would be left undone in the body were it not for the supportive gifts of helps which keep things from falling through the cracks. And what's more these people help us understand about the love of God.

Review again, before reading the suggestions below the definition of this gift. Keep it in mind as you read.

gifts of
helps

The gifts of helps refers to the capacity to unselfishly meet the needs of others through very practical means.

**CENTRAL THRUST - THE ATTITUDE AND ABILITY TO AID
OTHERS IN PRACTICAL WAYS.**

Here are some areas to work in to develop in this gift.

4 MAJOR GUIDELINES

1. **Bible Study.**
   Study the passages that deal with servanthood and serving. In your devotional life, work on developing your inner character so that you help cheerfully, willingly recognizing that your help is a ministry that you are offering up to God. Work to develop purity in your motives. Memorize 1 Peter 4:11 and remember when you use your gift in this way you are glorifying God.

2. **Develop A Lifestyle That Is Oriented Around Helping Others.**
   Let people know that you want to help. Make your services available. Learn to be creative in ways that you help people.

3. **Sensitivity.**
   Ask God to give you a keen sensitivity to needs in the body which need help. Meet the ones you can. But develop links to others with helps gifts so that together many needs can be solved.

4. **Understand Your Strengths And Weakness.**
   How can you help? What kinds of things can you do? What kinds of things can't you do? Are there any skills that you could pick up that would aid you in this type of ministry?

5. **Gain Ministry Experience.**
   This is not a theoretical gift. It is seen in practice.

SUMMARY

In this chapter, we have addressed the issue of development. It is obvious that we are stronger in the areas of development that we are familiar with. Some gifts have many things that you can do to help you develop. Other gifts primarily develop in the context of doing them.

We are continuing to do research, especially getting information from people with different gifts on how they have developed. We intend to continue revising the information you see in this chapter.

Remember two things: giftedness development is a process that occurs over time and involvement in ministry situations is the key to developing giftedness.

CHAPTER 11:
DEVELOPMENT TOWARD WHAT?

INTRODUCTION

What should be the end result of studying and using this manual? Let me digress a bit first and then give an answer to that question, which is the thrust of this closing word.

As I (Bobby) write this chapter I have been reminded of two incidents from my past. My mind flash backed to one of the first times I ever heard anyone teach on gifts. It was in my home church in Ohio about 1966. A missionary, I don't even remember his name, presented Ephesians 4:7-16. He was talking about the importance of interdependence. He didn't use that word. It wasn't in fashion then. But that was what he meant. He said the body needs all its gifts working together. And then he did an illustration. And it is that illustration that comes to mind as I write this chapter. He limped across the platform. He says when there are people not using their gifts in the body the body limps along at half speed. I can see him limping along in my mind's eye today. My practical experience with many churches over these 27 years since that illustration has confirmed his word. Most of the churches have limped along because many did not use their gifts productively. And then many of the churches I have been associated with, as a whole body, have limped along because of imbalance in the three clusters of gifts—word, love, power. We need all of these clusters; not necessarily in equal parts. But all do something that is needed by a church which is to impact its environment. This manual was written to help leaders mend their churches so they can walk and maybe even run.

A second flashback took me back to this past summer. I was visiting with my friend Dr. Robertson McQuilkin in Columbia, S.C. He knew I had done a lot of work on spiritual gifts. So he posed this question. How do you account for the fact that so many powerfully gifted people have such shoddy character? How come God allows these people to have powerful gifts when their lives have such flaws? It is a question well worth pondering. There probably is no answer that really satisfies everyone. But as I have pondered that very thing over the years I realize that we are dealing with two basic issues and how they relate: one concerns the gifts of the Spirit; the other the fruit of the Spirit. Let me distinguish between these in a chart which is based on some material I read long ago in an article, "Plumbline, Gift and fruit Hand in Hand," from the **Prairie Overcomer**. I now do not remember all the ideas in the article and even if I adapted the chart (I usually do). But here is the chart as I use it now.

Table. Distinction Between Gifts and Fruit of the Spirit

Gifts of the Spirit	Fruit of the Spirit
1. Related primarily to the body of believers.	1. Related primarily to individual believers.
2. Related to Ministry.	2. Related to Character.
3. May be classified as to order of importance (somewhat).	3. All are essential.
4. May be abusively exercised and cause discord and division in the body	4. Can never be misused.
5. Usually no one believer receives all gifts.	5. Any believer may bear all fruit all anytime.
6. No gift can be demanded of all believes.	6. All should manifest the fruit of the Spirit.

Both gifts and fruit are indications in a life of the working of the Spirit. When we glance at the table just given we recognize the tremendous importance of the fruit of the Spirit. All believers are being shaped by God toward bearing that fruit. Now back to Dr. McQuilkin's question. I think the ideal is for a person to evince the fruit of the Spirit and exercise the gifts of the Spirit with great power. That is the ideal.

But like most ideals few meet them entirely. So I hold that ideal but I recognize discrepancies. My natural response to hearing of someone who exercises powerful gifts but shows real lack in some areas of the fruit of the Spirit is that I wish God would not empower those gifts in such a weak character. But when I examine that notion and take it to the logical conclusion I am left with the fact that according to my natural standard only a person who manifested all the fruit of the Spirit perfectly would be allowed to exercise gifts of the Spirit. And most likely that would cut out all of us from exercising our gifts.

I am thankful that God allows gifts to be used by imperfect vessels. I wish we were all perfectly manifesting the fruit of the Spirit and using great gifted power. I know that God may exercise powerful gifts through apparently undeserving leaders with character flaws for His own purposes. I have seen it. And I don't want to deny, can't deny that it was God's power. But I also know that God is attempting to shape that character and will not use that person forever. There will be a season of discipline and if proper response a shaping of character and continued usefulness. But if not a proper response then I know God will usually set aside such an unresponsive leader. And maybe even remove them permanently. I am thankful that I don't have to judge when or why. Only God can do that. Only God can know the total answer to Dr. McQuilkin's question but at least this is my attempt.

Now both of these flashbacks lead me to answer the question I posed at the start of the chapter. What should be the end result of studying and using this manual? And the answer flows from both of the flashbacks. Balance. There should be a balanced approach to the body's giftedness. Bodies need not limp along. We would love it if a person having studied this manual would assess his/her group for appropriate balance of word, power, and love gifts. Balanced for their situation.

And there should be a balance between character and giftedness. And we would hope that a leader studying this manual would recognize the importance of operating at maximum potential in giftedness. As we said in the beginning of chapter 10, maximum potential is measured in several ways. First, a person operating in maturity in his/her giftedness <u>does it in a Godly way</u>. The character of God is revealed in all that is said and done. Secondly, the various elements of the giftedness set are operating in balance, harmony and synergistically. Thirdly, a person operating in maturity in his/her giftedness bears appropriate fruit and is accomplishing the things that God has set out for him/her.

Giftedness is extremely important. We have repeated a statement a number of times throughout this manual.

MINISTRY FLOWS OUT OF BEING.

Understanding our unique giftedness is a major step forward toward our ministry flowing out of our unique being. This knowledge provides a tremendous understanding which allows us:

- to be proactive in choosing roles that fit who we are,
- to see more clearly what our life purpose is all about,
- to see the potential contributions that we can leave behind as a legacy to God's involvement in our lives,
- to intentionally and deliberately prioritize our life around God's focus for it which will relate very strongly to our giftedness.

Giftedness is not the only factor that contributes to our attaining God's focus for us. But it is a very important one. And it has been the thrust of this manual.

Did we overstate the impact of our manual when we titled it?

DEVELOPING LEADERSHIP GIFTEDNESS

What Every Leader needs to know About
Spiritual Gifts To Develop
Themselves and Their People

I hope not. In any case I know we have helped you understand a little better your answer to our closing question.

When it is all said and done and you are standing before God, what kind of accounting do you want to give concerning the abilities, skills and gifts that God released to you?

References Cited

Blanchard, Tim
    1988   **Finding Your Spiritual Gifts.** Wheaton: Tyndale House.

Clinton, Dr. J. Robert
    1977   **Interpreting the Scriptures: Figures and Idioms.** Altadena: Barnabas Publishers.

    1985   **Spiritual Gifts.** Revisded edition of 1975 version. Beaverlodge, Alberta, Canada: Horizon House Publishers.

    1988   **The Making of a Leader.** Colorado Springs: NavPress.

    1989   **Leadership Emergence Theory—A Self-Study Manual for Analyzing the Development of a Christian Leader.** Altadena: Barnabas Publishers.

    1993   **Leadership Perspectives (formerly Handbook I.).** Altadena: Barnabas Publishers.

    1993   *The Paradigm Shift—God's Breakthrough Processing That Opens New Leadeership Vistas.* Altadena, CA; Barnabas Publishers.

Clinton, Dr. J. Robert and Dr. Richard W. Clinton
    1991   **The Mentor Handbook—Detailed Guidelines and Helps for Christian Mentors and Mentorees.** Altadena, CA; Barnabas Publishers.

    1994   **Unlocking Your Giftedness.** Altadena: Barnabas Publishers.

Davis, Stanley B.
    1987   **Future Perfect.** New York: Addison Wesley.

De Wet, Christian R.
    1981   **Signs and Wonders in Church Growth.** Pasadena: Fuller Theological Suminary, School of World Missin, special project.

Edwards, Robert Earl
    1986   *Leadership Develoment Process.* Unpublished research paper. Pasadena: School of World Mission of Fuller Theological Seminary.

Gee, Donald
    1949   **Concerning Spiritual Gifts.** Revised edition, 1972. Springfield, MO: Gospel Publishing House.

Harville, Sue
    1976   **Reciprocal Living.** Coral Gables, Fl: Worldteam.

Hummel, Charles
    1993   **Fire in the Fireplace—Charismatic Renewal in the Nineties.** This is a a revised and updated version of the earlier 1978 version. Downers grove, Il: InterVarsity Press.

Kiersey, David and Marilyn Bates
    1978 **Please Understand Me.** Del Mar, CA: Prometheus Nemesis Books.

Le Peau, Andrew T.
    1983 **Paths of Leadership.** Downers grove, Il: InterVarsity Press.

Loving, Richard
    1986 *Richard Loving—A Leadership Selection Process.* Unpublished research paper. Pasadena: School of World Mission of Fuller Theological Seminary.

Mager, R. F.
    1962 **Preparing Instrucitonal Objectives.** San Fransisco: Fearon Publishers.

Maranville, Randall R.
    1982 *Samuel J. Mills Jr.* Unpublished research paper. Pasadena: School of World Mission of Fuller Theological Seminary.

McConnell, C. Douglas
    1985 *Doug McConnell—A Leadership Selection Process.* Unpublished research paper. Pasadena: School of World Mission of Fuller Theological Seminary.

McCrae, William
    1976   **Dynamics of Spiritual Gifts.** Grand Rapids: Zondervan.

Senyimba, Michael
    1986 *A Lay Leadership Selection Process for Michael N. Senyimpa.* Unpublished research paper. Pasadena: School of World Mission of Fuller Theological Seminary.

Taylor, Mrs. Howard
    1964 **Behind the Ranges.** Chicago: Moody Press.

Tippett, A. R.
    1969 **Verdict Theology in Missionary Thought.** Lincoln, IL: Lincoln College Press.

Wagner, C. Peter
    1981 **Church Growth and the Wole Gospel.** San Francisco, CA: Harper and Row Publishers.

    1984 **Leading Your Church to Growth.** Ventura, CA: Regal Books
    Your Spiritual Gifts Can Help Your Church Grow.

Whitworth, Julia M.
    1989 *Giftedness Analysis and Development Strategy.* Unpublished Research Paper. Pasadena: School of World Mission of Fuller Theological Seminary.

Wrong, Dennis
    1979 **Power Its Forms, Bases and Uses.** San Francisco, CA: Harper and Row.

GLOSSARY
Primary location of definition is given in parenthesis at conclusion of definition, see underlined page number.

Acquired skills

part of the giftedness set; refer to those capacities, skills, talents or aptitudes which have been *learned* by a person in order to allow him/her to accomplish something. (p. 40, 74)

apostleship

a spiritual gift in the word cluster; refers to a special leadership capacity to move with authority from God to create new ministry structures (churches and para-church) to meet needs and to develop and appoint leadership in these structures. (p. 145, 183, 216, 267)

Balance

the term used to describe a proper relationship between manifestations of love, word, and power clusters operating in a given context so that God's witness in that situation can be adequate. (p. 125)

basic skills process item

refers to actual skills acquired and/or values learned in picking up those skills, during the foundational phase, which will later affect leadership skills, leadership attitudes, and leadership styles. (p. 83)

Christian role

an activity that every believer is commanded to be involved in due to being part of the Christian movement. Many roles have overlapping functions with spiritual gifts. (p. 123)

complementary giftedness-need indicator pattern

describes a giftedness recognition pattern frequently seen in potential leaders in which those potential leaders are intuitively attracted to leaders who due to weaknesses in ministry need giftedness which the potential leader has; the giftedness may be very embryonic. (p. 60)

continuum

a way of explaining and relating the notion of moving from one extreme to another extreme by a continuous movement from one to the other in which one extreme becomes less and the other becomes more. In the middle of the continuum there is some of each involved. (f p 42, examples: 42, 100, 154, 156, 164)

Consideration functions (relational behaviors)

one of three leadership functions; those things leaders do to provide an atmosphere congenial to accomplishment of work, affirmation of persons, and development of persons. (p. 20)

constellation

a term used to describe a cluster of elements and items on a Venn diagram which are tightly focused around some dominant element or item. (feedback p. 244, answer 3)

discernings of spirits

a spiritual gift of the power cluster; The discernings of spirits gift refers to the ability given by God to perceive issues in terms of spiritual truth, to know the fundamental source of the issues and to give judgment concerning those issues; this includes the recognition of the spiritual forces operating in the issue. (p. 163, 221, 222, 284)

dominant gift

part of the gift-mix; refers to that gift in the gift-mix or gift-cluster which is more central to the person's ministry. (p. 46)

evangelism

a spiritual gift in the word cluster; The gift of evangelism in general refers to the capacity to challenge people through various communicative methods (persuasion) to receive the Gospel of salvation in Christ so as to see them respond by taking initial steps in Christian discipleship. (p. 147, 217, 269)

exhortation

a spiritual gift in the word cluster; the capacity to urge people to action in terms of applying Biblical truths, to encourage people generally with Biblical truths, or to comfort people through the application of Biblical truth to their needs. (p. 143, 214, 215, 260)

faith

a spiritual gift of the power cluster; The gift of faith refers to the unusual capacity of a person to recognize in a given situation that God intends to do something and to trust God for it until He brings it to pass. (p. 157, 219, 220, 279)

focal element	refers to the element of a person's giftedness set that is dominant and to which the other two elements operate in a supportive way which enhances the dominant element. (p. 44)
Forced Role/Gift Enablement Pattern	describes the not so frequent pattern in which a person is placed in a role which requires some specific giftedness (especially a spiritual gift) not previously known or demonstrated and in that role is met by the Holy Spirit so as to demonstrates one or more of those needed gifts while the role is active. (p. 62)
gift, extant	A gift is said to be extant if it is available to today's church and can be seen in operation today. (p. 100)
gift projection	the tendency of strong gifted leaders to lay expectations (even guilt trips) on followers to operate in the same gifts in which these leaders are strong. (feedback, p. 45)
gifts of governments	a spiritual gift of the love cluster; The gifts of governments involves a capacity to manage details of service functions so as to support and free other leaders to prioritize their efforts. (p. 170, 223, 287)
gifts of healings	a spiritual gift of the power cluster; Gifts of healings refer to the supernatural releasing of healing power for curing all types of illnesses. (p. 159, 220,221,281)
gifts of helps	a spiritual gift of the love cluster; The gifts of helps refers to the capacity to unselfishly meet the needs of others through very practical means. (p. 173, 225, 290)
gifts identification continuum	a linear line, pictorial display, along which a given Bible interpreter can be located on his/her believe in how many spiritual gifts are available today—higher numbers go to the left; lesser numbers to the right. (p. 100)
gift-cluster	refers to a person's gift-mix which has matured in such a way that one gift is dominant and the other gifts harmonize with that gift in order to maximize the person's effectiveness. (p. 46)
gift-cluster ripening	the pattern describing the maturing of a gift-mix (p. 254)
giftedness awareness continuum	a linear display moving from the left with spiritual gifts to the right through natural abilities, expanded natural abilities, and on the right acquired skills. The continuum is based on the notion of awareness of God with sovereign intervention on the left and providential oversight on the right. When you move to the left your awareness of God increases. When you move to the right it decreases. (p. 42)
giftedness development pattern	the normal development pattern of a leader described in 12 stages (p. 53, 252, 253)
giftedness discovery process item	refers to any significant advancement along the giftedness development pattern and the event, person or reflection process that was instrumental in bringing about the discovery. (p. 51)
Giftedness Drift pattern	describes the tendency of a potential leader to most naturally respond to ministry challenges and assignments either that fit prior experience or acquired skills or perception of natural ability or intuitively, a spiritual gift. (p. 61)
giftedness set	a set of three elements seen in a leader's life: natural abilities, acquired skills, and spiritual gifts. (p. 5, 40)
giftedness time-line	a horizontal display of the discovery and acquisition of natural abilities, acquired skills, and spiritual gifts by identifying the actual date in which there was some recognition or discovery. (p. 55)
gift-mix	a label that refers to the set of spiritual gifts being used by a leader at any given time in his/her ministry. (p. 46)

giving	a spiritual gift of the love cluster; The gift of giving refers to the capacity to give liberally to meet the needs of others and yet to do so with a purity of motive which senses that the giving is a simple sharing of what God has given. (p. *171*, 223, 224,288)
Harvest leader model	a philosophical model founded on the central thrust of Jesus' teaching to expand the Kingdom by winning new members into it as demonstrated in the agricultural metaphors of growth in scripture. (p. *31*)
impartation	refers to the giving of spiritual gifts to a believer by the Holy Spirit. (p. *128*)
Initiation of structure function (task behaviors)	one of three major leadership functions; those things leaders do to focus on accomplishing the organization's mission such as clarifying goals, forming organizational units, and holding people accountable for achieving. (p. *20*)
Inspirational functions	one of three leadership functions; leadership activities that leaders do to motivate people to work together and to accomplish the ends of the organization. (p. *20*)
interpretation of tongues	a spiritual gift of the power cluster; The gift of interpretation of tongues refers to the ability to spontaneously respond to a giving of an authoritative message in tongues by interpreting this word and clearly communicating the message given. (p. *165*, 223, 286)
leader	a person with God-given capacity, and God-given responsibility who is influencing some of God's people towards God's purposes. (p. *8*, *14*)
leadership	a dynamic process over an extended period of time in various situations in which a leader utilizing leadership resources, and by specific leadership behaviors, influences followers, toward accomplishment of aims mutually beneficial for leaders and followers. (p. *18*)
leadership act	the specific instance at a given point in time of the leadership influence process between a given influencer (person said to be influencing) and follower(s) (person or persons being influenced) in which the followers are influenced toward some goal. (p. *12*)
leadership function	general activities that leaders must do and/or be responsible for in their influence responsibilities with followers. (p *20*)
Like-Attracts-Like gift pattern	describes an early giftedness recognition pattern frequently seen in potential leaders in which those potential leaders are intuitively attracted to leaders who have like giftedness even though the giftedness in the potential leader may be very embryonic. (p. *59*)
loose Venn diagram	describes a Venn diagram in which there is in general a lack of overlap between elements and items. Usually there will be some elements or items not relating to others. (p. *233*)
love gifts	a cluster of gifts; one of the three corporate functions of gifts; these are manifestations of God's love through practical ways that can be recognized by a world around us which needs love. They demonstrate the reality of relating to this God. (f. p. *9*, *125*)
major passage	one of 8 major passages in the New Testament concerning spiritual gifts; refers to any context in the New Testament epistles in which two or more gifts are listed either specifically or by a generic label and/ or the passage deals with the use or abuse of a gift or gifts. (p. *103*)
mercy	a spiritual gift of the love cluster; The gift of mercy refers to the capacity to both feel sympathy for those in need (especially the suffering) and to manifest this sympathy in some practical helpful way with a cheerful spirit so as to encourage and help those in need. (p. *172*, 224, 289)

metonymy	an emphatic figure of speech in which one word is substituted for another word to which it is closely related in order to stress the relationship. (f p. *103*)
ministry philosophy	refers to ideas, values, and principles whether implicit or explicit which a leader uses as guidelines for decision making, for exercising influence, and for evaluating his/her ministry. (p. *25*)
ministry skills process	from leadership emergence theory; refers to a definite acquisition of one or more identifiable skills which aids one in a ministry assignment. (p. *85*)
minor passage	refers to any context in the New Testament epistles in which one or more gifts are mentioned either specifically or by a generic label or by implication. (p. *105*)
natural abilities	part of the giftedness set; refer to those capacities, skills, talents or aptitudes which are *innate* in a person and allow him/her to accomplish things. (p. *40*, Tree Diagram *68*)
non-vested gifts	spiritual gifts that appear situationally and can not be repeated at will by the person. (p. *130*)
pastoring	a spiritual gift in the word cluster; The pastoral gift is the capacity to exercise concern and care for members of a group so as to encourage them in their growth in Christ which involves modeling maturity, protecting them from error and disseminating truth. (p. *146*, *216*, *271*)
power gifts	a cluster of gifts; one of the three corporate functions of gifts; a cluster of spiritual gifts that demonstrate the authenticity, credibility, power and reality of the unseen God. (f. p. *9*, *125*)
primary gifts	gifts that are vested gifts and are currently being demonstrated as a significant part of the gift-mix. (p. *132*)
process item	a technical term used in leadership emergence theory which describes the shaping activity of God. This shaping activity usually involves three kinds of formation: spiritual formation (leadership character), ministerial formation (leadership skills), and strategic formation (leadership values and direction). (f p. *51*)
prophecy	a spiritual gift in the word cluster; A person operating with the gift of prophecy has the capacity to deliver truth (in a public way) either of a predictive nature or as a situational word from God in order to correct by exhorting, edifying or consoling believers and/or to convince non-believers of God's truth. (p. *144*, 215, 265)
ruling	a spiritual gift in the word cluster; A person operating with a ruling gift demonstrates the capacity to exercise influence over a group so as to lead it toward a goal or purpose with a particular emphasis on the capacity to make decisions and keep the group operating together. (p. *148*, 218, 273)
secondary gifts	gifts that were at one time primary gifts but are no longer being demonstrated as part of the current gift-mix. (p. 132)
servant leader model	a philosophical model which is founded on the central thrust of Jesus' teaching on the major quality of great Kingdom leaders. That is, a leader uses leadership to serve followers. This is demonstrated in Jesus' own ministry. (p. *27*)
shepherd leader model	a philosophical model which is founded on the central thrust of Jesus' own teaching and modeling concerning the responsibilities of leadership in caring for followers as seen in the various Shepherd/ Sheep metaphors in scripture. (p. *29*)
spiritual gift	a God-given unique capacity which is given to each believer for the purpose of releasing a Holy Spirit empowered ministry either in a situation or to be repeated again and again. (p. 5, *40*)

stewardship model	a philosophical model which is founded on the central thrust of several accountability passages, that is, that a leader must give account of his/her ministry to God. (p. 25)
synergism	and related words (synergistic, synergistically) all refer to a process in which items work together to produce a united effort which is greater than just the sum of the individual efforts. (f p. 44)
teaching	a spiritual gift in the word cluster; A person who has the gift of teaching is one who has the ability to instruct, explain, or expose Biblical truth in such a way as to cause believers to understand the Biblical truth. (p. 142, 214, 256)
tertiary gifts	gifts that are now non-vested gifts or come and go due to spontaneous activity of the Holy Spirit. (p. 132)
tight Venn Diagram	A Venn diagram in which there is much overlap of elements and items with the major part of the diagram focused about the more important elements. (p. 233)
tongues	a spiritual gift of the power cluster; The gift of tongues refers a spontaneous utterance of a word from God in unknown words (to the individual giving the word) to a group of people. (p. 165, 222, 223, 286)
typology continuum	a linear continuum listing of five types of leaders in terms of sphere of influence: Type A, B (local), Type C(large local), Type D(regional/ national) Type E (international); (f p. 23)
Venn Diagram	A pictorial display of one's entire giftedness set which relates importance of elements and items by size, spacing, and symbols. Larger size means more relative importance. Overlaps means things work jointly. Non-overlap means they work exclusively. Rectangular is used for natural abilities. Triangles for spiritual gifts. Circles for spiritual gifts. (p. 229, examples: 110, 126, 232, 234, 237, 240, 243, 245, 247)
vested gifts	spiritual gifts that appear repeatedly in a person's ministry and can be repeated at will by the person. (p. 130)
word gifts	a cluster of gifts; one of the three corporate functions of gifts; they clarify the nature of this unseen God and what He expects from His followers. People using these gifts both communicate about God and for God. (f. p. 9, 125, 126)
word of knowledge	a spiritual gift of the power cluster; The word of knowledge gift refers to the capacity or sensitivity of a person to supernaturally perceive revealed knowledge from God which otherwise could not or would not be known and apply it to a situation. (p. 155, 219, 277)
word of wisdom	a spiritual gift of the power cluster; The word of wisdom gift refers to the capacity to know the mind of the Spirit in a given situation and to communicate clearly the situation, facts, truth or application of the facts and truth to meet the need of the situation. (p. 153, 218, 219, 275)
workings of power	a spiritual gift of the power cluster; The workings of powers, gift of miracles, refers to the releasing of God's supernatural power so that the miraculous intervention of God is perceived and God receives recognition for the supernatural intervention. (p. 161, 221, 283)

APPENDIX A
AN ANNOTATED BIBLIOGRAPHY

This bibliography has been gathered over the years from students who have done reading reports. We wanted to include them because they provide a viewpoint that we felt was valuable. We tried to select books which present a wide range of perspective on spiritual gifts. The comments recorded come from the students reports. They are certainly colored by their own perspective and background.

Basham, Don
 1971   **A Handbook on Tongues, Interpretation and Prophecy.** Monroeville, PA: Whitaker Books.

Comments:
This is a good book for understanding the standard charismatic position on speaking in tongues, interpretation of tongues and prophecy. The major weakness in the book is that it does not give very strong theological arguments for the positions stated. The questions answered in the book would probably only convince someone who already holds this position.

Baxter, Ronald E.

 1982 **Charismatic Gift of Tongues** Grand Rapids, Kregel.

Comments:
This book is basically covers the anti-tongues position.

Bell, Ora Melvin

 1984   **Gift Centered Ministry in the Seventh Day Adventist Church.** Pasadena: School of Theology, Unpublished D.Min dissertation.

Comments:
This dissertation covers the Seventh Day Adventist position on gifts.

Blanchard, Tim

 1988   **Finding Your Spiritual Gifts**. Wheaton: Tyndale House.

Comments:
This material is a manual on spiritual gifts which was written as a learning tool. The purpose of this manual is focused on finding, understanding and using spiritual gifts. It is written from a Conservative Baptist perspective. Blanchard selectively chooses the gifts he describes with clear criteria. He does exclude the Ephesians gifts saying that a defense of the gifts versus office is beyond the scope of the book.

Bridge, Donald and Phypers, David

1974   **Spiritual Gifts and the Church.** Downers Grove: Inter-varsity Press.

Comments:
A good book for understanding spiritual gifts in the New Testament. They teach that "no Christian is permanently endowed with any gift". It is written from a British perspective and is written for a college level audience. Usually Inter-varsity materials will be *middle of the road evangelical* but **open** to Christians of charismatic and non-charismatic persuasion.

Bryant, Charles

1986   **Rediscovering the Charismata.** Waco, TX: Word Books.

Comments:
This book provides illustrations of each gift. The perspective comes from a pastor (United Methodist) who has recently had an experience with the Holy Spirit and deliverance. There are useful resources in the back.

Clinton, J. Robert

1985   **Spiritual Gifts.** Beaverlodge, Alberta: Horizon House.

Comments:
        A practical and helpful self-study book on spiritual gifts. The focus is on the New Testament listing of spiritual gifts. Learning to identify your gift(s) and develop them is the strength of this book. It is based on solid Biblical hermenutical work. It is useful as a reference book and study manual.

De Wet, Christian R.
1981   **Signs and Wonders in Church Growth.** Pasadena: Fuller Theological Seminary, School of
            World Mission, special project.

Comments:
A good look through history at signs and wonders in each century.

Flynn, Leslie
1974   **19 Gifts of the Spirit: Which Do You Have?.** Wheaton: Victor Books.

Comments:
This book presents a well documented insightful discussion of nineteen spiritual gifts with clear definitions and many empirical examples. He has a weak section on the development of your gifts. He writes from a Conservative Baptist perspective and emphasizes using the gifts for serving the body of Christ.

Friesen, Harold
1979   **A Model for a Church in Ministry by Employing Spiritual Gifts.** Pasadena: School of Theology, unpublished dissertation.

Comments:
This dissertation is an attempt by a pastor to develop spiritual gifts into the life of a local church. It raises questions and points out issues regarding the practice of spiritual gifts in the church by comparing various viewpoints.

Gaffin, Richard B.

1979   **Perspectives on Pentecost: Studies in N.T. Teaching on the Gifts of the Holy Spirit.** Phillipsburg, NJ: Presbyterian and Reformed Publishing Company.

Comments:
Based on a biblical-theological perspective and exegesis, the author argues the cessation of the spiritual gifts, especially the gifts of prophecy and tongues. The basic strategy is to demonstrate the historical and "once for all" nature of the Pentecost event. Once the canon was closed, these gifts died out.

Gangel, Kenneth O.

1986   **Unwrap Your Spiritual Gifts.** Wheaton: Victor.

Comments:
A good book for understanding the concepts regarding the different books. The author covers 20 different gifts.

Gee, Donald

1972   **Concerning Spiritual Gifts.** Springfield, MO: Gospel Publishing House.

Comments:
This book was first published in 1949 and covers the classic Pentecostal perspective on spiritual gifts. It focuses on the 9 gifts of the Spirit mentioned in 1 Corinthians 12.

Gilbert, Larry

1987   **Team Ministry: A Guide to Spiritual Gifts and Lay Involvement.** Lynchburg, VA: Church Growth Institute.

Comments:
The author advocates the discovery and use of spiritual gifts to a primary audience of fundamental Baptists. Each chapter has "now what?" section which makes it very practical.

Gruden, Wayne
    1988   **The Gift of Prophecy in the New Testament and Today.** Westchester, IL: Cross Way.

Comments:
This book is about the nature and function of the gift of prophecy. The conclusions of the author are drawn from careful exegesis. While holding to the sufficiency of Scripture to every aspect of our lives, the author sees the blessings and the importance of exercising the gift of prophecy in churches today.

Hagin, Kenneth
    1981   **The Ministry Gifts.** Tulsa: Kenneth Hagin Ministries.

Comments:
This little book covers a popular Pentecostal approach to spiritual gifts.

Hubbard, David Allen
    1985   **Unwrapping Your Spiritual Gifts.** Waco: Word.

Comments:
This book provides a good overview of spiritual gifts. He stresses the gifts are to be used to strengthen the body. It is focused on encouraging people to get involved but doesn't provide much practical help. Not done with the thorough depth you would expect from this noted evangelical scholar.

Hummel, Charles E.
    1978   **Fire in the Fireplace: Contemporary Charismatic Renewal.** Downers Grove: Inter-varsity Press.

Comments:
This book is well written and covers the activity of the Holy Spirit and the body of Christ as it relates to the charisms throughout the history of the church. He writes this volume in order to provide a supportive foundation for the charismatic renewal. It is a helpful book in helping someone come up with a Biblical framework for thinking about the Holy Spirit and spiritual gifts. Though written so anyone can read it, you sense the scholarship behind it all the time. You may want to get both this edition and the revised editions which has just been released (1993) which brings his thinking up to date.

Jones, R. Wayne
    1985   **Using Spiritual Gifts.** Nashville, TN: Broadman.

Comments:
A compact and practical guide to discovering and using spiritual gifts written by a young Southern Baptist pastor.

Kinghorn, Kenneth Cain
1976   **Gifts of the Spirit**. Nashville, TN: Abingdon.

Comments:
Writing as a Methodist, the author demonstrates how Wesleyan theology can support spiritual gifts even though Wesley himself had a hard time with them.

Koch, Kurt E.
1975   **Charismatic Gifts.** Quebec: Association for Christian Evangelism.

Comments:
This is a book written by a pastor with 45 years of ministry experience. It has many stories both positive and negative concerning the use of gifts. He urges caution in the practice of the gifts. This is a reaction to the things that were happening in the early 70's in response to movies such as the "Exorcist." This man has done a good bit of research on what happens to those involved in exorcism type of ministries. I (heard him speak at the Jamaica Bible College in the 70s where he indicated many who get involved eventually go under.)

MacGorman, Jack W.
1974   **The Gifts of the Spirit**. Nashville, TN: Broadman.

Comments:
Even though Southern Baptists are far from agreeing among themselves as to what attitude they should take toward some of the spiritual gifts, one of their fine scholars and seminary professors sets forth a well balanced position in this book.

McRae, William T.
1976   **Dynamics of Spiritual Gifts**. Grand Rapids: Zondervan.

Comments:
The goal of the book is to encourage believers to identify their gift and use it to serve others. He writes from the classic dispensational perspective. He defines 18 gifts but says that only 9 gifts are still available today.

Packer, J.I.
1984   **Keep in Step With the Spirit.** Old Tappan, NJ: F.H. Revell.

Comments:
He provides a broad overview of the ministry of the Holy Spirit in the Bible and in history. He is weary of people trying to prove their various viewpoints with empirical evidence. He urges caution in regard to certain excesses in renewal movements that could be misunderstood or misguided. This is not a book about spiritual gifts as much as it is a book about renewal movements.

Purkiser, W.T.
1975   **The Gifts of the Spirit.** Kansas City: Beacon Hill Press.

Comments:
He writes from the Nazarene perspective and represents a common holiness perspective on gifts.

Pytches, David
1985   **Spiritual Gifts in the Local Church.** Minneapolis: Bethany House.

Comments:
The author is an Anglican minister involved in renewal in England. It gives a Pro-charismatic approach to bringing renewal in life less churches.

Sneck, William Joseph
1981   **Charismatic Spiritual Gifts: A Phenomenological Analysis.** Washington, D.C.: University Press of America.

Comments:
This work is an attempt to understand the expression of the charismatic gifts (particularly prophecy, healing, and deliverance) in the Catholic charismatic renewal from a research psychological perspective. The study was done in the Word of God community in Michigan. The strength of this book is that the author uses a different research methodology to approach the issue of spiritual gifts. The weakness is the lack of theological or Biblical perspective.

Snyder, Howard A. with Daniel V. Runyou
1986   **The Divided Flame: Wesleyans and the Charismatic Renewal.** Grand Rapids: Francis Asbury Press (Zondervan).

Comments:
An appeal to Wesleyans to become more open to contemporary Pentecostal and Charismatic phenomena with excellent historical insights and analysis of today's trends.

Stedman, R.C.
1972   **Body Life.** Glendale: Regal Books.

Comments:
His major perspective is that all the members of the church need to be involved if their is going to be revitalization of the Church. Using spiritual gifts is the primary method of getting people involved.

Underwood, B.E.
1967   **The Gifts of the Spirit**. Franklin Springs, GA: Advocate Press.

Comments:
This book is written from the Pentecostal Holiness perspective but is much broader than the classic Pentecostal viewpoint. He covers all of the gifts passages and has some helpful categories for understanding the practice and use of spiritual gifts.

Wagner, C. Peter
1979   **Your Spiritual Gifts Can Help Your Church Grow**. Ventura: Regal.

Comments:
This author looks at spiritual gifts from a church growth perspective. He defines spiritual gifts from both the New Testament lists, the Old Testament and experience. He identifies 27 gifts. The major usefulness of the book is to understand how and where spiritual gifts can influence the growth of the church.

Yocum, Bruce
1976   **Prophecy: Exercising the Prophetic Gifts of the Spirit Today**. Ann Arbor: Word of Life.

Comments:
A balanced view of prophecy presented from the charismatic movement. He emphasizes the need for discernment and a testing of the spirits. The first part of the book covers the function of the gift in the New Testament and the second part of the book focuses on how to start a Biblical prophetic ministry in the church today.

Yohn, Rick
1974   **Discover Your Spiritual Gift and Use It**. Wheaton: Tyndale House.

Comments:
This book is primarily inspirational. The author writes in order to encourage involvement in serving and building up the body. Some of the interpretations regarding various spiritual gifts are unclear.

APPENDIX B:
RANSACKING A GIFTEDNESS BOOK

introduction	When you are relatively familiar with certain topics, you may not need to read every chapter in a book but may choose to read very selectively. That is, you may read given portions to see if they add any new ideas or ideas different from those you are already aware of.
definition	*Ransack reading* refers to the technique of looking through a book in order to see what it says concerning a specific topic of interest or combing through a book on relatively familiar material to see if it has any new ideas not known to you.
definition	*Closed Ransacking* refers to rapid reading to compare or contrast what is said with some already known idea or ideas in mind.
definition	*Open Ransacking* refers to rapid reading to see if there is some new idea or new slant on an idea concerning some specific area of interest.
6 possible results	When you have ransacked a book you will have: 1. Noted a new idea on a pre-selected topic of interest to you, 2. Noted a contrasting or differing idea on some pre-selected topic of interest to you, 3. Determined that the book has nothing to add to your pre-selected topic of interest. 4. Gained something worth noting which is of interest to you on any topic. 5. Determined that nothing of interest to you can be gained from the book. 6. Made a tentative decision concerning reading the book at a deeper level.
3 hints	Here are three hints to remember when ransacking: 1. Books which deal with material already familiar to you normally should be ransacked. For example, once you have read a book on spiritual gifts, you can simply look at other books on spiritual gifts and compare and contrast them with the first book. Some books are more thorough on a subject and can form a standard for comparison. Such a book is called a **basal** book. Find and use basal books when ransacking. 2. Books which contain a series of papers or articles done by different authors is a natural one for ransacking. Rarely does such a book develop a coherent thesis. Hence it is not necessary to read everything in it. Just pick the topics and articles that are of interest to you. 3. The more narrowly you pre-select your topic of interest the more rapidly you can look just for perspective on those items.

INSTRUCTION FOR RANSACKING A GIFTEDNESS BOOK

We provide a form to follow for ransacking books on spiritual gifts. This is in essence a closed ransacking of books on spiritual gifts because we are asking you to compare and contrast information given in the books with what we have written in this manual. Answer each question in as much detail as you can. Give what the author's view is or isn't and the page number where information can be found. If extra writing space is needed, put overflow on the back of the page and identify the question.

RANSACKING A GIFTEDNESS BOOK

Name of student: _____ Date: _____
Name of the author and book: _____
Number of pages: _____

I. Overall Focus of the Book

1. What is the basic perspective of the author?

      A. Theological Perspective:
      ___ pentecostal
      ___ charismatic
      ___ main stream evangelical
      ___ main stream evangelical/sympathetic to charismatics
      ___ anti-pentecostal or anti-charismatic
      ___ other: explain

      B. Role in Ministry:
      ___ pastoral/local church
      ___ organizational/para-church
      ___ organizational/denominational position
      ___ apostolic/perspective for the international church
      ___ teaches in Bible College/Seminary
      ___ other: explain

2. Does the author emphasize one or two of the spiritual   yes   no
      gifts passages more than others (or even to the exclusion
      of others)?

      Check the passages which *are not* emphasized.

      ___ 1 Cor. 12:8-10   ___ 1 Cor. 14:26,27
      ___ 1 Cor. 12:28   ___ Romans 12:6-8
      ___ 1 Cor. 13:1-3   ___ Ephesians 4:11
      ___ 1 Cor. 13:8   ___ Hebrews 2:1-4
      ___ 1 Cor. 14:6   ___ 1 Peter 4:10,11

II. DEFINITIONS

3. Does the author actually define the term "spiritual gifts?" yes   no
      If yes, write the definition given.

4. Check the passages the author uses in defining any of the spiritual gifts:

___ 1 Cor. 12:8-10	___ 1 Cor. 14:26,27
___ 1 Cor. 12:28	___ Romans 12:6-8
___ 1 Cor. 13:1-3	___ Ephesians 4:11
___ 1 Cor. 13:8	___ Hebrews 2:1-4
___ 1 Cor. 14:6	___ 1 Peter 4:10,11
___ Other—List them:	

5. Does the author do a comparative listing of gifts between   yes   no
   two or more passages?

   If yes, indicate which ones.

___ 1 Cor. 12:8-10	___ 1 Cor. 14:26,27
___ 1 Cor. 12:28	___ Romans 12:6-8
___ 1 Cor. 13:1-3	___ Ephesians 4:11
___ 1 Cor. 13:8	___ Hebrews 2:1-4
___ 1 Cor. 14:6	___ 1 Peter 4:10,11

   If yes, which gifts are common between the passages? Indicate gifts and the passage references:

   Which gifts are distinct to one passage? (listed in only one passage) List the gifts and the references:

6. How many gifts does the author list as existing today?   _____
   How many extant? _____

7. Does the author define or discuss individual gifts in detail? yes   no

   If yes, which gifts. Please list them.

8. Does the author give Biblical evidence (such as word studies,   yes   no
   topical studies, contextual studies, etc.) for the origination of the
   gift definitions?

   If yes, which kind of evidence is used:

   If no, how does the author come up with his/her definitions?

9. Does the author *originate (come up with)* any specific gifts from passages other than the major gift
   passages?   yes   no

   If yes, list the gift with the Biblical references under the appropriate section:

   Old Testament:

   Gospels:

   New Testament:

10. Does the author *define* any specific gifts from passages other than the major gift passages?   yes   no

    If yes, list the gift with the Biblical references under the appropriate section:

    Old Testament:

    Gospels:

    New Testament:

11. Does the author *illustrate* any specific gifts from passages other than the major gift passages?   yes   no

    If yes, list the gift with the Biblical references under the appropriate section:

    Old Testament:

    Gospels:

    New Testament:

12. Is the author's research confined to Biblical study?   Yes   No
    Contemporary illustrations are indicative of
    empirical study.

    If no, describe the author's empirical data base and gifts which are illustrated, defined or confirmed via empirical evidence.

    Was the empirical evidence part of systemic research efforts or just the author's personal observations or opinions?

    ___ author's personal observations
    ___ systemic research efforts

13. Does the author treat "administration" (governments) in the Corinthians passage and "ruling" in Romans 12?   yes   no

    If yes, how are they treated?

    ___ sees them as identical gifts
    ___ sees them as different gifts

    If different, how are they seen as different?

    Administration =

    Ruling =

14. If the author sees Ephesians 4: 7-16 as a <u>spiritual gifts passage</u>, how is pastor and teacher treated?

___ pastor-teacher are seen as one gift,
___ pastor and teacher are seen as different gifts
___ other: explain.

If Ephesians 4: 7-16 is not seen as a spiritual gifts passage, how is the common overlap with other gift passages resolved (that is, Romans and Corinthians list two or three of these "offices" as gifts)?

15. Does the author treat the issue of <u>certainty of definitions</u>?   yes   no
(Be sure to note any delimiting remarks included in the book
which indicate aspects of certitude.)

If yes, list any gift definitions which are indicated as less certain than others:

If no, does he/she present all the definitions with the same certainty?

16. In the gift passages, does the author recognize differences between generic listing and specific listing of gifts? (Generic means categories under which various specific gifts can be grouped. For example, see 1 Peter 4:10,11 where some authors do recognize a generic listing.)   yes   no

If yes, how does the author threat these passages?

III. ORIGINS AND NATURE OF SPIRITUAL GIFTS

17. Does the author identify spiritual gifts as a Holy Spirit   yes   no
phenomena which is uniquely associated with the New
Testament Church? (That is, spiritual gifts, per se, are
not existent prior to the New Testament church?)

18. Does the author view any gifts as operative only for the   yes   no
early church and not today?

If yes, which ones and what rationale is given?

19. Does the author describe operative gifts today as   yes   no
vested/non-vested or some other view? (the issue
of possession, permanence, temporary, etc.)

IV. GIFTEDNESS SET AND DEVELOPMENT

20. Does the author treat the entire giftedness set?   yes   no

If no, does the author treat any aspect of the giftedness set?

If yes, which elements?

___ natural abilities and spiritual gifts
___ acquired skills and spiritual gifts
___ other: explain.

21. Does the author give helpful aids for identifying spiritual gifts for individuals?   yes   no

If yes, what kind of aids?

___ list of gift symptoms
___ some kind of questionnaire
___ a gifts test: simple or sophisticated (circle)
___ an outside form for confirmation
___ other: explain

22. Does the author suggest that giftedness can be developed?   yes   no

If yes, what development aids are suggested?

23. Does the author suggest some kind of a giftedness   yes   no
development pattern?

If yes, describe the pattern.

24. Give here any special insights or help received from the book or material.

25. Write a well integrated summary paragraph assessing the value of this book. Issues that could be a part of your summary include: the author's perspective, the focus of the book, comparisons with others, distinctive contributions of the book, strengths, weaknesses, etc.

APPENDIX C:
WRITING A GIFTEDNESS PAPER

INTRODUCTION

If you are using this manual with a class and want to get case study information from students in the class then the following is helpful. This is what we use with our students. We use a standard format when writing a giftedness paper. There are two different types of papers which are written. The most common is the paper in which a self-analysis of giftedness is done. The other type of paper is one which is done on another leader. In this appendix, we will cover the format and instructions for the self-analysis paper and include some forms that will help complete the paper.

THE SELF-ANALYSIS GIFTEDNESS PAPER

1. Format
    Use the following format for this paper.

    • A standard title page
    • The biographical information sheet (given in this appendix)
    • The Myers-Briggs sheet (if applicable, given in this appendix)
    • Section 1: Background
    • Section 2: Analysis of Your Giftedness Set
    • Section 3: Description of Development to Date.
    • Section 4: Future Development Plans
    • Section 5: Conclusion
    • Appendix: Include any material used to identify giftedness set.

2. Length of the Paper
    The length of the paper depends on the history of the individual, years of ministry experience and depth of analysis. The average student will write between 20 - 30 pages.

3. Description of each Section

    Section 1: Background (maybe 1 to 3 pages)
    This is a short section of the paper. In this section, you will want to give any important information regarding your background. This would include any previous personal perceptions concerning spiritual gifts, any teaching that you learned about spiritual gifts, your church's view on the use and practice of the gifts, etc. You basically want to cover where you first were exposed to the issue of spiritual gifts and their practice and what your thinking was concerning this issue before you started studying this material.

    Section 2: Analysis of Your Giftedness Set (maybe 12-20 pages)
    This should be the longest section of the paper. In this section, you should comment on how you identified your giftedness set. Describe the means that you used and what you learned from each one. (inward conviction, experience questionnaire, gifts tests, outside confirmation, etc.) You should display a giftedness time-line which reveals the process of discovery of each element of your giftedness set. You should also display your giftedness set using a Venn diagram. You should describe how you have identified each element of the giftedness set. You should indicate clearly the dominant gift of the gift-mix and how you see the other gifts operating in relationship to each other. You

should be able to describe the relationships of each of the elements of the giftedness set. You should be sure to identify the focal element of your giftedness set and why you see it as focal. You should mention any of the giftedness patterns that you have experienced to date. (giftedness drift, like-attracts-like, role-enablement, complementary gifted or some other unique pattern).

Section 3: Description of Development to Date (maybe 5-10 pages)

In this section, you will describe the development of each element. In the previous section you described how you identified the various elements. Now you will focus on how each of those elements has been developed. Using the development taxonomy given in chapter 10, list each component of your giftedness set and describe how it has been developed thus far. What development means have been used thus far?

Section 4: Future Development Plans (maybe 5-10 pages)

In this section, you will display a development plan and describe it. You should write a detailed plan for how you are going to work at developing some aspect of your giftedness set. You may want to begin by describing the area of ministry and type of role that you will be moving into after leaving seminary. Then, write a plan that will cover the next 2 years. At the beginning of the plan, include a short section describing why you are choosing to work on this aspect of your giftedness set. Describe the various development means that will be used and write a list of goals that would describe "ideal" development. In other words, what results would you want at the end of this development plan?

Section 5: Conclusion (maybe 1 page)

Summarize into a few paragraphs what you have learned in this paper.

Appendix

Include copies of the results, scores or information sheets of any material that you used to help you identify your spiritual gifts.

THE GIFTEDNESS BIOGRAPHICAL INFORMATION SHEET

Dates of interviews:

1. Person Studied: _____

2. Person Doing the Study: _____

3. Sex of the Person: M   F

4. Ministry Background

    a. ___ years of lay ministry involvement
    b. ___ years of full time ministry
    c. ___ total years of leadership ministry
    d. Has there been any formal training: Describe.

5. Date the Study was done: _____

6. Ministry Area of the person: location _____

7. Nationality: _____

8. Major Ministry Roles:

9. Giftedness Set:

    a. Natural abilities: _____

    b. Acquired skills: _____

    c. Spiritual gifts: Primary _____

                        Secondary _____

                        Tertiary _____

    Dominant spiritual gift: _____

10. Focal element of Giftedness set: _____

11. Other comments:

QUESTIONNAIRE FOR MYERS-BRIGGS/LEADERSHIP CORRELATION

Name: (optional) _____

1. What is your Myers-Briggs type?   _____

2. If you have taken the Myers-Briggs before, has your type changed? If so, what was it before?
    _____

3. How many years have you been in Christian ministry of any kind?

    Informal: _____   Formal: _____

4. Please list the kinds of ministry activities you have done and enjoyed: (For example, led small groups, helped work with the poor, preached, etc.)

5. Please list the formal positions that you have held in Christian ministry.

6. If known, please list the spiritual gifts, natural abilities, or acquired skills that God has given you for ministry:

7. What training for Christian ministry have you enjoyed and benefited the most from? (For example, seminary classes, informal seminars and workshops, on the job training, personal reading and study, etc.)